Fast-Track Management and Organizational Behavior

by

JAMES S. SAGNER, PhD

Fast-Track Textbooks

©James Sagner 2013

Copyright © 2013 James S. Sagner, PhD

ISBN: 1481958801

ISBN 13: 9781481958806

Library of Congress Control Number: 2013900673
CreateSpace Independent Publishing Platform
North Charleston, South Carolina

Fast-Track Management And Organizational Behavior
Table of Contents

Preface

Why do we need another book on management and organizational behavior (OB)? There are many good texts on these topics that are available for classroom use, but an instructor must explain and update most of the content. I know, because I've taught undergraduate and MBA management and OB at various universities for quite a few years. I was a banker for a dozen years (at First National Bank of Chicago, now part of J.P. Morgan Chase).

My responsibilities at the bank and in my private consulting practice have included any number of businesses including U.S. banks and other financial services companies, and industrial companies in North America, Europe and Asia. Management dynamics have been present in every business situation I have encountered. In fact, management is present any time three people come together for nearly any purpose.

There are several things one learns in teaching and practicing management theory.

1. Nearly all books that deal with management and OB are written by academics. The few exceptions deal with the mechanics of personnel management such as hiring practices or how to create a successful management-by-objectives program. What managers do each day varies significantly from the textbooks.

2. Much of what you'll find in other texts is irrelevant. For example, nearly every text on management discusses management history going back a century, communication theories about how people learn, and legal forms of structuring an organization. If you were to read a single book on all of these and other topics that arguably are relevant to a business, you would be holding 1,500 pages in your hands!

3. Much of what you'll find in other texts is padding. In some texts you'll find endless discussions, numerous references to practices in companies so obscure that your author has never heard of them, detours into topics not specifically related to management and organization behavior (such as strategy planning and decision-making, personal career

choices and organizations that support international business), and alternative management concepts that have been largely rejected.

At Fast-Track Textbooks, we aren't ivory tower academics, we focus on current issues, we present relevant concepts, and we are brief, use clear writing and go right to the point. You simply don't need 700 pages to understand management.

This book is one of a series of Fast-Track texts that are designed to simplify and clarify important business topics. Additional titles to be published include Fast-Track Finance and Fast-Track International Business. The series tries to make learning easy for the reader using several unique teaching aids. First, each section is identified with an icon indicating the level of difficulty. Here's what you'll see:

Content Level	**Icon**
Basic management and organizational behavior concepts	
Advanced management and organizational behavior concepts	
Important issues that should be addressed to bring modern management and organizational behavior concepts to an organization (and review and discussion questions)	

Second, important management terms in **bold** print and are defined at their first use. Some less important terms are included.

Third, each chapter begins with a list of the reader's expectations from the material ("After reading this chapter you will be able to ...."), and ends with a list of questions to consider for your organization. In other words, this is a hands-on book that you can use to improve your management practices and not just to earn a grade in a college course.

Fourth, we write with a U.S. perspective although the book is intended for anyone seeking this information. As the result, we praise and fault U.S. companies, we note U.S. government agencies, and refer to U.S. law. However, we reference senior managers - see, for example, Appendix A - and companies in other countries, many which parallel U.S. experience. The various individuals were selected to represent good and bad practice in managing business organizations. Readers should also consider reviewing biographies of leading public figures, and some references are provided in footnotes.

Fifth, Chapters 11 and 12 address current problems faced by managers but not fully addressed in management texts. Chapter 11 discusses the multiple issues of interpersonal dynamics, a relatively new sub-field of organizational behavior. Chapter 12 reviews management in a time of change.

Sixth, management and OB cases are included in Appendix B. The issues raised are based on actual company experiences and require the application of certain of the concepts developed in this book. Suggested solutions are available for your instructor through our website (www.fasttracktextbooks.com).

The term "company", "organization" and "business" (or their plural forms) are meant to be used interchangeably throughout. Any management concept applying to a for-profit is equally relevant for a not-for-profit organization. Many examples of companies and other organizations are presented to illustrate specific points being discussed in the text.

The reader should not infer any positive or negative connotation for a company under its current management. For example, the Disney Company is favorably mentioned at various places, yet Disney has made serious mistakes, including the planning and execution of EuroDisney (Disneyland Paris) and quite possibly, the hiring of Michael Eisner as it chairman. (The current chairman is Robert Igor.) However, Disney has attempted to correct and learn from past mistakes as have all successful organizations.

Thanks to Fast-Track Textbooks, particularly my colleague Ward Thrasher; to my University of Bridgeport colleagues; and to the staff at Sagner / Marks.

James Sagner
New York City
January 2013

CHAPTER 1

The Changing Environment for Management

After reading this chapter, you will be able to:

- Understand the concept of management
- Appreciate what managers do and why it is important
- Consider the role of management in a global environment
- Be aware of the basic management functions of planning, decision-making, organizing, leadership and controlling

Do Companies Understand the Critical Nature of Management?

Before attempting to define and explain the topic of management, let's consider the plight of one of the largest manufacturing companies in the world. In his former life as a banker, the author called on General Motors (GM) in the 1980s and early 1990s to discuss credit and various financial issues. Conversations and meetings were always pleasant and dignified, but it was clear that the company – at that time the first or second largest in the world – was out of touch with evolving customer demands, modern theories of business practice and the inevitable change to a mixed demographic of management, staff and automobile buyers.

Every meeting followed the same pattern: five to as many as fifteen senior managers would be present, all white, all male and all politely listening and then refusing to consider any of the ideas suggested by the bank's team. Even when the practices and successes of companies in similar industries was explained and demonstrated, the GM executives shook their heads "no".[1] On returning from GM (in Detroit) to Chicago, the question from my management usually related to how the company appeared to be doing (as we were a significant part of their very extensive banking relationship). Inevitably my answer was that GM was out of touch with their customers, stuck in out, out-of-date ideas, and probably likely to fail within a decade.

While my timing was wrong (GM was insolvent by 2009 and then rescued by the U.S. government),[2] the inevitability of the decline was clear. In 1954, GM sold 54% of the vehicles sold in the U.S.; by 2010, that market share had fallen to 17½%. In 2007 alone, GM lost nearly $40 billion! A great company and the city of Detroit (and neighboring towns) were nearly destroyed, yet it was not until the Ford Motor Company surpassed GM in sales (in 2010) that a complete change in the structure and mix of senior management began.

Lessons Learned and Lessons Ignored

Management is directly responsible for an organization's success or failure. In the case of GM, the lessons disregarded included ignoring customer complaints about quality (American vehicles were manufactured to begin to deteriorate and require replacement by about the fourth year of ownership); mileage concerns as gasoline prices rose steadily higher beginning in the 1970s; innovation (computer technology originated with Japanese automobiles); size, particularly for urban driving and parking; safety (read Ralph Nader's *Unsafe at any Speed*, 1965, his account of the danger of the GM Corvair); and price (Germany's Volkswagen could be bought for less than $2,000 in the late 1960s). Furthermore, only the American male bought cars – if you review GM's advertising from that period.[3]

---

1 The author was an officer of the First National Bank of Chicago (now part of J.P. Morgan Chase), the largest bank in the Midwest. No confidential client information was ever disclosed.
2 On June 8, 2009, GM filed for protection under Chapter 11 of the bankruptcy laws.
3 There have been several good accounts of the recent period of GM and the American automobile industry. See, for example, R. Carter, *What Really Happened to General Motors (2011), and* B.Vlasic, *Once Upon a Car:The Fall and Resurrection of America's Big Three Auto Makers--GM, Ford, and Chrysler* (2011).

Lessons learned are what this textbook addresses. We will look at the tasks of management, the creation of a corporate culture, how subordinates respond to various directions and stimuli, and a large variety of critical factors seemingly ignored by GM. We'll consider the role of competitors, the government, employees, and the most important constituency[4] of all, the customer. We'll review managing in midsized and smaller companies, noting that the biggest organizations can delay implementing good management practice for long periods – think GM's decades of mistakes – while smaller businesses can disappear overnight because of a single mistake. And we'll try to answer our question that opened this section: do companies understand the critical nature of management?

What is Management?

While there is no single, universally accepted definition of management, it is generally thought that **management** coordinates and directs the activities of employees and members of other constituent groups to accomplish the organization's goals efficiently and effectively. The work of management cuts across the lives of many participants, and can bring enormous wealth and prosperity to an area and an entire country, as GM did in the years from its founding to about 1960, or decline and unemployment as that same area experienced beginning with loss of market share and profitability.

Because companies compete globally and rarely control the industry in which they operate, management must be efficient and effective in its use of scarce resources.[5] **Efficiency** means deriving the highest degree of output of goods and services from the fewest units of input. There are various techniques used by management to accomplish this objective. For example, in manufacturing, plant managers may control inventory quantities by economic order quan-

---

4 In business, the term "constituent" refers to a group affiliated with and directly affected by the activities and results of a company or other organization. As an example, a corporation like GM will have various constituencies dependent on its success, including vendors, employees, union (the United Auto Workers), the government, citizens and stock- and bondholders, as well as all of the families supported by members of those groups.

5 Economists refer to these resources as "factors of production" and include land, labor, capital and entrepreneurship.

tity (EOQ). In finance, decisions are made on the investment of funds (money) using such capital budgeting procedures as net present value or internal rate of return. In marketing, the design of a salesperson's optimal (best) customer route may involve an operations research procedure like linear programming. The choice of advertising media (broadcast, telecast or publications) may be through a media planning model.

Effectiveness is concerned with the accomplishment of an organization's goals. For example, do we make an environmentally friendly automobile that is low on fuel consumption and is safe to drive? The measurement of effectiveness has often been accomplished through reference to the company's mission, which translates into goals, and then finally into a management-by-objectives (MBO) system.

Mission Statements

A **mission statement** is an announcement to the stakeholders[6] of the broad purpose and intentions of a company. The chapter began with a comment on General Motors. Here is their mission statement:

GM is a multinational corporation engaged in socially responsible operations, worldwide. It is dedicated to provide products and services of such quality that our customers will receive superior value while our employees and business partners will share in our success and our stockholders will receive a sustained superior return on their investment.[7]

The reader could rightly wonder what this contributes to our understanding of the business of GM, its strategic plans or organizational objectives. The statement could apply to any organization providing any kind of product or service.

Three more thoughtful mission statements follow:

- McDonald's vision is to be the world's best quick service restaurant experience. Being the best means providing outstanding quality, service, cleanliness, and value, so that we make every customer in every restaurant smile.[8]

6 "Stakeholders" are discussed later in Chapter 1 and are revisited in Chapters 8 and 12.

7 See www.slideshare.net/hasilzaheer/gm-presentation3-presentation, slide 5 (mission statement)

8 :"One World, One Burger-McDonald's," PowerPoint presentation October 28, 2007. at www.slideshare.net/guest47c65d/mcdonalds.

- Google's mission is to organize the world's information and make it universally accessible and useful.[9]
- The Walt Disney Company's objective is to be one of the world's leading producers and providers of entertainment and information, using its portfolio of brands to differentiate its content, services and consumer products. [10]

These statements briefly describe each business and how the company expects to be an industry leader.

Goals and Objectives

Management will work from this "mission" to develop **goals** which are specific statements on how the mission will be accomplished. Possible goal topics could include profitability (often defined as return-on-equity results), sales, new product development, maintaining the company's credit rating, energy conservation, actions in diversity hiring and promotion, world-class manufacturing, and various other initiatives. Typically, the goals are full statements, such as "implement world-class manufacturing technologies in our North American operations" or "develop meaningful programs to conserve energy use in our production facilities". Companies usually focus on those several goals that are particularly important in accomplishing the coming years' strategies, encompassing any aspect of its operations.

Objectives are specific expectations for a company or a significant business segment. In developing these objectives, the two most important factors are measurement using specific quantities, and a stretch or an expansion from normal results. For example, an objective could be "to increase sales by 15,000 units or 20%" or "to have 60% of the management group attend a seminar on and be certified in diversity management". Both of these statements contain quantifiable targets and may be considerably greater than normal results. The stretch element is important to focus efforts on those objectives that are important to support the success and growth of the business.

---

9 Statement on the company website at www.google.com/about/company (2011).
10 Statement on the company website at thewaltdisneycompany.com/investors (2012).

What is Management-by-Objectives?

Management-by-objectives (MBOs) is a managerial technique through which specific divisions or units of a company are assigned their share of the company's objectives, which are then translated into specific assignments for each senior manager.[11] The managers in turn assign the MBOs to each of their subordinates, resulting in a specific expectation for each person to accomplish his or her portion of the total objective.

An Application of MBOs

Here's an example of an MBO application. A company has an objective of increasing sales by 15,000 units. This may seem overwhelming, but assigning an incremental 3,000 to each of five divisions may be attainable. And then having each salesperson accept some portion of that objective, such as an additional 300 units (if there are 10 persons with sales responsibility) may make the objective quite reasonable. Once accepted, the salespeople now have an agreement with their manager.

If the extra units are sold during the contract period, normally one year, that constitutes "acceptable" performance for that MBO. Of course, there are several MBOs for each employee: support for product development, furtherance of a graduate degree or certification, assistance in training new employees, a quality performance objective and other business activities. Each activity is attained, surpassed or not met, and each receives a rating ranging from superior to failing. (Many organizations use a numerical ranking scale rather than a descriptive grade.) The totality of the effort of the employee is an objective evaluation of performance and the basis for promotion, reassignment or remedial work.

The entire process should not be mechanically used as too many companies have done. There are numerous situations where MBOs have become an imperative to an organization's culture and are mindlessly applied. Some of the flaws of MBOs are noted in Figure 1-1.

---

11 Peter Drucker is widely credited with popularizing the MBO process in his landmark book, P.F. Drucker, *The Practice of Management* (1954).

Figure 1-1: Problems in the Use of Goals/Objectives/MBOs

Relevance of the Goals, Objectives and MBOs. Achievement of these company purposes can become an end in itself, without regard to changing business conditions and organizational priorities. Thirty sales calls may not be enough if they are not bringing in new business, and they may be unnecessary if several major contracts have already been signed. The author participated in bank sales visits ("calls") when a second, third or fourth bank representative attended but did not participate. The purpose of these extra attendees was to establish a call for that day to be counted against the MBO quota.

Quantity Not Quality. The objectives and MBOs measure quantity, but do not measure the quality of performance. For example, a sales call can be perfunctory, five minutes long, without any real exchange of information, and made merely to count toward the MBO. Or it can be carefully planned, researched and developed, with materials, a script, "leave-behinds" (such as a brochure) and follow-up (such as a "thank-you" letter). Should these calls be counted as equivalent?

Validity of Objectives. Who knows if a set of MBOs is the right set of objectives, or if some non-quantifiable objective is more important to the success of the organization? A valid activity may be to do a better job managing people through work interaction, counseling, and the advocacy of training. Yet none of these are easily measured, unless one counts the number of contacts or the number of minutes devoted to being a better manager.

Change in Goals/Objectives/MBOs. During the course of a year, downsizing, reassignments, and new business initiatives may change management's allocation of resources. Many employees have had the experience of working diligently toward fulfillment of their MBOs, only to be asked to take on projects for which there is no MBO criterion. In today's chaotic business environment, yesterday's priorities can quickly become irrelevant to the company's success. What happens at the end of the year when the MBO goal is not met but there has been progress on the new and quite important project?

Irrelevance of Aggregated MBO Results. MBOs only work in situations when an employee has fairly close control over his or her accomplishments or failures. When MBOs are applied to managers responsible for groups of employees, the aggregation of results from these individuals makes it difficult to equitably attribute goal accomplishment to those managers. He or she may claim successes for the work actually done by others, and may avoid responsibility for failure using the same strategy.

Soft MBO Targets. An employee may soften his or her objectives to assure success in meeting or exceeding the MBO expectations. Unless the manager demands stretch MBOs, the process is subverted so that even mediocre performance may be rewarded. One trick from banking days was to postpone reporting a result until the next period if the banker had met/exceeded the MBO for the current period.

Source: Based on and revised from J. Sagner, *Cashflow Reengineering*, AMACOM, 1997, pages 29-30.

The mission/goal/objective/MBO process is a commonly accepted procedure to quantify and establish expectations for business organizations: measurements of efficiency to operate the business, and measurements of effectiveness to manage the employees. This suggests that we spend much of our time in comparing actual results to standards; however, there are other critical management functions, which are addressed in the following section.

What are the Functions of Management?

Managers perform several functions as they perform their daily activities of attempting to be efficient and effective in utilizing company resources. We will be devoting chapters of this book to the details of each of these activities, and the cases in Appendix B address each topic. The functions of management are briefly reviewed in this section; see Figure 1-2.

Planning

The activities of **planning** involve setting goals, developing strategies to achieve goals that have been accepted by the company, and choosing methods to coordinate and integrate the use of company resources. Essential components of planning include problem identification, evaluating relevant factors in solving the problem, and the process of decision-making including specific techniques used by 21st century managers.

Decision-Making

An important activity of management is **decision-making**, which uses knowledge and analysis to select a course of action among various alternative scenarios. Decisions require the specification of the critical problem, that issue that must be solved before any other activity can be considered. Finding that problem, developing possible solutions and choosing a course of action requires an integrative view of the organization's mission and current position.

Organizing

The process of **organizing** requires that managers structure work so that the company's goals can be accomplished. The manager must decide what must be done, what resources are required, how the resources will be assigned to the tasks, which reports will summarize the actions taken, and other elements of getting the job completed. In order to be efficient and effective, the appropriate organizational structure must be selected, a significant decision point in the life of a company. Furthermore, the individuals and teams or groups who work in the company must be managed to provide motivation and adequate compensation.

Directing

Directing (or leading) involves accomplishing work through the managers and employees of a company. This activity requires motivation, resolving conflicts, selecting communications channels, and developing equitable procedures to resolve employee performance issues. Organizational behavior studies (see Chapter 2) are particularly useful in understanding worker attitudes and in developing insights to personality, so as to create learning environments and instill leadership traits to extend the reach of the business into new markets at home and globally.

Controlling

Many managers report that much of their energy is expended on control, which determines if a business is producing results consistent with plans. **Controlling** involves monitoring and evaluating performance, and taking any necessary corrective actions to revise plans or to bring additional resources to bear to accomplish the plan. The controlling of work has become largely quantitative, with financial and statistical procedures important components of the manager's job. However, the writing of memos and the reporting to senior executives on the progress of a planned activity are inevitable elements in any manager's day.

Figure 1-2: The Five Management Functions

Planning	Decision-Making	Organizing	Directing	Controlling	RESULT IN
Set goals, establish strategies, develop plans	Determine critical factor in problem, analyze alternatives, make decision	Resolve needs to achieve goals, how strategies will be done, who will do these tasks	Motivate, lead and act to complete tasks through employees	Monitor activities to determine that plans are accomplished, and make necessary adjustments	Accomplishing the Organization's Mission and Goals

What are the Skill Requirements of Supervisors and Middle Managers?

Anyone who wants to work in a business or not-for-profit organization probably aspires to be a manager. Many of us who have work experience have probably thought at one time or another that we could do a better job than the person who has the "manager" title. The skills necessary to be in that position will vary by management level in an organization.

First-Line Managers

First-line (supervisory) managers typically are responsible for employees who have some production objective, as broadly defined. This means that these workers are required to do something to make the company accomplish its objectives, and can range from selling to manufacturing to accounting to information technology to just about any activity that one can imagine. A Disney worker is expected to make guests happy by serving food, performing in a show, cleaning restrooms, answering questions or just about anything that occurs at an amusement park.

The first-line manager of these workers primarily needs **technical skills**, which are job-specific techniques to accomplish the tasks. The manager can coach and counsel the worker to do a job in the best (and usually company-mandated) manner, so that the food is served quickly and according to accepted standards of hygiene, or so that the actor playing Mickey Mouse has the proper enthusiasm and gusto in greeting children and posing for pictures. One way to be a good first-line manager is to have previously worked in food service or as a Disney character.

First-line managers should have human relations skills (described below) as a secondary competence. However, most large companies have fairly rigid sets of requirements for their workers and do not expect supervisors to provide much human resource assistance. Smaller companies may be more flexible and encourage first-line managers to provide both technical and human resource skills.

Mid-Level (Middle) Manager

The **mid-level (middle) manager**, who has responsibility for several first-line managers, certainly needs technical skills, but also must possess human resources and conceptual skills. **Human resources skills** involves the ability to direct individual and groups toward assigned objectives for his or her business unit. It is at this level of management that there is no manual or pre-defined method of accomplishing objectives. Instead, the manager must work through his first-line managers as in creating an event for corporate attendees at a convention held at Disney, or to provide appropriate support services when Disney has a press event to highlight a new ride or other attraction.

Conceptual skills require thinking through difficult, often new situations. The manager must be able to envision the company (or at least his or her part of the company) as an entirety, to bring to bear all of the necessary talents to stage the event for corporate attendees or the press event. In some ways, it is more difficult to be a mid-level manager than a senior manager or executive, because that person must have some competency in all three skill sets. For this reason, many companies require mid-level managers to regularly attend training sessions, while encouraging the pursuit of college and graduate degrees. Close records are maintained of their successes (and failures).

What are the Skill Requirements of Senior Managers?

Senior managers – the leaders of companies – need fewer technical and significantly greater conceptual skills than mid-level managers. Although there have senior managers with excellent technical skills such as Walt Disney and Bill Gates (Microsoft), the generation after the inventor typically is a conceptual and human resources manager. Examples include former chairman Louis Gerstner of IBM who came from RJR Nabisco (a food company) and American Express; and Alan Mulally, president of Ford Motor whose career had been spent with the Boeing Company (aircraft) although his engineering background has been an important asset. The exception to this trend is a specialized industry like insurance and banking where most senior managers came up through the middle manager ranks. Jack Welch of General Electric (profiled in Appendix A) is the exceptional manager who demonstrated conceptual and human resources skills as a senior manager.

The variation in skill sets required by various management levels is presented in Figure 1-3. The first-level manager needs very different skills from the senior manager, which may explain why so few supervisors ever become chief executive officers. The reader of this text may wonder why senior managers typically receive compensation far in excess of first-level and mid-level managers. These higher salaries are primarily justified because the senior manager is responsible for the future of the company based on their insight and conceptual skills. When they are successful, as with Disney, innovations can be developed that astonish the world. When they fail, as with Enron, the company fails and employees find themselves unemployed and stockholder value destroyed.

Figure 1-3: Manager Skills Sets (by primary and secondary skills required)

Primary Skills	Conceptual			Human Resources	Technical
Secondary Skills	Analytical			Technical	Human Resources
	Planning	Decision-Making	Organizing	Directing	Controlling
1st-Level				✔	✔
Mid-Level	✔	✔	✔	✔	✔
Senior Level	✔	✔	✔		

Concerns of Senior Managers

The senior manager no longer has only conceptual skills to consider in managing the modern corporation. Managing an organization is not simple and requires enormous energy, knowledge and even inspiration. Previously successful managers may fail in new assignments; consider Robert Nardelli at

Home Depot.[12] Some of the issues that senior managers encounter are briefly noted below and considered in depth in Chapter 12.

- Technology. How do we deal with robotization and automation, mass customization, information technologies including mobile computing, contacts from and demands by customers for immediate responses including pricing, and a variety of other technological applications that impact a company's existence?
- Ethics and Law. World governments have passed laws and regulations that seriously constrain the freedom of companies to utilize their resources.
- Global Competition. The development of the industrial age may have started in the West, but competitors now exist in nearly part of the globe. The U.S. automobile industry in general and General Motors with which we started this chapter may have only been the first to lose market share in competition with international companies.
- Security Threats. There are various security threats that can attack an organization to destroy, steal and eavesdrop on confidential information. We discuss some of these situations in Chapters 9 (on controlling) and in 12 (on other security threats).
- Sustainability and Stakeholder Expectations. **Sustainability** is the ability of a business to accomplish its mission and goals while being socially, environmentally and socially responsible. The **stakeholders** of a company include all of the constituencies that may be affected by corporate decisions, including employees, stock- and bondholders, vendors, vendors, customers, the public and government.

---

12 Nardelli became the chief executive officer of Home Depot in 2000, despite having no retail experience. He refocused the management structure of the company and replaced its entrepreneurial culture. He changed the decentralized management structure, by eliminating and consolidating division executives. His blunt, critical and autocratic management style angered employees and the public. Nardelli was criticized for cutting back on knowledgeable full-time employees replacing them with part-time help with little relevant experience, hurting customer service. The board of directors ousted him in 2007.

What are the Issues You Should Address?

In considering your organization's management activities, here are some issues to review.

- Are we using efficient and effective techniques to manage our company's resources? Or, are we continuing past practices that are no longer relevant to our needs or that do not meet competitive pressures?
- Do we have a company mission statement? Is that statement still relevant or have environmental factors changed so that a revised mission may be necessary?
- Has the company established goals and objectives? Are they reflective of the mission or are they merely being used to satisfy a company requirement? Are they stretch but realistic, or are they so unlikely of success as to cause employees to lose their motivation?
- Have we established MBOs for employees that can measured, are reasonable and allow for flexibility as company requirements change during the year? Are the MBOs stretch objectives or too easy to attain?
- Are we planning, organizing, directing and controlling so that goals and objectives are properly set, strategies are thoughtfully developed and decisions made based on modern management principles?
- Are our senior managers concerned about the multitude of issues now confronting business?

Discussion and Review Questions

1. How do managers contribute value to their organizations?
2. Could organizations effectively and efficiently function without managers to provide the various activities associated with management?
3. What is efficiency? What is effectiveness?
4. Why do organizations publish mission statements, and how do they assist in managing?

5. What is a management goal? An objective? What does it mean to "manage by objectives" (MBOs)?

6. Are there any problems in using MBOs? If there are problems, why are MBOs used?

7. What are the specific functions of management and how do they differ?

8. How do the responsibilities of first-line, middle and senior managers vary?

CHAPTER 2

The Behavior Of Individuals In Organizations

After reading this chapter, you will be able to:

- Understand the meaning and current situation of organizational behavior
- Appreciate influences on the behavior of the individual
- Consider theories of individual motivation
- Be aware of how individuals make decisions, and how the organization can negatively constrain those actions

What is Organizational Behavior?

Organizational behavior (OB) is the analysis of the attitudes and behaviors of people as they participate in the mission and goals of an organization. Implicit in this activity is the concept of a systematic study, that is, observations of individuals and groups under controlled conditions and interpreted to determine cause and effect. Behavior is critical to understanding the contribution made to a company by humans. Other resources ("factors of production" in economic language) are largely known by and subject to the direction of managers.

For example, materials used in a manufacturing process do not differ sig-nificantly in their physical configuration. The single greatest variable is cost, which can be partially controlled through hedging[13] or a long-term pricing arrangement with vendors. People vary continuously, and can be tardy or absent from work, can be high or low energy from day-to-day, can be productive or accomplish little, can change jobs with little warning, and can manipulate others or be manipulated to positions contrary to the best interests of the company.

The Recent Decline in OB

Until the global economic recession that began in 2008, the most significant problem businesses faced was managing people. A listing of these concerns might have included:

- motivation
- communication
- compensation
- conflicts
- resistance to change
- organizational restructuring

The past five years have seen a significant decline in the discussion of the concerns noted – or others – as employees worry about keeping their jobs, the effects of outsourcing and offshoring (to be discussed in Chapter 7), personal bankruptcy, the loss of savings in a retirement plan and other concerns.[14] This has led to various societal problems including alcoholism and other addictions, family problems, interpersonal conflicts and even suicide. OB problems are no longer a major concern but are likely lying in wait for the time when prosperity returns.

---

13 **Hedges** are transactions that reduce exposure to risks by taking positions opposite to the initial positions. For example, a farmer could hedge his investment in a corn crop by selling the corn at a specified price for delivery at a future date. The transaction would occur on an organized commodities exchange, such as the Chicago Board of Trade. The cost of the hedge would be the commission to a dealer for the sale of the commodity, and the farmer would not participate in any increase should there a rise in the price of corn.

14 Indeed, one leading author on OB wrote a section in the first chapter of his textbook on "Declining Employee Loyalty". It is difficult today to find a manager who worries about the problem. S.P. Robbins, *Essentials of Organizational Behavior,* Pearson Prentice Hall, 8th ed., 2005, page 14.

What Influences Behavior of the Individual?

The values (or value system) of the individual are the essential qualities that a person brings to a work environment or any other important aspect of his or her life, including friendships, school, religion, marriage or relationships, and leisure. These values are often derived from childhood lessons and experiences ("nurture") but may also reflect inherited traits ("nature"). Some values may be acquired after childhood such as discipline and loyalty, as in military service; responsibility, as with one's family; and hard work, as in an employment situation.

Global Cultural Values

The pioneering work on values across cultures was done by Geert Hofstede in the 1970s.[15] While his findings are arguably no longer current, he was the first OB researcher to determine that values are not consistent globally. In fact, the leading OB researchers until that time were fairly consistently examining North Americans, mostly U.S. We will examine several of their theories in the next section. Hofstede organized his values into four important categories:[16]

- Power distance: the unequal distribution of power in organizations, ranging from relatively equal to unequal
- Individualism vs. collectivism: collectivism represents low individualism, which is the concept of the importance of the individual
- Achievement vs. nurturing: achievement effectively relates to money and materialism, while nurturing concerns the value of relationships and the feelings of others
- Uncertainty avoidance: the preference for structure or an absence of structure, with the latter situation often leading to anxiety

15 G. Hofstede, *Culture's Consequence: International Differences in Work Related Values*, Sage, 1980; G. Hofstede, *Cultures and Organizations*, McGraw-Hill, 1991. It should be noted that all of the observations were based on interviews with 115,000 IBM employees in 40 countries, and cannot be considered as either current or representative of the global workforce.
16 Hofstede actually notes a fifth value: long-term vs. short-term in orientation, which has largely been ignored by management researchers.

The results are specific by nationality and are scored by measurements from 0 to 100. Without showing all of these metrics, it is perhaps sufficient to report that certain countries scored low on power distance (e.g., the U.S. and Australia) but high in Arab countries; Asian countries were particularly collective in values; high achieving countries can be observed by their economic growth (e.g., Germany); and certain countries (e.g., Japan, Mexico and South Korea) score high on uncertainty avoidance.. Important changes to the global economy have occurred since Hofstede's research, including the fall of communism, the globalization of capitalism and the rise of China as a world power. Subsequent research has extended rather than replacing these findings.[17]

Employee Satisfaction

Is financial compensation the most likely response that the reader has when deciding what satisfies employees? The evidence indicates that work challenges, rewards that are fairly distributed, and supportive organizations are the important factors.

- Work Challenges. Employees appreciate the opportunity to address a task or a problem, and to apply their mental skills and experiences to develop solutions. This is a primary reason that the early management theorists fell out of favor. For example, Frederick W. Taylor developed scientific management to find the "one best way" for a worker to do a job repetitively, using the precise tool, motions and rests to maximize output. See Figure 2-1 for further information on this and other "classical approaches" to worker efficiency, that largely eliminate the creativity of a job and results in a workday of tedium. Endlessly repeating relatively menial tasks creates boredom, frustration and negative attitudes toward the employer.

- Equitable Rewards. While compensation is important, research indicates that a more important factor is equitable pay among workers, consistent with expectations, and not subject to undue manipulation for favored employees. Many companies recognize this situation, have

17 See, for example, R. House, M. Javidan and P. Dorfman, "Project GLOBE: An Introduction," *Applied Psychology*, October 2001, pages 489-505, describing national values and culture from 62 countries.

developed compensation systems that attempt to measure job requirements and employee efforts, and objectively allocate financial rewards
and promotions.

- Supportive Organizations. Much of OB focuses on the work group and
on the organization; see Chapters 3 and 4. Employees expect to derive
more from work than pay; they want contact with others, the opportunity for social interaction, and the sense that one's productivity is the
result of collaboration with intelligent, motivated co-workers.

Figure 2-1: Classical Management Approaches to Worker Efficiency

---

Scientific Management: Based on his profession as a mechanical
engineer, Frederick W. Taylor developed a precise approach to
worker efficiency, using tools, work motions and rests to maximize
output. His theories were implemented at steel mills in PA, focusing
on the specific principles of a pre-determined work method, worker
selection and training, and the allocation of work tasks between
managers and employees. Taylor's efforts consistently resulted in
a doubling or more of output, and the increased productivity was
shared with workers through higher wages.[18]

Time and Motion Studies: Frank and Lillian Gilbreth studied
and extended Taylor's work to eliminate tools and bodily motions
that were inefficient. Among their contributions were a device that
recorded these motions (the microchronometer) and a classification
of hand motions (called therbligs).[19]

Administrative Theory: Henri Fayol identified the essential
managerial functions: planning, organizing, commanding,
coordinating and controlling. He developed the principles of
management that have been used for a century in organizations,

---

18 F. W. Taylor, *Principles of Scientific Management*, Harper, 1911. A recent analysis of Taylor's
work can be found in R. Kanigel, *The One Best Way: Frederick Winslow Taylor and the Enigma of
Efficiency*, Viking, 1997.
19 F.B. Gilbreth, *Motion Study*, Van Nostrand, 1911, and F.B. and L.M. Gilbreth, *Fatigue Study*,
Sturgis and Walton, 1916.

including division of work, unity of command, authority from top management to workers (the Scalar principal) and various others.[20]

Bureaucracy: Max Weber was a German sociologist who developed a theory of authority structures in organizations which he called a bureaucracy. This form of organizing required certain of Fayol's principles, with the resulting structure capable of being displayed on an organization chart; see the discussion in Chapter 7.[21]

What is Motivation?

Motivation is having a desire or being willing to take an action that satisfies an individual need. A **need** is a deficiency in our existence, either physiological (of the body) or psychological (of the mind), and in some cases with joint effect. As an example of the latter situation, we have a physiological need to exercise to overcome inertia and a lack of movement of our body, but we also derive psychological (mental or emotional) pleasure from participating in a sport. These needs are satisfied for a relatively brief period; with the need for food, three meals a day are required for most people. Working in the decades after World War Two, various researchers have attempted to use these relationships to explain individual behavior in a work environment; we note the more well known of these theories.

---

20 H. Fayol, *Industrial and General Administration*, Dunod (Paris), 1916. We discuss certain of these principles of management in Chapter 7.

21 M. Weber, *The Theory of Social and Economic Organizations*, in translation (by A.M. Henderson and T. Parsons) from the German, Free Press, 1947.

Maslow's Hierarchy of Needs

The hierarchy of needs concept suggests that people prioritize their needs, and that when a need becomes substantially satisfied, the next need in the ranking becomes the focus of that person.[22] The essential focus of Abraham Maslow's work is that motivation does not work for satisfied needs which, in fulfillment order, are:

- Physiological needs: hunger, thirst, shelter, sex, other bodily needs
- Safety needs: protection and security against physical and psychological harm
- Social needs: affection, acceptance, interpersonal contact, acceptance, friendship
- Esteem needs: self-respect, status, recognition, attention
- Self-actualization needs: becoming the person that one is capable of being, personal growth, self-fulfillment

The lower order needs of physiology and safety are met by external actions of others, including employers, government and family, while higher order needs must be satisfied by the efforts of the person.

The popularity of the Maslow hierarchy has not been supported by objective research on the concept, as there is little evidence that need structures are organized as proposed or that satisfaction of a need leads to a focus on the next higher need. Despite these findings, employers have attempted (at least in the past) to provide opportunities for higher order need fulfillment through social interaction in the workplace, recognition, and personal and professional development.

McGregor's Theory X and Theory Y

Theories X and Y view the process by which managers view employees as either negative (X) or positive (Y).[23] Theory X assumptions about employees include:

---

22 A. Maslow, *Motivation and Personality*, Harper & Row, 1954.
23 D. McGregor, *The Human Side of Enterprise*, McGraw-Hill, 1960.

- A dislike for work and attempt to avoid it
- The requirement to be coerced, threatened and controlled to achieve goals
- The need to be directed and forced to face responsibilities
- Security as the highest priority with only slight personal or professional ambition

Theory Y assumptions about employees include:

- Seeing work as natural like rest or leisure
- Self-directed if committed to work objectives
- Accepting and even seeking of responsibility
- Able to make decisions and develop innovative solutions to problems

Douglas McGregor concluded that employees are basically Theory Y and can be motivated by work challenges and participation in decision-making. As with Maslow, there is no evidence that there is any validity to these concepts.

Herzberg's Hygiene Factors

Frederick Herzberg's hygiene theory assumes that workers cannot be positively motivated by factors like pay, their manager, company policies or working conditions. However, they can be unsatisfied ("dissatisfied" in Herzberg's theory).[24] Positive motivators are the same as Maslow's self-esteem and self-actualization factors. The impact of this theory is that job "hygiene" factors are neutral in terms of motivation. Various methodological problems have been noted with regard to these findings although Herzberg has been credited with the movement toward job enrichment and greater worker responsibility for the structure of a work assignment.

---

24 F. Herzberg, B. Mausner and B. Snyderman, *The Motivation to Work*, Wiley, 1959.

McClelland's Theory of Needs

David McClelland's need theory proposes three motivations in working:

- Achievement (nAch)
- Power (nPow)
- Affiliation (nAff)

The nAch and nAff needs are similar to Maslow's findings. The nPow need or its equivalent was new to the results reported in post-War research, and reflects the desire to be influential and to control others.[25]

These motives are measured through psychological tests usually requiring the subject to write a brief story based on a picture he or she has been shown. A possible picture could be a family, with the resulting story that refers to how the a spouse and children influences or hinders the observer. The expectation is that unconscious motives will be discerned and scored based on the three needs (nAch, nPow and nAff).

There may be some validity to the testing procedure; for example, high nPow and low nAff people are likely to become successful managers. The two problems with the theory of needs are: 1.) the ease with which a subject can cheat by consulting various websites and other references on the testing procedure and likely scoring; and 2.) the totally subjective evaluation of the story that has been written by the subject (although McClelland does provide analytical guidelines).

---

25 D.C. McClelland, *The Achieving Society,* Van Nostrand Reinhold, 1961.

What are other Theories of Motivation?

There is no generally accepted theory of motivation that applies to managers and employees across global cultures. For selected motivational theories, see Figure 2-2.

Figure 2-2: Selected Motivational Theories

Alderfer's ERG theory. Clayton Alderfer, working from Maslow's hierarchy of needs, developed the ERG theory. His three groups of core needs are existence, relatedness, and growth. Existence is concerned with basic material requirements and includes the needs that Maslow considered to be physiological and safety needs. Relatedness is the desire we have for maintaining important interpersonal relationships, and aligns with Maslow's social need. Growth needs are an intrinsic desire for personal development, and include the intrinsic component from Maslow's esteem self-actualization hierarchy.

Self-determination theory (SDT). Developed by Edward Deci and Richard Ryan, self-determination theory focuses on intrinsic (internal) motivation in driving human behavior. Like Maslow's hierarchical theory, SDT suggests a natural tendency toward growth and development with requires active encouragement from the workplace. The primary encouragement of motivation is autonomy with constructive feedback.

Temporal Motivation Theory (TMT) organizes the primary aspects of several other major motivational theories into a single concept, simplifying the findings of motivation theory and allowing findings from one idea to be translated into terms of TMT.

Achievement Motivation is integrative assuming that motivation results from how components of personality are oriented towards performance. The theory includes dimensions that may be relevant to success at work but which are not usually regarded as being part of performance motivation.

Goal-Setting Theory is based on the concept that individuals drive to reach a clearly defined end, which may be a reward in itself. A goal's efficiency is affected by three features: proximity, difficulty and specificity. A goal should be capable of being accomplished, not too hard or too easy. Most people are not optimally motivated, as many want a challenge with a reasonable likelihood of success.

Job Characteristics Model (JCM) attempts to use job design to improve employee motivation based on five key job characteristics: Skill Variety, Task Identity (completion of a whole and identifiable piece of work versus a partial task), Task Significance, Autonomy (the degree of independence or freedom allowed to complete a job), and Task Feedback. JCM links these job factors to critical psychological states to attain desired personal and work outcomes.

Theory Z consists of Japanese and American philosophies and cultures. The Japanese focus is on a standardized structure with heavy emphasis on socialization of its members. The American focus retains a formal structure among members and the organization.

Cultural Limitations

The various motivational theories noted are primarily based on U.S. experience. It is unrealistic to apply a theory like Maslow's hierarchy of needs (or the others noted) to cultures that value leisure, family and social needs more highly than safety needs. For example, Latin American, Mediterranean and certain Asian cultures have a completely different set of needs priorities, and are not primarily motivated by individual rewards and promotional opportunities. The concept of organizational culture is so essential to this discussion that Chapter 3 is focused on that topic. As previously noted, the current economic climate has significantly reduced the fixation on how to best motivate employees.

How Do Individuals Make Decisions?

The previous section discussed individual behavior, with a general theme that such conduct varies by person and by culture. If we do not fully understand behavior in the workplace, do we at least know how managers and workers make decisions? When you study economics, you may observe that economic theory generally assumes that decisions are presumed to be rational, that is, the costs and benefits from a purchase or sale are weighed and thoughtfully acted upon.

Behavioral economists know that people do not act in this manner except for certain very significant buying decisions, such as a home, a computer or perhaps an automobile. More often, we tend to respond to such stimuli as advertising, brand appeal, and packaging; to the choices of peers; and to the real decision-maker in a household – ask any parent, and you'll be told that it is often the child who decides.

Bounded Rationality

Individuals behave in much the same manner in organizations, with most managers and employees content to find a solution that is acceptable and does not require too much investigation. Judgment is the usual method of proceeding rather than a careful statement of the problem, a review of all feasible solutions, and a rational decision based on a long-range vision of the mission and goals. In Herbert A. Simon's phrase, workers "satisfice", accepting solutions that are good enough without necessarily being optimal.[26] This behavior is necessary to cope with the complexities of life; for example, we simply could not shop all of the automobiles available for sale, every place to take a vacation, or each potential marriage partner!

---

26 H.A. Simon, *Administrative Behavior,* Free Press, 3rd ed., 1976.

In facing a multi-faceted problem, most people tend to use **bounded rationality**, that is, they reduce the situation to a simple two-dimensional model (perhaps on paper or at least in the mind). Once the problem is defined, criteria are established to bound or limit the decision to allow a solution to be chosen. Since you cannot shop every automobile, you set criteria regarding price, gasoline mileage, certain features and the convenient location of the dealer, allowing you to efficiently narrow and refine your search. For most people, car shopping is exhausting and time consuming, and so you will likely choose the satisficing choice, which is the first acceptable vehicle meeting your criteria.

Biases

Decisions are often influenced by biases or "rules of thumb" that may be gut feelings or intuition, or simply a desire to move beyond the conflict to an easier situation. The biases that may occur are as follows:

- Overconfidence. Individuals are frequently mistaken in matters of judgment because of relative certainty about an issue, particularly when the person's skill set is weak! More informed workers tend to not be overconfident in their knowledge, and will seek additional information before proceeding.
- Anchoring. Individuals may fixate on a set of assumptions and fail to include new data in their reasoning. Suppose you are conducting an employment interview and the candidate is on time, well dressed and has a firm handshake. This appearance tends to anchor the perception and subsequent information exchange could be irrelevant to the first positive impression made.
- Confirmation/Refutation. Individuals select which information to gather, often focusing on what is easily available and on whatever confirms our previous experience. As a corollary, new information that might change our mind tends to be refuted. When the author was a banker, he asked the treasurer of a large insurance company who their lead commercial bank was and why they choose to do business with that bank. The response was that Bank X had been their banker for 75 years, so why consider a change? The idea that there might be a better, cheaper or more efficient bank was refuted and outside of his thinking.

- Commitment. Individuals stay with decisions despite clear evidence that it is wrong, particularly when they may be held responsible for any failure. Lost causes should be abandoned, but they are often supported with additional time, money and other resources to prove that the original decision was correct.

We may not fully understand individual motives, but we do know that the decisions people make are subject to various biases that should be considered, analyzed and perhaps made subject to review. In a hiring decision or an employee review, are there biases present that could lead to the wrong choice or an unfair assessment? In a decision regarding a vendor, are there biases of anchoring (they have done good work for us in the past) or commitment (we contracted with this supplier to perform this work and "they will get it done!"). When preparing forecasts, does a commitment to an outcome interfere with objective analysis? Biases influence much of the work of an organization; the manager's responsibility is to review and try to neutralize such attitudes.

Constraints Imposed by or on the Organization

The organization may constrain manager decision-making by forcing actions that are reflective of the performance evaluation and reward system. This problem is endemic in large companies, where the senior level of managers do not receive factual information about activities perhaps two or three levels below their position level.

For example, customers are not buying certain products because of high prices, poor service, unsatisfactory service or other factors. The sales reports may disguise the actual problem if the marketing vice-president does not want to hear unpleasant news, does not travel to talk to customers or listen to salesmen, and prefers to stay in his or her office. In some industries, it can take many quarters of slow sales before the "critical problem" is uncovered. Dell Computer lost market share for years because of poor customer service, yet no one wanted to tell the founder and principal shareholder, Michael Dell.

A company may reward "yes-men" and repress those with different opinions or ideas. This can be fatal to an organization, as we discussed in Chapter 1 about General Motors. Another example is the disastrous 2002 Hewlett Packard (HP)-Compaq merger, when the CEO Carly Fiorina refused to listen to certain managers who strongly advised against diluting the strong HP reputation by combining with a company perceived to produce products of lower quality. During Fiorina's leadership, the stock market value of HP was halved and heavy job losses were incurred. The HP Board of Directors finally asked her to leave, and she resigned in February 2005.

Other constraints imposed by or on organizations include:

- Company regulations that force managers to follow certain rules and regulations regardless of market opportunities or the need to serve customers. Here's an example of bending the rules: The author recently traveled to Berlin and arrived at his hotel at 10 a.m. (local time). Of course, the sleeping room was not ready. Hotel reception graciously allowed a stay in an empty junior suite for a greatly discounted price as an accommodation (and to allow for some needed sleep!).
- Time constraints that artificially cause poor decisions and the reporting of those actions. As an example, companies that establish a closing date for sales contests may force salespeople to advance or delay the reporting of a sale occurs to improve their chances to win a particular prize. Assume April's prize is a weekend in Las Vegas, and May's prize is a new car – a rational salesperson would report everything that he or she could in May.
- Historical precedent often drives decisions about the next period. A budget nearly always begins with last period's numbers, rather than starting from a zero base (referred to as "zero-based budgeting"). For further material on this point, review the material on the organizational culture of company founders in Chapter 4.
- Regional constraints, particularly in global companies. As we discussed earlier in this chapter, cultures vary significantly by national origin, and these differences may interfere with a strategic view of a company's mission and how it can be accomplished.

What are the Issues You Should Address?

In considering the behavior of individuals in your organization, here are some issues to review.

- Does your organization continue to focus efforts on organizational behavior, particularly in attempting to influence how individual managers and workers perform?
- Is there an awareness of global variations in behavior and motivation, especially for global or multi-country companies?
- Do we utilize any of the classical approaches toward employee efficiency? Are these approaches relevant in our 21st century business organization?
- Are we aware of and use any of the theories of individual motivation? If so, are they being properly applied and can we determine if these theories have been successful in motivating our employees?
- Are we supportive of decision-making by individual managers and workers? Do we make any effort to extend and document the process and to neutralize biases that may lead to inferior decisions?

Discussion and Review Questions

1. Why is the study of organizational behavior relevant to our understanding of management?
2. What has been the experience since the beginning of the current recession (in 2008) in concerns for OB in companies and not-for-profits?
3. What are the important influences on the behavior of individuals?
4. How do cultural values vary across regions of the world and degree of economic development?
5. What are the various approaches that developed during the period of classical management theory?
6. What contributions have been made by the study of individual behavior and motivation?

7. How do individuals make decisions? Does the organization impose constraints on the individual that may lead to suboptimal results?

CHAPTER 3

Group And Team Behavior

After reading this chapter, you will be able to:

- Understand the relevance of group and team behavior to managing organizations
- Appreciate the importance of the Hawthorne studies in group theory
- Consider norms of behavior in groups and teams, and how positive and negative behaviors can be influenced
- Focus on attributes of group behavior
- Be aware of issues in managing and structuring teams

Why Are We Concerned About the Behavior of Groups?

OB theory has extensively studied the behavior of the group in business and not-for-profit organizations, largely because it has long been known that motivation is both individual and group-based. As we have noted, a person's value system partially defines how he or she acts, but so too do the groups to which that person belongs or to which membership is desired.

As children, we brought our value system to school, play or worship, and then we absorbed what our peers did and altered our value system to match their behavior. For example, if we cried or had a tantrum when angry or frustrated, we probably realized in these group interactions that tears and screaming were not a good way to make or keep friends. However, if some of the other children did something well outside of our value system, such as cursing or hitting, we likely rejected that group and found others who were more compatible. These alterations of values are an essential form of **socialization**, the ability to become an accepted member of a civilized world.

Work and Non-Work Groups

At work, the group that sets behavioral standards may be formal, as defined by the organization, with structure and tasks oriented to the mission and goals. An example of a formal group association is a department, division or business unit that is assigned specific tasks critical to the mission of the organization. More often, the group is informal, without an organizational mandate but necessary to accomplish work and provide socialization. The informal group often meets the needs of the individual that are not a "formal" part of work, such as eating lunch, carpooling, organizing a football pool, and meeting for a beer after work.

Individuals are members of various groups, including those at work, school, recreation or leisure, and a house of worship. In some groups we are followers; in others we may be organizers and leaders. And we certainly experience conflict in these roles: we may not be able to drive at our assigned time to children's soccer practice if we have to meet with our work colleagues to discuss a problem. The resolution of these conflicts is an essential element in managing our lives and progressing toward our individual goals.

The group survives because it establishes standards or norms of behavior. As children, we found out that we had to take turns, to not be too much of a "teacher's pet", to learn the rules of games and to follow the media (television, pop singers, etc.) that were important to others. As workers, we follow standards on how much work is to be accomplished, how to communicate with others, how to get assistance with difficult tasks, how to relate to our manager, and how to conform to group standards. The basis of our modern understanding of work group behavior is the Hawthorne studies, discussed next.

What Caused the Focus on Group Behavior?

The early management theorists like Taylor, Gilbreth and Fayol (discussed in Chapter 2) were entirely focused on efficiency and cost effectiveness. After these engineers made their contributions, several other management analysts came to believe that people were an important asset in organizations and not merely extensions of tools and production processes. The most important of these "people" advocates are noted in Figure 3-1.

Figure 3-1: Advocates of Behavior in the Success of Organizations

Early **social workers**, including Robert Owen, Jacob Riis, Jane Addams and others, who argued for the improvement of the quality of life and well being of people through a variety of helping interventions. Some of these social workers were advocates for improved living *and* working conditions, while others focused on family sanitation, health, nutrition, problems of alcoholism and gambling, literacy and recreation

Industrial psychologists such as Hugo Munsterberg, who attempted to scientifically study people at work and advocated psychological testing, the use of learning theory, and the study of worker motivation

Group behavior advocates, such as Mary Parker Follett, who recognized the influence of the group on the behavior of individuals in work situations

Social organization advocates, such as Chester Barnard (an actual large company manager), who suggested that companies were social systems and that the manager's job was to communicate and stimulate employees

The Hawthorne Studies

The Hawthorne studies were conducted at the Western Electric Company (the manufacturing division of AT&T, at that time the telephone monopoly), in Cicero IL, beginning in 1924. The purpose was to determine the effect of lighting on the productivity of workers in producing telephone relays, which were entirely hand-assembled electrical connections. The hypothesis of the studies was that the optimal lighting conditions in the relay assembly work areas would result in the greatest output and to this end, control and experimental groups were established.

While the engineers assumed that there was an optimal level of light beyond which the vision of the workers would be affected, the findings indicated that illumination increases resulted in higher output for both groups. The degree of light was then decreased, but the output continued to increase. The surprising conclusion was that light did not correlate with output, and that worker involvement with these studies was the driving force to greater productivity. The studies lasted through 1932, and encompassed a variety of job redesigns, including the length of the workday and work week, the number and length of rest periods, and various wage incentive plans.

The results from the Hawthorne studies, as later supervised and analyzed by Harvard professor Elton Mayo, were that group factors have considerable influence on individual behavior, including worker output, attitudes and feelings of security. Essentially the Hawthorne studies began an intense interest in individual and group behavior in organizations, including businesses, including realization that the group provides substantial influence through various admonitions:

> *Don't be a rate buster, a chiseler or a squealer*
> *Do follow the group's rules or you'll be ostracized, subject to ridicule,*
> *and physically abused*

Mayo's work has survived as human behavior or behaviorism, leading to various studies of the impact of the organization and groups within the organization on the behavior and motivation of the individual worker.[27] The Hawthorne studies were the first to systematically research and analyze group

---

27 E. Mayo, *The Human Problems of an Industrial Civilization*, Macmillan, 1933. Mayo's work was extended and explained by F. J. Roethlisberger and W. J. Dickson, *Management and the Worker*, Harvard University Press, 1939.

influences on worker behavior. Previously, the assumption was that the organization could control the individual worker if the proper procedures were utilized. After Mayo, the futility of this pursuit began to be realized, especially once worker organized in labor unions and rose above struggling for subsistence employment.

Norms and Group Behavior

While the Hawthorne studies have been discussed for decades in management courses, the focus usually is on explaining the influence of the group rather than other pioneering findings. Just as crucial to understanding worker performance in organization is the concept of the **norm**, which is the expected outcome or standard of behavior determined by the group (and not the company).[28] In discussing norms, a short case is often used that places a college student (call him "Lloyd") in a summer work situation where the group establishes norms of work effort (usually in a repetitive, boring task) that are far below what is attainable by average people making a reasonable effort.

The case attempts to solicit reasons that people who do a menial job – for example, loading and unload boxes and shipments all day – would be uninspired and unwilling to either worker harder or to accept Lloyd. The norm of work effort is set by the group and unless managed or threatened with discipline,[29] that norm is unlikely to change. There are various group agendas: to establish contempt for the organization, management, the work task (and subconsciously, for themselves); to extend the amount of time required to complete the work to guarantee that the jobs will continue; and others we will note shortly.

The intention is to try to find ways to enhance self-respect within the group, and suggestions often include work redesign to extend the job responsibilities. This can be accomplished through various strategies:

- Have the group self-schedule the work tasks, and extend job tasks by including packing, preparing boxes for shipment and handling simple customer service issues

---

28 There is an extensive body of literature on norms in business organizations. See, for example, D.C. Feldman, "The Development and Enforcement of Group Norms," *Academy of Management Review*, January 1984, pages 47-53.

29 Such threats typically do not accomplish very much, and may result in sabotage and other undesirable outcomes.

- Vary the worker's tasks so that repetitive, boring tasks are encountered less frequently and so that the members of the group are distributed throughout the company
- Affect the cohesion of the existing group; see the comment in the next section

The student hopefully will begin to appreciate the impact of the group on the setting of the norm of performance.

What are the Attributes of Group Behavior?

The researcher Solomon Asch focused on the influence of the group on behavior, determining through many experiments that individuals will conform to group norms even when those norms are wrong. Asch determined that a basic human desire is conformity, that it is the exception for individuals to refuse to conform even when facing ostracism (being an outcast), and that we do not desire to be viewed as different.[30]

The desire to conform can wipe away basic values; an extreme case is that of Nazism when German values taught in the home, schools and church were suppressed in the effort to satisfy the demands for proscribed individual behaviors as set by Hitler and the German government. It should be noted that conformity is essential in times of a threat to existence, as in wartime or when a hospital or airline emergency dictates that workers follow a pre-established series of tasks.

Status and Cohesion

Groups develop various roles, rituals and points of differentiation for its members that convey status and a position within the group. There are several sources of status: the member's power over others, usually by having access to necessary resources; the member's contribution to group goals, often

---

30 S. Asch, "Effects of Group Pressure upon the Modification and Distortion of Judgments," in H. Guetzkow (ed.), *Groups, Leadership and Men*, Carnegie Pres, 1951, pages 177-190.

manifested when that involvement is above average; and the member's personal characteristics, particularly attractiveness and personality.

In simplistic terms, a position of status in a group of children may be because of a child is the natural leader, because he or she is a good athlete, or because he or she is handsome or pretty. The power position is particularly important in work groups, with contribution and personal characteristics of lesser significance. The group depends on those individuals in positions of status to make decisions, to be assertive and to drive the group toward certain behaviors, even those that are undesirable.

Status varies by national culture. Americans may deny that they are concerned about their position in society, but any quick look at advertising or lifestyle will indicate their status consciousness.[31] Cultures manifest status through various mechanisms; for example, status may derive from family, membership in certain organizations, graduation from prestigious schools, or other factors. In addition, status is age-specific; for example, a 50 to 60 year old in Japan or China will likely follow traditional status symbols, such as the formal role in the employer's organization, while the generation of teens and early 20's will follow Western styles and derive status from possessions.

Composition and Groupthink

One finding from various research studies that might help Lloyd, the summer worker previously discussed, is that groups comprised of individuals who are somewhat dissimilar (are **heterogeneous**) are more likely to have the various skills and experiences that the accomplishment of its tasks require. **Homogeneous** groups – those with similar individuals – are generally less effective.[32] Diversity increases the likelihood that the skills to perform a task will be present and increases the views and opinions of group members, thereby reducing the possibility of conformity.

Managing a group toward accomplishing the organization's mission is a challenge, but overcoming the natural cohesion of the group may be necessary to achieve productivity. **Cohesion** is the attraction of the members to

---

31 A best seller in the 1950s was V. Packard's "exposé" of this phenomenon, *The Status Seekers*, McKay, 1959.

32 There are various studies on the impact of diversity in improving group performance. See, for example, S.E. Jackson, K.E. May and K. Whitney, "Understanding the Dynamics of Diversity in Decision-Making Teams," in R.A. Guzzo and E. Salas (eds.), *Team Effectiveness and Decision-Making in Organizations,* Jossey-Bass, 1995, pages 204-261.

each other and the group. In the case of Lloyd, we have established some ideas to overcome the group's largely destructive cohesiveness. As to why he was not accepted, the group will not allow its "solidarity" to be threatened by a worker so obviously different from themselves, and so it bands together for self-protection.

As Mayo and Asch reported, groups are useful in accomplishing work and in setting values. However, groups are likely to continue a pattern of actions that may lead to failure. This outcome has become known as **groupthink**, when the drive for consensus leads to the wrong conclusion as different courses of action and minority views are not adequately considered. Successful businesses have later failed when insufficient attention is paid to alternative strategies, as with Eastman Kodak or the U.S. auto industry.

A tragic situation of groupthink was the U.S. involvement in the Vietnam War. Other examples include the 1961 Bay of Pigs invasion of Cuba in a futile effort to overthrow the Fidel Castro government, the 1986 Challenger and the 2003 Columbia space shuttle disasters when engineers and scientists ignored various safety issues and warnings, and the invasion of Iraq in 2003 to destroy non-existent weapons of mass destruction. These were consensus-driven decisions to proceed with unrealistic programs that in hindsight could not have succeeded.

What are Important Work Team Issues?

Companies today extensively use work teams to solve complex technology, manufacturing, marketing and financial decisions that require access to a variety of skills and experience sets. A **team structure** consists of workers brought together (usually on a temporary basis) to accomplish the organization's mission and goals. The concept differs from classical management concepts (to be discussed in Chapter 7) as there may not be a direct relationship from senior managers to workers. Past organizational structures depended on permanent configurations of managers and workers (called departments, divisions, groups or other terminology) that impeded cooperation among those sub-organizations.

A team coordinates efforts from previously separate functions, geographic locations and products, to solve problems and take advantage of competitive opportunities. There can be a **synergistic** result, with employees acting together to produce a result that is not independently obtainable. Instead, the teams organize and produce the work as is deemed appropriate, with team members empowered to make decisions, use resources and accept responsibility for the results. Teams may disband when a specific purpose no longer exists. See Figure 3-2 for a comparison of groups and teams.

Figure 3-2: Comparing Groups and Teams

	Groups	**Teams**
How organized	Informally organized by members to enforce norms established within the group	Usually formally organized by a company to accomplish a specific task
How focused	Norms may be consistent with or contrary to the mission of the organization	Objectives are consistent with mission of the organization
Impact on productivity	Can restrict productivity to assure permanent employment for group members	Objective is synergistic, to perform in a coordinated manner
Accountability	Accountable to the group's established norms	Accountable to the team and to the organization
Composition of skill set	Comprised of similar skill and experience sets	Comprised of complementary skill and experience sets

Types of Teams

There are various types of teams used in today's global companies.

- Problem-solving. Much of the favorable publicity for the team format is due to the structure that focuses on improving quality, most commonly known as the **quality circle** (QC). The concept is attributed to W. Edwards Deming, an American statistician, and Kaoru Ishikawa, a Japanese management professor, who consulted with several companies beginning in the early 1960s, at a time when Japan's manufactured products were of suspect quality. Research indicates that QCs with top-management support solve significantly more problems than those that are voluntary meetings of workers who attempt to solve a management issue. The idea has spread globally although the largest usage is in Asia, particularly Japan and China, where the culture supports team rather than individual initiatives.

- Self-managed. Self-managed teams are workers who take on management responsibilities, including the various activities discussed in this text that would ordinarily be performed by first-level supervisors. There have been astonishing successes using this approach, but in times of economic recession, as at present, the self-managed team has generally not been willing to make the hard decisions, such as downsizing by eliminating team members. Global applications are another problem, as certain cultures require hierarchal structure and a certainty of the work objective.

- Cross-Functional. Large companies often encounter the typical bureaucratic problem of the lack of communication among various sub-organizational units except at the senior management level. A popular solution has become the use of cross-functional teams to allow participation in planning and decision-making for a particular project or activity. When this approach is used, teams are provided staff support through the traditional functions, usually organized as departments. Hewlett-Packard, Boeing, the auto manufacturers and several high technology and biotech companies have implemented this concept. A significant difficulty in using cross-functional teams is that each member is often a strong advocate for his or her "home" discipline and may not consider the interests of the team effort.

- Virtual (where communication is by computer, teleconferencing and other technologies). Many global companies use virtual teams to exchange information, discuss problems and do the business of a team without face-to-face meetings. While the advantages are probably obvious — barriers due to time, space and distance disappear as do the expense and exhaustion of travel — the virtual team loses the communication provided through eye contact, nonverbal cues and body language as well as the satisfaction from social contact. However, there is no more practical approach when international workers must collaborate, as many companies have discovered.

How Can Effective Teams Be Created?

Teams have become so pervasive in organizations that many managers are struggling with methods to make them effective. The concept is relatively new, and unlike athletic teams where success is defined by a victory in competition usually decided in a matter of hours, work teams may not see the end result for months or even years. Furthermore, the "final score" may be elusive: do we measure victory by getting the idea operational regardless of cost; is it determined by meeting an arbitrary time deadline; or is it a satisfied client (whose contact is with and who gives praise to the senior manager in charge)? These are difficult issues, particularly when success is no guarantee that team members will retain their jobs given today's weak economy.

The Necessary Components for Team Success

The team requires certain factors to succeed; a manager cannot simply request a competent worker from each relevant area of a company and expect Herb, Jane, Jorge, Maria and Anne — who may not even know each other — to work together to accomplish a work task. Research suggests that the company make the following elements available.

- Resources. Workers cannot function without access to adequate resources. Work teams are often established off-budget, that is, not in the formal structure of a company. Teams may fail because sub-organizational units that have contributed personnel to the team may resist providing equipment, budget, office or factory space, critical information, technology or other assets. The senior manager(s) who established the team must determine how to overcome this common problem.

- Structure. Recall the five team members who were assigned to work on a project. How will they structure themselves in this new team? Will a natural leader evolve? Will Herb or Jorge assume control? Will Maria or Jane be reticent and reluctant to demonstrate their knowledge?

- Size. Teams should be relatively small in size, no more than about eight members. Too many members exponentially increase problems of coordination, cohesiveness and communications. The author has worked with corporate teams that were created to select financial service providers (including commercial and investment banks). The team could not work effectively when there was a representative of every affected unit within the business, often as many as 15 or 18!

- Trust. If the team members hardly know each other, why would they trust one another? Who will take credit for team achievements? Will that same person place the blame for failure on a weaker member? Will there be sufficient trust that each member will do his or her fair share?

- Evaluation. Where is the accountability for performance and how does the reward system acknowledge successes and/or failures? Since MBOs typically are assigned to individuals in traditional sub-organizations, how will that process be managed? Too many senior managers ignore this critical issue, promising to make rewards equitable later on. This is inappropriate.

- Skills. Herb, Jane, Jorge, Maria and Anne may be among the most competent from their work areas, but do they have the necessary skills for team success? Technical skills do not necessarily translate to communication skills, or problem-solving skills, or interpersonal skills. Having the most skilled engineers, information technology experts and accountants may doom the team to failure if the other skills are inadequate.

How to Create Successful Teams

Although teams may be the newest concept in management, the extent of problems and concerns should force a careful investigation of how to make them function. It is quite obvious that the individual worker has only slight control over his or her performance, and that organizational unit, group and/or team will define success or failure. Workers who are alienated from the company because of this diminution of the role of the individual do not help themselves, their groups or teams, or the organization, and in this economic environment, should not expect much permanence in their jobs.

To make teams successful, senior managers should consider the issues previously discussed regarding national cultural differences; see the discussion on Hofstede in Chapter 2. In this regard, individualistic cultures like the U.S. will likely create the most problems in team situations. Cultures that value collaboration will have the fewest challenges with team cooperation, such as those with Asian and Latin American workers. Where the culture requires a hierarchal structure, the absence of a leader designated by the organization can also present difficulties.

Training Work Teams

There has been some limited success with training programs that support team cooperation and team building. The types of educational activities include group exercises, case studies, role playing, verbal exercises and situations using hypothetical situations led by a trainer (often called a "facilitator"); see Figure 3-3 for specific training ideas.

Figure 3-3: Ideas for Work Team Training

For team building to be effective, leaders must first identify the issues being faced. They can then plan activities to address these challenges directly — and make sure that the team will actually gain some benefits from the event. Make sure that the team-building exercises are not competitive, as the desire to win tends to make one person or team work against another.

Objective: To Improve Communications
Back-to-back drawing — Divide the team into pairs, and have each pair sit on the floor back to back. Give one person in each pair a picture of a shape, and give the other person a pencil and pad of paper. Ask the people holding the pictures to give verbal instructions to their partners on how to draw the shape without actually telling the partners what the shape is. After finishing, ask each pair to compare their original shape with the actual drawing, and consider whether there were problems with both the sending and receiving parts of the communication process.

Survival scenario —Tell your team that their airplane has just crashed in the ocean. There's a desert island nearby, and there's room on the lifeboat for every person — plus 12 items in total that they will need to survive on the island. Instruct the team to choose which items they want to take. How do they decide? How do they rank or rate each item?

Objective: To Eliminate Stereotypes and Labels*
Stereotype party —Write on nametags many different personality types (see the list below), and pin or tape one tag to each person's back. Don't show people which tag is on their back — they'll be able to see everyone else's tag, but not their own. Here are some personality types you could consider: auto mechanic, banker, Olympic athlete, lawyer, sanitation worker, professor, fast-food restaurant worker, postal worker, actor/actress or police officer.

Ask each person to figure out which personality type is on his or her back by asking stereotype-based questions of other people – "Am I a man?" "Am I an athlete?" "Am I an entertainer?" and so on. Allow group members to answer only "yes" or "no", and encourage participants to ask questions to as many different people as possible.

Objective: To Build Interdependence and Trust
Mine field –Set up an obstacle course using chairs, balls, cones, boxes, or any other object that could potentially be a barrier to trip someone. Leave enough space between the objects to walk through. Divide your group into pairs. Pay attention to who you match with whom. This is a perfect opportunity to work on relationships, so you might want to put together people who have trust issues with each other.

Blindfold one person, the 'mine walker', who is not allowed to talk. Ask his or her partner to stay outside the mine field, and give verbal directions, helping the mine walker avoid the obstacles, and reach the other side of the area. Before starting, allow the partners a few minutes to plan how they will communicate. Make sure there are consequences when people hit an obstacle. For example, perhaps they have to start again from the beginning.

   *We discuss stereotyping in Chapter 11

Source: Developed from "Team-Building Exercises: Planning Activities that Actually Work," at www.mindtools.com/pages/article/newTMM_52.htm.

A rigorous form of team building is variously known as a ropes course, an Outward Bound® event or by other names,[33] and usually involves a short, mostly physical set of exercises that require a team effort for a successful outcome. For example, a team may be required to get every member over a smooth five foot barrier, so climbing it individually is impossible. The solution is to push

33 Name variations include obstacle course, challenge course and even commando course.

one lighter-weight member over (sometimes by climbing on the shoulders of larger individuals) and then having that person sit on the barrier and pull the others over, perhaps using a rolled-up shirt for an assist.

Other obstacles may include a trust fall[34] and a ropes course that requires the individual to walk on a rope path between trees perhaps 20 feet off the ground. Disadvantages of the more physical team training exercises are that they may be too strenuous or intimidating for certain individuals, they can be fairly costly particularly when offsite, and any lessons learned are likely to be quickly forgotten.

What are the Issues You Should Address?

In considering the behavior of groups and teams in your organization, here are some issues to review.

- Are we aware of the groups that have formed in our organization? Are these groups supportive or are they negative influences on the accomplishment of our mission? Are the norms established by the group acceptable to management?
- Do we accept or even know of seriously underperforming groups that have established their own norms of performance?
- Have we allowed homogeneous groups to develop, limiting diversity and reinforcing conformity?
- Are we so obsessed with conformity that we are experiencing or have had situations of groupthink?
- Do we use teams to deal with business problems? Have we considered how these teams were organized, how they function and whether they are performing satisfactorily?
- Have we provided the necessary elements for team success, including resources, structure, size, trust, evaluation and skills? Have issues of national culture and the possible gains from training been considered?

---

34 A trust fall is a group exercise in which an individual deliberately allows themselves to fall backwards from a perch several feet off the ground, relying on the other members of the group to catch the person.

Discussion and Review Questions

1. What is the role of the group in understanding of behavior in a work organization?
2. What contribution did the Hawthorne studies make to understanding worker motivation?
3. How did the Hawthorne studies refute the idea that the organization could control the individual worker if the proper procedures were utilized?
4. What are positive and negative results of group behavior in a work situation?
5. How do teams support the work of the organization? When are they preferable to groups?
6. How can work teams be structured and supported to increase the likelihood of team success?

CHAPTER 4

Organizational Culture

After reading this chapter, you will be able to:

- Understand the concept of organizational culture
- Recognize the influence of the founder or chief executive officer on the organizational culture
- Appreciate the role of the culture of an organizational unit
- Consider how cultures are perpetuated and how they are changed
- Identify recent influences on organizational culture

What is the Culture of an Organization?

In Chapter 7, we will discuss the formal elements of organizational structures that enable managers and employees to accomplish work. We note that certain formal processes are commonly established to assist this activity, such as line-and-staff and chain of command. However, it has been recognized for the past three decades that companies accomplish as much through informal as through formal processes, which we refer to as organizational culture.

Organizational Culture

Various management texts use this term but definitions vary. It is probably simplest to consider **organizational culture** (OC) as a shared attitude and respect for the history and traditions of the business. Within the culture, there may be sub-cultures that develop to manage problems specific to an organizational unit or a geographic location.

OCs often arise because of the work attitude and influence of the founder. The culture becomes a motivational tool to accomplish the company's mission and goals, and is openly promoted or reported on by the media. Or, it becomes an insidious demoralizing force, destroying managers and quite possibly the company.

Founders' Positive Cultures

The founders or important leaders of Du Pont, Disney, Berkshire Hathaway represent positive OCs and personal/business values. Their companies are frequently mentioned in rankings of admired and socially responsible businesses.

- Éleuthère I. du Pont (1771–1834), the founder of the Du Pont Company. Du Pont was a man of ethics long before it was fashionable. As one example, in March 1818 his manufacturing facilities were destroyed by an explosion that killed 40 men. The laws of the time provided no payment to the survivors or the families of the deceased. However, du Pont compensated the victims. His sense of obligation to customers and employees was different from the behavior of other businesses. Many times he risked his business and his personal fortune to fulfill a promise. This philosophy has continued to the present day, with Du Pont considered as an ethical and socially responsible company.

- Walt Disney (1901 – 1966), the founder of the Disney Companies. Walt and his brother Roy started with a core set of conservative moral principles that included honesty, truth, respect for others, fellowship and optimism, and a belief in the heroic capabilities of humankind. They continually integrated their company's operating culture into this moral framework, which was informally codified as "The Disney

54

Way". Disney never compromised on quality, service to his audience and constant product innovation, and this orientation continues in the company operations in theme parks, entertainment and various other businesses.

- Warren Buffett (1930 -). The chairman of Berkshire Hathaway. Warren Buffett constantly reiterates his ethical position: to zealously guard Berkshire's reputation, that Berkshire can afford to lose money but they cannot afford to lose any of its reputation. The notion that others are unethical does not provide justification for a business decision, and any activity or decision that has the slightest odor of impropriety should be avoided.

Founders' Negative Cultures

The founders or important leaders of Ford Motor and Montgomery Ward represent negative cultures.

- Henry Ford (1863 – 1947), the founder of Ford Motor. The first Henry Ford was tyrannical, obsessed with control, and unwilling to accept the opinions of others. A famous quote was "Any customer can have a car painted any colour that he wants so long as it is black."[35] Ford's attitudes led to a fixation with prejudice, hatred of trade unions, and distrust of many of his executives, and may have hastened the early death of his son and likely successor Edsel (at age 49). Faced with the potential failure of the company in the mid-1940s, pressures from various stakeholders led to the appointment of Henry Ford II (Henry Ford's grandson) as the chairman.
- Sewell Avery (1873 – 1960), the chairman of Montgomery Ward. Avery is perhaps best known as defying the Franklin Roosevelt Administration during World War II. Avery would not comply with government orders to allow unionization efforts. As a result, National Guardsmen carried him from his office in 1944. "To hell with the government," he blurted out at the U.S. Attorney General.

---

35 Ford's remark about the Model T Ford in 1909, published in his autobiography *My Life and Work*, 1922, page 71.

Avery's opposition to laws permitting collective bargaining is summed up in his words when asked what he intended to do after the government had seized Montgomery Ward: "… the government has been coercing both employers and employees to accept a brand of unionism which in all too many cases is engineered by people who are not employees of the plant…these devices… are a disguise for leading the nation into a government of dictators."[36] The company announced that it was ceasing operations in 2000 after years of weak leadership including a slow response to the movement of the American middle class to suburban locations.

The Culture of the Organizational Unit

Departments and other company units sometimes create their own cultures to cope with their position in the organization, and often develop protocols to enhance respect or raise visibility. These business unit cultures are informal, that is, not stated in any company literature. As an example, during the years of prosperity prior to the current recession, some manufacturing business units limited output to assure adequate and permanent employment. This was often enforced by peer pressure and occasionally stronger methods of persuasion.

A major U.S. bank encouraged the development of a culture within one of its departments. Components included sales contests, incentive awards, recognition at an annual banquet, special off-site meetings and other motivators. The other parts of the bank did not participate, were not particularly incented to the same goals, and were not motivated to coordinate their efforts with the department that had this special culture. The downside that became apparent in time was the emphasis of the culture and goals of the unit and not that of the entire enterprise.

Some organizational units typically do not develop their own cultures. For example, marketing (particularly sales) is generally self-motivated to solve problems and customer objections that may prevent sales success. Another unit that does not usually have a separate culture is information technology, as the focus is on operating computer systems and overcoming technological challenges.

---

36 J. Grant, *Money of the Mind*, Farrar, Straus and Giroux, 1995, page 26.

How is Culture Perpetuated or Changed?

Strong culture organizations tend to select new hires that are likely to accept the culture and are willing to learn the routines and rules. During the 1950-1970 period, IBM insisted on a standard of dress, haircut and demeanor for its employees.[37] That same appearance and dress code requirement is used by the Walt Disney Company at its theme parks to provide a uniform and clean look. Some management researchers believe that senior management (after the founder departs) has an important influence on culture, but this is unusual. Employees do not tend to have contact with corporate executives and would not likely choose nor could they afford to emulate their behaviors.

Culture is maintained through various devices including stories, rituals and symbols.

- An example of a "story" is the entrepreneurial innovation of Microsoft, which Bill Gates and Paul Allen started in a garage to create an operating system for a mid-1970s computer. The business drive and technological focus of Microsoft are part of the legacy of the company, and employees receive orientation on this focus.
- American companies do not tend to employ "rituals". However, a famous example of a company that uses rituals is Wal-Mart, which has a morning chant by employees that spell the name of the company. Japanese companies use short, mandatory exercise periods as a bonding ritual.
- "Symbols" include the design of company offices, the size of and furniture in manager offices, the company car assigned to the executives, first-class airline tickets for senior managers (at least before the current recession) and other visual markers.

---

37 P.R. Smith, *Strategic Marketing Communications: New Ways to Build and Integrate Communications*, Kogan, 1999, page 24.

Changes to the Culture

It should be apparent from our discussion that the implicit purpose of OC is conformity. This tends to become a liability as business conditions demand new ideas and responses which require "thinking out of the box" and a risk-taking orientation. Companies may recognize that these situations require responsiveness to the changing environment, and may act to move the culture to a new position.[38] This can be accomplished by a combination of several actions.

- Changing leadership, to bring a different management style to an organization that cannot otherwise change its cultural style. This sometimes works, as in the case of Apple, which brought back founder Steve Jobs when the company was floundering under Gil Amelio and his predecessor, John Sculley. As is widely known, Jobs turned the company around through astonishing technology including the iPod and iPad.[39] This sometimes does not work, as in the case of Home Depot which hired Robert Nardelli only to find the disruption and focus on cost-cutting alienated customers and employees. Nardelli was replaced seven years later by Frank Blake.
- Selectively acquiring businesses or eliminating those parts of the company that resist change. Many merger and acquisition (M&A) transactions are specifically to improve the culture; for example, Time Warner bought AOL to change a staid entertainment/media company, but the merger was unsuccessful and the companies separated. A successful merger was Pepsi and Frito Lay to diversify the product line and instill a marketing orientation in a conservative beverage business.
- Creating a new mission for the organization that redefines its purpose and intent. For example, when IBM realized that its dominant position of the 1950-1970 period was eroding, largely due to the PC, it brought in Louis Gerstner, Jr. from RJR Nabisco. Gerstner started by making the company solvent by cutting billions in expenses and raising cash by selling assets. He decided to tie employee compensation to the performance of the whole company rather than to the employee's particular division.

---

38 However, recall the discussion of General Motors in Chapter 1.
39 See *W. Isaacson, Steve Jobs,* Simon & Schuster, 2011.

This would force workers to cooperate and venture outside of the organizational units in which they operated. Using IBM's technological expertise to provide solutions for customers in addition to just creating technology was also a key to its new strategy. One of IBM's most successful initiatives has been to become a major application-service provider (ASP), which provides computer-based services to customers over a network.[40]

- Communications, to explain the need for change and to deal with misinformation that may have been disseminated through rumor ("the grapevine"). Unfortunately, senior management may massage the information in its short-term interest, and subsequent revelations may cause distrust and increased resistance.

- Participation, to give various organizational participants the opportunity to structure and formulate a new idea, operational method or other change. The author's experience in many situations has used a representative *ad hoc* group to discuss, review and approve a change. At the point of such consensus, it is difficult to later resist the change.

- Support and a reward system, to provide positive reinforcement for the acceptance and implementation of a change. Such rewards do not always require a financial payment; often employees need recognition through mention in a company newsletter, at a meeting or through a commendation letter.

Why Do Organizations Resist Change?

A nearly universal truth is that organizations resist change. The idea of "new" requires altering accepted views and attitudes that have become comfortable and generally in harmony with the established order. In a sense, this is positive, because constant change would become chaotic, making life difficult if not impossible. Individuals and combinations of people (groups) in organizations resist change through various methods. The current economic recession has

---

40 See L. Gerstner, *Who Says Elephants Can't Dance?: Leading a Great Enterprise through Dramatic Change*, HarperBusiness, 2003.

forced individuals and organizations to respond to competitive and efficiency demands considerably more rapidly than in normal times; it remains to be seen whether this will be a permanent situation.

Resistance by Individuals

Reasons that individuals resist change include the following:

- A perceived threat to one's security, particularly concerning employment status or if a worker is required to learn new skills to keep his or her job. Today's economy has resulted in job cuts and a reduction in wages for some workers. Managers report that employees required to add new responsibilities to their job routines have made the necessary adjustments due to the fear of unemployment. An example is when an accounts payable clerk is asked to also handle accounts receivable, finds six reasons not to embrace the additional responsibilities, but decides that a larger job at no increase in pay is better than no job.
- Habit, in that the magnitude of stimuli and pressures an individual encounters each day requires an established schedule. There is comfort in following a pattern of behavior; learning a different route to work or dealing with a new manager requires adjustments and coping mechanisms.
- Discomfort with new information, in that people only hear what they choose to hear and reject new data until they are forced to listen and adopt. For example, many addicts refuse to acknowledge that they have a drinking or a drug problem and believe that they can quit at any time. Workers who are required to learn a computer routine to control a previously mechanical manufacturing process will resist until forced to change.

Resistance by Organizations

Organizations try to prevent change because of possible challenges to established procedures. This partly explains why a company may be an industry leader but eventually decline to a lesser position or even fail. In the word processing industry, Wang Labs was the dominant company in word processing in the 1980s but eventually failed when the PC business made the process simpler and available at every worker's desk.

The term **inertia** is from physics (as described by Isaac Newton), and refers to the resistance of any physical object to a change in its state of motion or rest, or the tendency of an object to resist any change in its motion. This state of inactivity typically overwhelms any organization, even those with individuals or groups that desire to change to meet competitive pressures or to implement new technology. The decline of the labor union movement illustrates this situation; unions have long resisted changes in their effort to maintain the existing status.

Companies that continually stress the importance of learning and training tend to be able to sustain a flexible, "living" OC. Large combinations of people cannot function without a mission, goals, objectives and a philosophical focus. OC can accomplish these purposes if properly managed and if capable of responding to environmental threats, challenges and opportunities.

However, changing an OC is not a single initiative. Successful changes occur when most or all of the change factors noted in this chapter are used in a coordinated manner. It is not enough to publicize the change, or educate managers and workers, or reward successful participants, or provide a mechanism for participation in planning the change. An integrated plan must be developed and implemented, or the organization may continue to resist, eventually threatening its survival.

What Are the Recent Influences on Organizational Culture?

The rapidly changing pace of business and management's response has pressured OCs to adapt accordingly. Cultures that had been accepted for decades have been altered to conform to societal pressures to meet new requirements. In this section, we discuss five of these influences: ethics, the economy, customer service, workplace diversity and globalization. We say more about certain of these topics in Chapter 12.

Ethics

The ethical behavior of companies like Enron, WorldCom and many others have forced managements throughout the world to establish an atmosphere of corporate governance and ethical behavior. While laws have been enacted requiring such actions,[41] companies have extended their OCs to demand high ethical standards by managers and employees. Examples of such actions occurred even before the recent governmental emphasis.

- Johnson & Johnson. A leading pharmaceutical company with high ethical standards, J&J was faced with a near-disaster when some of its Tylenol (used for headaches) bottles in a Chicago drug store were found to contain poison. J&J employees immediately pulled the drug from store shelves even before management had issued a statement on the tampering. The company's employees knew what was expected and acted accordingly.
- Tyson Foods. This food products company known for chicken and other poultry products has made corporate ethics part of its core mission. Tyson has worked to relieve childhood hunger, tying new media approaches to this campaign, including providing 100 pounds of chicken to a Texas food bank for each comment it received on its blog. Over 650 responses were received on the blog in two hours, and Tyson filled two trucks with chicken for the hungry. The company has repeated the donation idea in Boston and San Francisco.
- Google. During the G. W. Bush Administration, the Department of Justice attempted to gather information from Google's search-engine database. The company believed that the request was too intrusive, violated fundamental constitutional guarantees, and refused to comply. When the issue was brought before a federal court, the ruling was in Google's favor. "We will always be subject to government subpoenas, but the fact that the judge sent a clear message about privacy is reassuring … What this ruling means is that neither the government nor

---

41 In the U.S., these include the Foreign Corrupt Practices Act of 1977 (preventing bribes to secure international contracts), the Sarbanes-Oxley Act of 2002 (with various provisions regarding the behavior of publicly-traded companies), and the Dodd-Frank Act of 2010 (limiting the trading activities of banks and establishing a financial consumer protection bureau).

anyone else has carte blanche when demanding data from Internet companies."[42]

It is difficult to "script" ethical behavior. As a result, the problem has been addressed by establishing codes of ethics, requiring attendance at seminars and other training, establishing the office of ombudsman[43] to anonymously report possible violations, and other measures.

The Economy

OC exists in an economy experiencing alternating cycles of prosperity and recession, and since 2008, the latter has been dominant. In difficult economic times, companies must attempt to balance the requirements of its various stakeholders, and inevitably, certain (or even all) will be adversely affected. Some recent statements by companies explaining their positions include the following:

- Pepsico. "Many of the countries in which we operate, including the United States, have experienced and continue to experience unfavorable economic conditions… we cannot predict how current or worsening economic conditions will affect our critical customers, suppliers and distributors and any negative impact on our critical customers, suppliers or distributors may also have an adverse impact on our business results or financial condition."[44]
- Bosch Group (manufacturing technology). "Where 2009 brought recession on a historic scale, 2010 proved a year of historic recovery. We can now say we have emerged from the crisis with renewed strength. Not just in the shape of new orders and gains in market share, nor solely in the further expansion of our presence in growth regions like Asia Pacific; we are also stronger in the solidarity shown across the

---

42 Statement by Google's associate general counsel, Nicole Wong, in Chris Gaither, "U.S. Is Denied Google Queries," March 18, 2006, at articles.latimes.com/2006/mar/18/business/fi-google18.

43 An **ombudsman** is a person who acts as a intermediary between an organization and some internal (i.e., employee) or external constituency. A Danish, Norwegian and Swedish term, *Ombudsman* essentially means "representative".

44 2010 *Annual Report*, at www.pepsico.com/Download/PepsiCo_Annual_Report_2010_Full_Annual_Report.pdf, page 54.

company. Part of this we owe to the principles and measures we embraced in steering our company through the economic and financial crisis."[45]

These attempts to manage a difficult economic situation are necessary to demonstrate a compassion for the problems faced by every stakeholder and to provide motivation for continuing efforts at success.

Customer Service

The current business climate has driven many companies to follow such long-time leaders as FedEx, Nordstrom, Walt Disney and others in creating a customer service OC. Poor service has probably happened to most readers; certainly the author's treatment at a resort property owned by a European firm and by a U.S.-based communications company are experiences that will be remembered and repeated to acquaintances and business colleagues. Companies that recognize the long-term negative implications of these incidents have worked to create a culture of listening, responding in a positive way, and attempting to resolve any problems. Certain cultural attributes appear to be required for this approach to succeed:

- Employee friendliness and a genuine interest in the customer
- Flexibility in using the company's resources to address customer issues
- Concern for the creation of a lasting relationship rather than for single transaction

In the past, companies could assume that one unhappy customer did not matter. Today, the Internet provides countless venues to report the perceived or real bad behavior of a company and to effectively trash a reputation that may have taken decades to establish.[46] Here are two examples:

---

45 *Annual Report* 2010, at www.bosch.com/worldsite_startpage/flashbook/GB2010_EN.pdf, page 2.
46 As one example, see complaints about Progressive Insurance at www.consumeraffairs.com/insurance/_progressive_insurance.htm. The company was attacked for defending the driver who apparently killed a 24 year old Maryland policyholder and for refusing to pay the resulting claim. See, "Internet Outrage grows around Progressive Insurance," CBS *This Morning,* August 16, 2012, at www.cbsnews.com/8301-505263_162-57494354/internet-outrage-grows-around-progressive-insurance.

- Nestlé. The international food company provided free milk formula for babies in undeveloped countries, primarily in Africa. Critics contended that the promotion of infant formula over breastfeeding has led to health problems and deaths among infants because of the use of contaminated water to mix the formula. Because of the low literacy rates in developing nations, some mothers were not aware of the sanitation methods needed in the preparation of bottles. In addition, breast milk has many natural benefits lacking in formula. Advocacy groups began an anti-Nestle campaign including claims that "Nestlé kills babies", obviously harming the company's reputation and causing collateral damage to its other products.
- McDonald's Corporation. *Supersize Me* is a 2004 U.S. documentary directed by and starring Morgan Spurlock that follows a thirty-day period during which he ate only McDonald's food. The film shows the effect on Spurlock's physical and psychological condition, and explores the fast food industry's influence, including how it encourages poor nutrition for its own profit. Spurlock ate at McDonald's restaurants three times per day, eating every item on the chain's menu at least once. The film helped to raise consciousness about obesity and diet.

The solution is to establish an OC that anticipates such problems through marketing research, **Beta-site testing** (first customer trial use prior to general release to the public) and other proactive information gathering; responding immediately at the slightest indication of a problem; and taking whatever actions are necessary to make things as "right" as possible.

Workplace Diversity

Some countries are not culturally similar (are heterogeneous), with the U.S. a leading example of diversity based on national origin, religion, race or other characteristics. Organizations would hire based on their perceived needs but could — at least in the past — choose to arbitrarily exclude Asians, Jews, African-Americans, women, Italians, the handicapped, gays and lesbians, or members of any class. Workers today cannot be denied employment because of such factors, and managing diversity has become a global concern. See Figure 4-1 for a listing of governing legislation. The old assumption that workers want to assimilate has become one that recognizes and embraces these differences.

Figure 4-1: U.S. Law Governing Employment Discrimination

Equal Pay Act of 1963 (amending the Fair Labor Standards Act), prohibiting employers and unions from paying different wages based on sex.

Title VII of the Civil Rights Act of 1964, prohibiting discrimination based on race, color, religion, sex or national origin.

The Pregnancy Discrimination Act of 1978 amended Title VII, specifying that unlawful sex discrimination includes discrimination based on pregnancy, childbirth, and related medical conditions.

The Age Discrimination in Employment Act (ADEA) of 1968 (amended in 1978 and 1986) prohibiting employers from discriminating on the basis of age.

The Rehabilitation Act of 1973, prohibiting employment discrimination on the basis of disability.

The Bankruptcy Reform Act of 1978, prohibiting employment discrimination on the basis of bankruptcy or bad debts.

The Immigration Reform and Control Act of 1986, prohibiting employers from discriminating on the basis of national origin or citizenship status (except an unauthorized immigrant).

The Americans with Disabilities Act of 1990 (ADA), prohibiting discriminatory barriers against qualified individuals with disabilities, individuals with a record of a disability, or individuals who are regarded as having a disability.

The 19th Century Civil Rights Acts, amended in 1993, ensure all persons equal rights under the law and outline the damages available to complainants in actions brought under Title VII of the Civil Rights Act of 1964, the Americans with Disabilities Act, and the 1973 Rehabilitation Act.

The Genetic Information Nondiscrimination Act of 2008, prohibiting employers from using individuals' genetic information when making hiring, firing, job placement, or promotion decisions.

The labor force in the U.S. and many other countries is notable for its changing demographic profile. U.S. statistics on gender are provided in Figure 4-2, and it is useful to note the population trends of the past few decades. These statistics on female participation do not address the astonishing increase in manager and senior manager ranks among women, who three decades ago were largely in secretarial and assistant roles. Estimates are that women now constitute between 10 and 20 % of Western senior management and boards of directors. This is far more diversity than in Asia, where countries like Japan and South Korea have less than 5% in equivalent positions, and gender diversity in that region is not seen as a priority.[47]

The percentage of Hispanics or Latinos in the U.S. has increased by just 43% in the past decade, now constituting 16.3% of the total population. The age cohort of those 62 years and above has increased 21.1% during those ten years. Managers have been forced to address the mix of workers by recognizing diversity and by being proactive in preventing conflict.

Figure 4-2: Selected U.S. Data, by Gender of Workers

% of the Population	1970	2000	2010
Male	62.2	49.1	49.2
Female	37.8	50.9	50.8

Source: Various U.S. Census documents; the 2010 and 2000 data are at www.census.gov/prod/cen2010/briefs/c2010br-03.pdf

47 "Untapped Talent," *The Economist*, July 7, 2012, page 62, citing a study by McKinsey, a global consulting firm.

Globalization

The world has become a global village.[48] Consider for a moment your daily routine. Your coffee comes from Colombia or perhaps from Indonesia. The company that makes your electric razor is headquartered in Germany. Your working apparel is manufactured in a developing country such as Thailand or China, with the cloth woven in other areas of the world. Your cell phone alarm that tells you to get going was produced in Finland, your car in Sweden, and the news show on the radio is gathered from such global sources as the BBC and Reuters. Most of the oil that is refined into gasoline for your car comes from the Middle East, and the company you work for may very well have international ownership like InBev that owns Anheuser-Busch (Budweiser).

Capitalism inevitably drives business activities to countries with lower cost labor and a supportive attitude toward free enterprise. The move of manufacturing and assembly activities offshore greatly increases the complexity of managing a company's employees and contract workers, in dealing with other cultures and motivations, and in coping with workers in the home (headquarters) and host countries.

What are the Issues You Should Address?

In considering the culture of your organization, here are some issues to review.

- Does our organization have a culture? Was it created by the founder or a significant chief executive? Is it relevant to current conditions or does it interfere with the natural progress and improvement toward our mission?
- Do organizational units have their own cultures? Do they support or are they in conflict with the mission of the organization? Are these cultures condoned by senior management?

---

48 "Global village" is a term closely associated with Marshall McLuhan, and refers to the real-time movement of information across the world through technology. See his *Understanding Media: The Extensions of Man,* McGraw-Hill, 1964.

- Do we have mechanisms to perpetuate our culture? Do they continue to be relevant?
- If cultural change is appropriate, do we have the necessary mechanisms to instigate the change?
- Do we understand recent influences on our organizational culture? Are we responding to these influences in an suitable manner or have we essentially ignored these factors?

Discussion and Review Questions

1. What is organizational culture? Why is the concept relevant to our understanding of organizational behavior?
2. What is the relevance of the influence of the founder or chief executive officer on organizational culture?
3. Give examples of positive and negative cultures in organizations. What was the resolution of the negative organizational cultures?
4. What devices or procedures are typically used to perpetuate organizational cultures?
5. How are organizational cultures changed?
6. How has the current economic recession affected organizational and individual resistance to change?
7. What are recent influences on organizational culture?

CHAPTER 5

Entrepreneurship And Planning

After reading this chapter, you will be able to:

- Understand the issues in entrepreneurship and intrapreneurship
- Determine the activities and steps in operational and strategic planning
- Recognize what SWOT and the BCG matrix require and how they are used
- Appreciate the insights of scenario analysis
- Consider how managers make decisions and how decision-making can be improved
- Be aware of issues in risk management and other concerns of 21st century decision-making

What is Entrepreneurship?

Managers should think of themselves as **entrepreneurs**, businesspeople who create opportunities by change, revolution, transformation and "creative destruction".[49] Entrepreneurship is necessary to bring new products to new markets, to cut costs, and to bring competitive advantages to companies

---

[49] "Creative destruction" has become popular jargon although its author, Joseph Schumpter, intended a different usage of the term; J. Schumpter, *Capitalism, Socialism* and *Democracy*, Routledge, 1942, page 139. It now refers to the destruction of established companies by new, entrepreneurial, innovative businesses.

by being lean, anxious to succeed, and willing to take risks. Unfortunately, large companies tend to focus on what was successful in the past rather than to continuously innovate and question the conventional wisdom. Those businesses that are entrepreneurial on a continuing basis are the exception and are so beyond normal practice that they tend to receive enthusiastic press coverage (except when they stumble) and interest by stock investors. Current outstanding entrepreneurial companies include Google, Apple and Starbucks, while recent examples have been Best Buy, Southwest Airlines and eBay.

Entrepreneurs have many issues to resolve in starting a business or in bringing an entrepreneurial attitude to an established business. In this section, we review typical start-up considerations; in the next section we discuss **intrapreneurship** ("inside entrepreneurship"), an attitude or responsibility in an existing company that takes charge of turning new ideas into a profitable product or service through risk-taking and innovation.

Entrepreneurship Issues

The idea that leads to a new business may be complex, as in the case of Google which uses advanced mathematical modeling to conduct high-speed web searches, to relatively simple, such as McDonald's offering a limited menu of fast-food at low prices. There may be competition or the idea may be unique; regardless the successful entrepreneur must find a method of delivering value added that is not currently accessible to customers. Often, the idea results from changes in demographics or income in a specific market. An example of the former is any of several of clothing retailers (e.g., Justice, Aéropostale, American Eagle) that dress teenage girls who have strong opinions about fashion; of the latter, Wal-Mart which emphasizes a low-price policy focused primarily on households at or below middle class.

A formal evaluation of the idea is presented in a feasibility study or business plan, which discusses specific actions necessary to start the new business.[50] The study or plan is used to structure the start-up, focusing on raising capital, forms of organization, management, marketing and other essential components; see Figure 5-1. The essential purpose is to describe the proposed business in a brief, concise manner, and to explain why the need that you perceive is not being fulfilled at the present time. Although a business may change its le-

---

50 Numerous websites provide business plan templates, some at no cost.

gal form at any time during its existence, the time to consider the appropriate structure of organization is at start-up. See Figure 5-2 for information on alternative legal forms of ownership.

Figure 5-1: Feasibility Study Elements or Business Plan for a Start-Up Venture

1. Introduction
    A. Explanation of the idea
    B. Description of the industry and/or market
    C. Economic conditions that may impact the venture
    D. Requirements for future development of the idea (including research, obtaining patents or copyrights, and trademarks)
    E. How the product will be manufactured or prepared for the market
    F. How will competitors likely respond
2. Accounting and finance
    G. Financial statements (pro forma balance sheet and income statement)
    H. Financial statement projections and cash requirements for three years
    I. Start-up costs and working capital required
    J. Source of capital (loans, equity investments, Small Business Administration [SBA])
3. Management
    K. Experience of entrepreneurs
    L. Staffing requirements
4. Marketing
    M. Target market
    N. Channels of distribution to get product or service to market
    O. Pricing
    P. Promotion (advertising, personal selling, other)

5. Legal
    Q. Discussion of the business structure (see Figure 5-2)
    R. Insurance
    S. Future buyout and succession
    T. Contracts, licenses, permits

Figure 5-2: Legal Forms of Business Structures (in the U.S.)

Sole Proprietorship: The owner maintains complete control of a business and is personally liable for its debts. No approval or charter is entailed except for any local licenses or permits that may be required, such as for a restaurant or for a hair salon. Income and losses pass through to the owner and are taxed at his or her tax rate as calculated on the Internal Revenue Service (IRS) Form 1040, Schedule C.

Partnership: Two or more owners share the risk of unlimited liability, the management and the income or losses from the business. Many partnerships have written agreements binding the partners to specific obligations and to prevent future disputes. Although partnerships must file an IRS return (Form 1065), there is no tax paid by the business. Instead, the gains or losses flow through to the partners.

    Limited Liability Partnership (LLP): A partnership with a general and limited liability ("limited") partners as owners. The general partner has unlimited liability and the limited partners are usually passive (nonparticipating) owners. The LLP must provide an IRS Form K-1 to the limited partners, and income or losses is treated as any partnership.

Corporation: The owners organize a distinct legal entity and receive a charter from the state in which the company is registered, in most jurisdictions through the Secretary of State. The advantages of this ownership form are that the business is considered as a separate ("artificial") being[51] and debts cannot be assessed against the individual owners; and that funds can be raised from numerous investors (stockholders) who only risk the amount of that investment. The corporation files its own tax return – IRS Form 1120 – and pays taxes on its income.

> S Corporation: A corporation that permits its owners to be taxed as a partnership so long as certain criteria are met, including limits on the number of stockholders (75) and other restrictions.

> Limited liability corporation (LLC): A mix of characteristics of partnerships and corporations, including limited liability and tax treatment as a partnership. The LLC is complex to establish.

Note: "Hybrid" forms of ownership (shown in indented text) were created to permit greater flexibility to owners in structuring their businesses in the early years of operation and to minimize restrictions.

Intrapreneurship

The concept of intrapreneurship sounds like a positive idea, but only a few companies have actually institutionalized the development of new business innovations into their cultures. A leading example is 3M (formerly Minnesota Mining and Manufacturing), which gives freedom to employees to create their own projects and funds for development. Intel and Google also have traditions of intrapreneurship. In the days of its founders, Hewlett-Packard *had* similar policies when the founders led the company.

---

51 In the case of Dartmouth College v. Woodward, 17 U.S. 518, 4 Wheat. Rep. 626 (1819), American Chief Justice John Marshall described a corporation to be "an artificial being, invisible, intangible, and existing only in contemplation of law. Being the mere creature of law, it possesses only those properties which the charter of its creation confers upon it, either expressly or as incidental to its very existence... The most important are immortality, and if the expression may be allowed, individuality properties by which a perpetual succession of many persons are considered, as the same, and may act as the single individual, They enable a corporation to manage its own affairs." Marshall based his opinion on English law.

The most difficult issues are overcoming inertia, the expectation that the existing business model will continue to be successful, and the lack of a direct financial incentive to the intrapreneur. As a result, the company must deal with organizational change issues (see the discussion in Chapter 4) and with creating a bonus plan, stock option or other compensation specifically designed to reward successful innovation. It appears that intrapreneurship can only work when senior management includes the concept in the company's mission statement and in its goals.

Unfortunately, the departure of the entrepreneurial founder(s) often ends the intrapreneurial culture and "freezes" the values and traditions that originally made a success and now may make the company simply one of many in its industry. This nearly happened at Apple when co-founder Steve Jobs (with Steve Wozniak) and CEO John Sculley became rivals in a power struggle in 1985, with the board of directors siding with Sculley. Jobs resigned and did not return to Apple until 1996 to bring the company back from the brink of failure.

What is Planning?

Planning involves defining the goals of an organization based on its mission. Once the goals are known, strategies to achieve those goals are developed, and plans are made to coordinate resources and company activities to accomplish those goals. You may wish to review the mission/goal/objective/ MBO process discussed in Chapter 1. As we will see from this explanation, the planning concept is not a single activity; rather, it encompasses many business functions to provide direction to managers, reduce uncertainty, maximize efficiency and establish a control system to measure whether plans are successful. The two types of planning in any organization are strategic and operational; see Figure 5-3.

Figure 5-3: Planning by Managerial Level

Managerial Level	Types of Planning Activities
1st-Level	Operational
Mid-Level	Operational and Strategic
Senior Level	Strategic

Strategic Planning

The **strategic plan** is the organization's set of comprehensive goals based on its mission. Strategic planning has been through various phases of importance particularly since World War Two, with advocates finding a receptive audience primarily in the years of prosperity. As the global economy is largely in recession, the field has recently declined in importance.

There are various methodologies used in strategic planning, from straight forward analysis of a company's position with its industry (e.g., SWOT analysis), to complex simulations (e.g., Monte Carlo, involving computational algorithms that rely on repeated random sampling to compute results, and various proprietary models). SWOT components are noted in Figure 5-4. Other planning procedures are summarized in Figure 5-5.

Figure 5-4: SWOT Analysis Components

- Internal <u>Strengths</u> and <u>Weaknesses</u>
  - o Controllable activities performed especially well or poorly
  - o Arise in functional areas of the business:
    - Management
    - Marketing
    - Finance
    - Accounting
    - Production/operations
    - Research and development
    - Information technology
  - o Core Competencies
  - o Building competitive advantage involves taking advantage of distinctive competencies
  - o Strategies are designed in part to improve on a firm's weaknesses and turn them into strengths
- External <u>Opportunities</u> and <u>Threats</u>
  - o Significantly benefit or harm the organization in the future
  - o Include the following trends:
    - Economic
    - Social
    - Cultural
    - Demographic
    - Environmental
    - Political
    - Legal and governmental regulation
    - Technological
    - Competitive trends
  - o Largely beyond the control of a single organization
  - o Strategy formulation to:
    - Take advantage of external opportunities
    - Avoid or reduce impact of external threats

Figure 5-5: Selected Planning Procedures

Environmental Scanning: The screening of information about global external factors (see Figure 5-4) to anticipate and plan for changes that might affect an organization. Companies that use this approach monitor non-traditional sources of data. Examples include job ads which could indicate a competitor's new strategic initiative; demographic data that may reveal increased or decreased opportunities for retailing (such as changes in age cohorts or family formation); closures of businesses or increases in available commercial real estate space indicating weakening economic conditions in specific markets.

Competitive Intelligence: The screening of information about competitors using public documents, such as filings with the investment regulatory agency (in the U.S., the Securities and Exchange Commission [SEC]), public relations releases, background stories in print media, changes to products and services sold in retail operations, brochures and other handout material at industry conferences, and information from business data providers such as Dun & Bradstreet (D&B), Moody's, Standard & Poor's (S&P), and statements by vendors and customers. A long-established strategy is **reverse engineering**, which involves a company purchasing a competitor's products and having its engineers studying them to understand the technology and design. It is critical to understand that the theft of a competitor's proprietary information or trade secrets is a crime under the Economic Espionage Act of 1996 (U.S.).

Forecasting: The data developed from environmental scanning and competitive intelligence, when layered onto recent financial results, can be used to forecast possible future results. These forecasts are based on mathematical algorithms that provide a range of outcomes that reflect various economic possibilities. For example, a company might consider sales and profits in a continuing global recessionary climate, and develop a forecast that reflects improvements and/or deterioration in specific indicators such as employment, the value of the home country currency, the expectations for economic growth (usually measured as real gross domestic product [GDP] and other factors).

Scheduling: This activity involves the allocation of human, financial and physical asset resources to the operations of an organization, the sequencing of those operations and other issues of arranging work. An early technique that continues to be used is the GANTT chart, developed by Henry Gantt about a century ago, that visually presents activities to be done and those that have been completed. The concept shows managers the status of work at a glance; see the example that follows. The stage of completion of each activity can be by percentage (as is shown) or by time units.

There are several variations on the GANTT chart, such as complex scheduling by a PERT network analysis. PERT (an acronym for Program Evaluation Review Technique) shows the sequencing of activities and includes the associated costs. PERT requires the manager to not only determine the various tasks but also to determine which events depend on other events, allowing the identification of potential bottlenecks or trouble spots.

Illustrative GANTT Chart

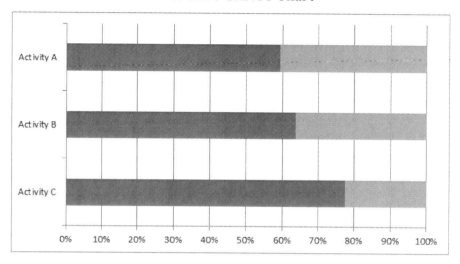

Medium Gray: Completed Work
Dark Gray: Work-in-Process
Light Gray: Targeted Future Work Completion

What is Operational vs. Strategic Planning?

Operational planning specifies methods to achieve short-term, largely process objectives. Examples of operational plans include a new configuration of manufacturing tasks to reduce vertical movement of raw materials and work-in-process, or the acquisition of equipment that can produce different products by changing fabrication tools. In sales, an operational plan could be a realignment of sales territories or a new media plan to change the mix of advertising messages and the target audience.

Assumptions in the Operational Plan

There is only limited similarity between organizations at the operational level, and so companies generally must plan based on their specific needs rather than on a general methodology. The significant commonality is that operational plans are the basis for and justification of an annual operating budget request, including staffing and other resource requirements. Bounded rationality (see Chapter 2) dominates most decisions.

The normal activities in an operational plan would not help in the unexpected situations a business may encounter. The essence of management is dealing with possibilities ("contingencies" has been a popular buzzword)[52] that are in the environment but whose occurrence is not predictable. In fact, many businesspeople admit that a first-level manager's job is about 98% repetition and boredom, and perhaps 2% panic. As an illustration, a fast food operation follows rules and procedures for nearly every activity – but what happens when electricity goes down due to a storm, or there is an health emergency at the store (such as a customer's heart attack), or a utility pipe breaks and there is no water for coffee or to clean utensils? The concept of possibilities requires rapid responses to unpredictable crises that could prove disastrous unless properly handled. For these situations, we need contingency plans, such as a call to 911 for a medical emergency, the use of a back-up supply of bottled water, or having stand-by generators to produce electricity.

The Assumptions in the Strategic Plan

Unlike operational planning, the evaluation of strategic plans is a multi-step process that begins with past experiences but then requires some research into new processes. The number of steps will vary by organization, and what we present here is a possible template for general use.

1. Relevance of the Current Mission Statement. What is our mission statement? Have we identified our customers, markets and products or services; our commitment to ethical and socially responsible actions; our concern for our image, our employees and our stockholders; or other relevant factors? Have we addressed new customers and prospects, new markets and new delivery systems?
2. Analysis of the External Environment. Are we current on legislative issues; changes in government policy or attitudes in our global markets; innovative products offered by competitors; and numerous other actual or potential changes in our business?

---

52 See, e.g., L. Donaldson, *The Contingency Theory of Organizations,* Sage Publications, 2001.

3. Internal Analysis. Are we adjusting to competitive pressures by cost efficiencies and improved product design; are new technologies being considered; and do we understand the situation with regard to the Figure 5-4 internal strengths and weaknesses?

4. Strategy Formulation. Should we focus on growth, stability or retrenchment? Ideally, companies would prefer growth to increase the size of the corporate "footprint" into new global markets. However, the weak economy may force a more prudent strategy, to either stabilize sales and profits (as some consumer products companies are doing) or to retrench, by cost cutting and the closing of some operations (as is the situation in many global banks). One popular approach is the BCG matrix (of Boston Consulting Group); see Figure 5-6. The four sections of the schematic are overly simplistic in making decisions on business strategy, but they do assist in focusing on alternative strategies.

5. Strategy Implementation and Evaluation. The formulation of a strategy necessitates its implementation which must be assigned to a sub-organization or team in the company. We will discuss methods of evaluating corporate decision-making in Chapter 6.

Figure 5-6: BCG Matrix

	Market Share	
Growth Rate	Stars	Question Marks
	Cash Cows	Dogs

In the BCG Matrix, the four cells represent the following strategies for a business unit, product or other component of a company:

- Stars – heavy investment
- Question marks – careful analysis and observation
- Cash cows – "milk" (take cash from) these units and limit future investments
- Dogs – sell or liquidate

What are Current Issues in Strategic Planning?

Current economic conditions have led to necessary refinements of traditional planning, including scenario analysis, zero-based budgeting (or its equivalent in planning) and adaptation to global concerns.

Scenario Analysis

Industries, companies, and products are trapped in interrelated lifecycles. These patterns are not linear; they rise and fall driven by a variety of factors. A critical aspect of the work of Clayton Christensen, an important strategic planning researcher, is the notion of disruptive innovation that alters the lifecycle of a business and its environment.[53] Acknowledging these inevitable changes with a contingency process is a necessary development in planning.

In its most fundamental format, **scenario analysis** applies probabilities to various future outcomes and a joint expected value is calculated. The technique is used in finance for risk management and in structuring portfolios of investments, but managers do not generally apply it in the consideration of alternative (particularly worst case) business strategies. The issue is: "what could go wrong?" While acts of God are random,[54] a company should attempt to list and prepare for any event that can reasonably be predicted.

It is recommended that at least three "cases" be considered based on the base or existing case:

- A most likely case representing a defensible expectation for future results.
- A worst case that represents the greatest dangers and threats to the company's attaining its goals.

---

53 C. Christensen, *The Innovator's Dilemma*, Harvard Business School Press, 1997.

54 Examples include the 1989 Exxon Valdez oil spill in Alaska, the 2001 terrorist attacks on the World Trade Center and the Pentagon, the 2011 Japanese tsunami and near nuclear meltdown and the 2012 Super-Hurricane Sandy.

- A best case showing optimistic results from an improving economy and customer acceptance.

The forecast of financial results is then assigned probabilities for each scenario, which will vary depending on the company's perception of likely outcomes. For example, the most likely could be assigned a 60% probability, while the worst case could receive a 25% probability and the best case a 15% probability. The result provides a range of possible results, and defines the riskiness of the venture.

Scenario analysis can be applied to any business organization; Figure 5-7 shows the three scenarios developed for a fast food business focusing on a potential strategic investment in a developing global market, perhaps China. The following assumptions were made in developing the most likely case, and others were constructed for the best and worst cases.

- Sales assumes growth at a slightly higher rate than the company as experienced from 2009 to 2011
- Cost of goods sold assumes improvements in cost control through inventory and purchasing management programs
- Fixed costs (depreciation expense, interest expense) do not vary as these amounts would be incurred regardless of sales volume
- Operating expenses are assumed higher due to marketing and legal costs

Figure 5-7: Scenario Analysis for a Chinese Fast-Food Business

(Applied to Expected 2012 Results)

(in millions of $)

	Most Likely	Worst Case	Best Case	Probable Outcome
Probability	60%	25%	15%	100%
Sales	$317	$308	$340	$318
Less: Cost of goods sold	$226	$257	$238	$235
Gross profits	$91	$51	$102	$83

Less: Selling and administrative expense	$50	$42	$55	$49
Less: Depreciation expense	$11	$11	$11	$11
Operating profit	$30	- $20	$36	$23
Less: Interest expense	$7	$7	$7	$7
Earnings before taxes	$23	- $9	$29	$16
Less: Corporate taxes (at 35%)	$8	0	$10	$6
Net income after taxes	$15	- $9	$19	$10

The probable outcome shows net income after taxes of $10 million and a worst case of a $9 million loss. These results would be used to calculate financial ratios, and the managers could then determine how to proceed.

How Does Entrepreneurship Relate to Strategic Planning?

We started this chapter with an explanation of entrepreneurship and related issues. Entrepreneurship and strategic planning are essentially identical activities, except that the former begins with a base case of zero with all outcomes based on probabilities for various possible outcomes. Strategic planning uses a base case of current business operations as adjusted for these results. A better strategic planning procedure would be to start at zero (in government, this is known as zero-based budgeting [ZBB]) and challenge every revenue and cost assumption. Unfortunately, few companies attempt this because of several factors:

- ZBB is more time-consuming and requires more expertise than traditional (incremental) budgeting
- Justifying every item can be difficult for organizations with intangible outputs (such as customer service or a government-run social agency)
- In a large company, the amount of information supporting the budgeting process may be overwhelming

In the current economic climate, it is difficult to pursue ZBB or an equivalent strategic planning process due to cost efficiency limitations.

Global Issues in Planning

In theory, there should be no difference in planning regardless of the global location. However, we know from Chapter 4 that national cultures have a significant effect on organizational behavior. Successful international companies understand that such differences exist, and plan accordingly. For example, our fast-food operation in China must develop menus that urban Chinese will patronize, that meet local rules and regulations, and that are compatible with the provisions that vendors can provide.[55] Global decisions must be consistent with the values, beliefs attitudes and behavior of local people.

A decision in international markets is inevitably made on the basis of limited information. We simply do not know what another culture will accept or if our data is credible. As a result, we must be willing to act based on a limited understanding of the marketplace, and when we err, we must be willing to "call it quits" or quickly adjust. In order to do this, we must build a business that can see the unexpected and respond to any environmental surprise. Western companies are not good at being this flexible, particularly in cultures in any of the developing economies.

This situation is why the chapter began with a comment on contingency. Planning is an iterative process, that is, one that learns and improves from actual results. This is particularly important as plans are implemented, and is often accomplished by flattening the organizational structure so that first-level supervisors are actively involved in goal setting and plan implementation. The planner must be a participant in the entire process, which makes a separate planning department or function significantly less relevant than previously.

What are the Issues You Should Address?

In considering your organization's planning activities, here are some issues to review.

- Does our organization have an entrepreneurial (if a start-up) or an intrapreneurial (if an existing company) attitude toward innovation and

---

55 We'll continue this example in Chapter 6.

risk-taking? Do we encourage or discourage new ideas and the development of new ideas and methods of doing business?

- Have we prepared a business plan or feasibility study? Have we addressed the relevant issues with regard to the important components of the company?
- Does our company have a process for operational and strategic planning? Who has responsibility for planning and is there a formal process including specific deadlines, report format, access to external and internal information, and other critical inputs?
- For strategic planning, do we use SWOT or other planning techniques?
- Do we plan using a logical sequence of steps to assure the inclusion of appropriate data and the review of logical alternatives?
- Do we use scenario analysis or other assignment of probabilities to develop outcomes that reflect various future outcomes?
- Do we use zero-based budgeting or an equivalent process in strategic planning?
- Have we considered global planning issues including national cultures and limitations on available information?

Discussion and Review Questions

1. What is the concept of entrepreneurship? Of intrapreneurship? Cite recent examples of each.
2. How do demographic and/or economic trends impact the opportunities in entrepreneurship and intrapreneurship?
3. What are the components of a feasibility study or business plan?
4. How does a businessperson select an appropriate legal form of ownership?
5. What are the two important forms of planning in an organization, and how do they differ?
6. How does scenario analysis assist in strategic planning?
7. What are the significant global issues in planning?

CHAPTER 6

Decision-Making

After reading this chapter, you will be able to:

- Understand the various steps required to objectively make management decisions
- Appreciate the significance of the definition of the critical problem as an initial step in decision-making
- Focus on the use of a weight and point system to quantify alternative actions and reach a decision
- Consider how risk management has affected decision-making
- Be aware of decision-making issues in the 21st century

What is Managerial Decision-Making?

Making decisions should not be merely choosing among alternatives, which is the process too many managers seem to use. Instead, **decision-making** should be viewed as a process of thoughtfully investigating all reasonable alternatives. The material that follows is developed in part from the writings of leading management thinker Peter Drucker.[56] A basic approach to problem-

---

56 His *The Practice of Management* was referenced in footnote 11; see particularly Chapters 5 through 7 and 28. Another recommended Drucker classic is *Management: Tasks, Responsibilities, Practices*, Harper & Row, 1974.

solving involves several deliberate steps which we discuss in this section of the chapter.

Step 1. Definition of the Problem

What is the critical problem? In other words, what is that thing which must be changed or altered before anything else can be changed? Too often, we focus on symptoms of the problem and not the underlying problem. The most visible symptoms are usually the least revealing ones. For example, management may see a clash of personalities; the real problem may be poor organizational structure or responsibilities that have not been clearly defined.[57] Management may see an unacceptable level of manufacturing costs and start a cost-reduction drive; the real problem may be poor engineering design.

The first task in discovering the problem in the case is to find the factor that must be changed before anything else can be altered, improved or acted on. Here's an example: A large diversified company (actually a conglomerate)[58] found itself in many unrelated businesses chosen because of the philosophy of the president/founder of investing in unique profitable companies. Senior management was located in plush corporate headquarters in a major Midwestern city in the U.S. These executives attended meetings and read reports but rarely visited any of the operating companies that were in somewhat grimy industrial locations throughout North America. For about 15 years, profits were acceptable to the conglomerate's bankers and investors, and so the stock price was steady and attractive (if not spectacular).

Eventually, competitors began to seize market share with innovative products, better pricing and aggressive marketing, and the conglomerate's profits began to decline. Careful analysis revealed that the portfolio of companies were now only marginally profitable, with the one "star" (see Chapter 5) producing most of the profits. However, the star was beginning to lose market share and the overall situation was deteriorating. When the critical problem was finally determined — a flawed strategy in selecting and managing the operating companies — the bankers, investors and the board of directors insisted on a new mission for the business, including selling or closing the marginal companies that could not be saved and focusing on a few, potentially profitable operations including the "star".

---

57 We note this very situation in the Balto/Nectis case in Appendix B.
58 The conglomerate organizational structure is discussed in Chapter 7.

To find the critical problem, ask these questions: "What will happen if nothing is changed?" and "What could have improved the situation when the problem first appeared?" In the situation just described, if no changes are made the conglomerate will eventually deteriorate and perhaps cease operations. The problem first appeared when the previously profitable operating companies began to lose market share and the ability to generate acceptable net income.

Step 2. Analysis of Facts and Issues

The author advised a large manufacturing company and discovered that parts were being purchased in anticipation of pricing increases or shortages. This problem surfaced when metrics were developed on materials utilization that showed a significant increase in the days of inventory. A loan was requested from the author's bank to finance this growing and largely obsolete inventory which led to the discovery of the situation. The problem could have been avoided years earlier if appropriate purchasing practices had been established.[59]

Data should be assembled from the company's internal records and is available from print and Internet sources. Information must be scrutinized for underlying patterns that indicate that the problem has been correctly or incorrectly defined. For example, if you suspect that a financing is supporting an inappropriate policy on inventory (the critical problem), you could compare the company's inventory turnover ratio to its competitors and to results of earlier years.[60] In addition, you can investigate whether modern inventory management techniques are being used, such as economic order quantity (EOQ) or just-in-time (JIT).[61]

Students often remark that certain critical information is missing from a business situation or a management case (such as those in Appendix B). However, managers seldom obtain all of the facts about any situation. Most decisions are based on incomplete knowledge — either because the data is not available or because it would require too much time or cost to obtain.

---

59 This example is explored in greater detail in J.S. Sagner, *Essentials of Working Capital Management*, Wiley, 2010, pages 119-120.

60 A **financial ratio** is a relative magnitude of two selected numerical values taken from a company's financial statements. The **inventory turnover ratio** is measured as cost of goods sold (an income statement account) divided by inventory (a balance sheet account).

61 **Economic order quantity** (EOQ) is the order quantity that minimizes total inventory holding costs and ordering costs. **Just in time** (JIT) is a production technique that attempts to reduce in-process inventory and associated carrying costs by having raw materials and components delivered just prior to being placed into production.

Decisions in the real world are often made with important information missing. The thoughtful manager will determine which data are missing in order to judge the risk of a decision.

A public utility was considering several international investments, some of which were in countries where information on business practices, employee training and retention, local regulations and other factors was sketchy. The company pursued several sources to obtain the necessary data, including on-site visits, discussions with local and global banks and attorneys with appropriate expertise, a review of documents published by government ministries, and discussions with companies doing business in the counties. Inevitably, the utility had to make commitments with some critical data missing. A risk premium investment return[62] was developed reflecting the extent of hazardous conditions in each country for each possible alternative. Decisions were made based on the expectation that each alternative would or would not exceed that return.

Step 3. Formulation Of Alternative Actions

Once the critical factor is determined, the next step is to determine the conditions for its solution based on the company's missions and goals. These goals should always focus on business performance and results, but may require changing established practices. In the situation of the diversified conglomerate (described in step 1), appropriate business performance was a rational assignment of duties and responsibilities among the members of senior management based on a logical organizational structure. The change eventually required removing the founder/president and choosing a new chief executive officer.

The development and testing of alternative actions is the heart of the scientific method. The **scientific method** is a set of procedures for investigating observable activities, acquiring information, or correcting and integrating previous knowledge. The method of inquiry must be based on an accepted experimental procedure and evidence that can be measured subject to specific principles of logic. The scientist always considers alternative explanations for observations, no matter how familiar and commonplace.

---

62 A risk premium is the amount by which the expected return on a risky asset must exceed the return on a risk-free asset in order to induce an investor to hold the risky asset rather than the risk-free asset. In finance, we use the concept in the Capital Asset Pricing Model (CAPM) and measure the risk of a publicly-traded company using beta (ß). It is the minimum return that the investor requires as compensation for the risk.

In management, as in science, an observer should never focus on what is obvious, but expand his or her imagination to fully consider various approaches to any problem. For example, when your television stops working properly, is the problem related to cable TV box, the cable TV feed, the electrical connection, or the TV? Or did you forget to pay the cable TV bill? Companies are particularly difficult to subject to the scientific method because of the many variables that can affect a situation. There are numerous avenues of investigation when a company's earnings are below that of its peer companies. Is the problem our pricing, our costs, our product mix, our market penetration, our productivity, our engineering or some other factor?

A clothing manufacturer's production facilities had become obsolete: one building had originally been a canning facility build about 80 years earlier, and the other building had been constructed some three decades ago. Neither structure was capable of meeting environmental requirements, was air-conditioned except in the executive offices, offered adequate power for electrical cutting machines, sewing machines or computers; and both were generally unattractive places to do business or present to customers. The situation threatened the company's market position in a highly competitive industry.

Management concluded that it had to move, and decided to build a new consolidated manufacturing plant. This decision eventually bankrupted the company. Actions that were never considered included sub-contracting production (which is common in the industry, particularly to developing countries); leasing an existing facility; closing the older building and moving some production to the other structure with the rest sub-contracted; or selling the business to a competitor. Unfortunately, management did not think of these alternatives until it was too late.

Step 4. Do Nothing!

One possible action that should be considered in any business situation is to *do nothing*. To take no action is a decision fully as much as to take specific actions, and the analyst must specify the consequences of not acting. Occasionally the problem will self-correct, and a decision to do nothing may be entirely appropriate. Here's a "do nothing" example: A law firm based in New York had established a Washington office primarily to provide on-site contacts with government, including Congressional offices and regulators.

The expectation was that legal business would be developed for clients with the contacts that were developed, despite the very limited corporate activity that was likely to be awarded to the firm through that office. Eventually the lease on the Washington space was up for renewal at a much higher rate. The firm decided that any Washington activity could be handled through New York, and to save on rent, overhead and other costs, the lease was not renewed – the "do nothing" solution. Staff was allowed to move to New York, to work out of their residences (but on a part-time rather than full-time basis), or to leave with a generous severance.

Step 5. Analysis of Alternative Courses of Action

Criteria for selecting the appropriate course of action include the following:

- The Risk. The risks of each action must be weighed against the expected rewards, and the action that has the highest risk/return relationship should be chosen. However, no action should be selected that would jeopardize the future of the company.
- The Effort. The analysis has to consider the investment of time, money and persuasion necessary to effectuate each alternative.
- Timing. Urgent situations require quick actions, which may have to be followed by more permanent solutions. Strategic situations allow more thoughtful, long-term actions, which may involve a commitment of significant financial or other company resources.
- Limitations. Who will carry out the action? The analyst has to work with the organization in the company, and cannot simply recommend that teams of high-powered MBAs can be hired and put to work on the problem.

Step 6. Recommendation

The development of a recommendation should logically follow from the analysis in the preceding sections. Always try to select an action that is practicable rather than heroic, particularly given the resources, time and risk constraints faced by the company. The organization needs a plan for implementation or "road map" as a guide to the correct actions; too often this element is missing from the process. The plan should include specific tasks, manager responsibilities and criteria to determine the degree of success. See Figure 6-1 for an example of such a recommendation. Note that the write-up includes a statement about industry practice, specific statistics on current practice at the company (ABC Corporation), a calculation of benefits and the requirements for implementation.

Figure 6-1: Example of Implementation Plan

Action: End the Practice of Early Release of Accounts Payable Checks

Findings: Vendor payments are made as payment terms dictate or earlier, after the taking of all cash discounts. Many U.S. corporations are paying in 40 to 50 days regardless of terms, and vendors of ABC Corporation would logically expect equivalent treatment. Statistics provided by Accounts Payable indicate the following payment practices during the first half of 2012:

Invoice Date to Payment Date	# of Invoices	Cumulative % Distribution
0 - 5	3,313	2%
6 - 10	9,761	8%
11 - 15	21,168	20%
16 - 20	19,191	31%
21 - 25	17,191	41%
26 - 30	33,028	60%
31 - 35	42,209	84%
36 - 40	7,393	88%
41 - 45	4,274	90%
46 - 50	2,513	91%
51 - 55	1,220	92%
56 or More	13,020	100%

Some 60% of all invoices are paid prior to 30 days, with nearly 300,000/year invoices paid early by an average 62 days. It is recommended that payables be extended by 5 days, to 35 days, to gain 112 days of float. With payables of about $23 million/day for Divisions 1-3, the savings would be approximately $22 million a year at a 10% cost of capital, and would simply involve instructing Accounts Payable to institute the change. Divisions 4-6 experience payables of about $400,000/day. For the entire corporation, the savings would probably be in the range of $3 million/year if a mechanism were developed to diary manual payments. (Each additional day of delay is worth in excess of $350,000.)

Required: A senior management decision to implement a policy of paying all invoices on day 35 (after invoice date) or later if the item is in dispute. Records should be developed to indicate how payments are actually processed. The Accounts Payable Manager should be tasked with preparing the necessary policy directives and informing payables clerks as to the new procedure.

How do Managers Make Decisions?

In Chapter 5 we outlined a logical process for strategic planning that should lead to thoughtful actions, and suggested scenario analysis as a procedure to assign probabilities to best, likely and worst case outcomes. An important issue in planning is managerial decision-making; that is, the process of choosing between alternatives once a strategy has been set. We previously noted (toward the end of that chapter) an investment in China by a fast-food company. Now the company must decide on locations, whether to joint venture with a local partner, who the vendors of food ingredients and supplies will be, how to advertise and market the stores, and other business decisions. The process should be logical and deliberate, and specific actions are discussed in this section.

Identify and Assign Weights to Decision Criteria

In the China fast-food decision, various factors are important, including population at the location, accessibility of vendors, cost and freshness of ingredients, availability of marketing channels, the potential pool of management and food service workers, issues with regard to local regulations and licenses, and various other concerns. We need to determine which the "must" factors are and which are less important but desirable, assign weights to each criterion and point values for each alternative (perhaps on a 1 to 5 scale, with 5 as the highest).

Make a Final Decision

Weighting each criterion (including "musts") and multiplying them times the point value provides a weighted score, which when summed effectively makes decision-making relatively objective. Of course, the criteria and/or the weights can be the wrong choices, so participation by management and, if necessary, by outside advisers, is certainly appropriate. A matrix of decision factors for the China decision is provided in Figure 6-2. As can be seen, the first choice is a location in Beijing, with Shanghai a second alternative.

The first-round of this analysis may result in a prioritization of choices that is not consistent with *a priori* expectations.[63] Suppose the fast-food managers had previously visited the three locations and expected that Shanghai would be the first choice. The managers can then examine the weights and points assigned in the analysis and make adjustments to either affirm or revise the original calculations. In addition, it may be necessary after further review to add additional criteria, such as the proximity of potential sites to rapid transit stations, or the likelihood that the local population will be receptive to the items planned for the menu.[64]

This system allows for directed marketing research on such specific issues as public acceptance of specific menu items or price/demand alternatives. See Figure 6-3 for the results of second-round modifications that now show Beijing and Shanghai to be in a virtual tie. It may be that the optimal decision is to

---

63 *A priori* knowledge or justification is independent of experience or data. In contrast, *a posteriori* knowledge or justification is dependent on experience or empirical evidence.

64 Indeed, the author participated in one such exercise for an insurance company where the number of alternatives grew from six to more than two dozen!

open two locations to spread various costs and to allow experimentation with menus, pricing and other issues at one of the restaurants.

Figure 6-2: A First-Round Decision Matrix for a Fast-Food Location in China

	Locations and Points Assigned		
Criteria and Weights	**Beijing**	**Shanghai**	Guangzhou
Population size (10%)	5	5	3
Access to vendors (20%)	5	5	4
Cost/freshness of ingredients (15%)	5	4	4
Marketing channels available? (15%)	4	4	3
Pool of potential employees (15%)	5	5	4
Local regulations and licenses (15%)	4	3	4
Other criteria (site cost, receptivity to Western products, etc.) (10%)	4	4	3
Criteria and Weighted Point Assignments			
Population size (10%)	0.50	0.50	0.30
Access to vendors (20%)	1.00	1.00	0.80
Cost/freshness of ingredients (15%)	0.75	0.60	0.60
Marketing channels available? (15%)	0.60	0.60	0.45
Pool of potential employees (15%)	0.75	0.75	0.60
Local regulations and licenses (15%)	0.60	0.45	0.60
Other criteria (site cost, receptivity to Western products, etc.) (10%)	0.40	0.40	0.30
Weighted Points	4.60	4.30	3.65

Figure 6-3: A Second-Round Decision Matrix for a Fast-Food Location in China
(added criteria are shown in italics)

Criteria and Weights	Locations and Points Assigned		
	Beijing	Shanghai	Guangzhou
Population size (5%)	5	5	3
Access to vendors (20%)	5	5	4
Cost/freshness of ingredients (15%)	5	4	4
Marketing channels available? (15%)	4	4	3
Pool of potential employees (10%)	5	5	4
Local regulations and licenses (10%)	4	3	4
Proximity to transit stations (10%)	*3*	*5*	*5*
Reception for menu items (10%)	*4*	*5*	*4*
Other criteria (site cost, receptivity to Western products, etc.) (5%)	4	4	3
Criteria and Weighted Point Assignments			
Population size (5%)	0.25	0.25	0.15
Access to vendors (20%)	1.00	1.00	0.80
Cost/freshness of ingredients (15%)	0.75	0.60	0.60
Marketing channels available? (15%)	0.60	0.60	0.45
Pool of potential employees (10%)	0.50	0.50	0.40
Local regulations and licenses (10%)	0.40	0.30	0.40
Proximity to transit stations (10%)	*0.30*	*0.50*	*0.50*
Reception for menu items (10%)	*0.40*	*0.50*	*0.40*
Other criteria (site cost, receptivity to Western products, etc.) (5%)	0.20	0.20	0.15
Weighted Points	4.40	4.45	3.85

How has Risk Management Affected Decision-Making?

The single issue that confronts companies more than any other today is risk and uncertainty, and risk management has become an important discipline within the toolbox of managers. Because of the huge potential for loss and even the destruction of a business from a bad decision, various approaches to risk management have developed to support management.[65] While risk is essentially a financial sub-discipline, there are various processes that apply to all managers.

Risk

Risk is the possibility of loss or injury. The measurement of risk has traditionally been the frequency of human or property loss in specific categories, such as death or disability by age, sex and occupation or the frequency of fire damage to specific types of construction at various locations. In the past, we managed many risks using insurance, with the policyholder accepting a small certain loss – the premium expense – rather than the possibility of a large catastrophic loss. Other types of risk have been generally recognized but, until recently, were not included as a formal management function.

Those now considered are generally known as operational risks. **Operational risk** is inherent in business activities as it arises from problems with technology, employees or operations. These risks are often managed by the establishment of policies and procedures to govern the conduct of ongoing activities. Realistically, behaviors cannot be regulated by proclamation. However, assigning specific duties states the company's position on responsibilities, sets a charter for responsible corporate behavior and assesses penalties should violations occur. Finance-based risks include:

- **Credit risk** concerns the failure of customers to pay amounts owed and due in a timely manner.

---

65 An entire chapter (Chapter 12) is devoted in risk management in the author's *Fast-Track Finance*, Fast-Track Textbooks, due in 2014.

- **Liquidity risk** is a company's inability to pay obligations as they come due, resulting in financial embarrassment, a negative impact on the company's credit rating and vendor relations and potential bankruptcy.
- **Information reporting risk** is the receipt of inaccurate information from a financial institution or vendor, most usually in the daily transmission of bank account entries, balances or transactions.
- **Foreign exchange/interest rate/commodity risk** involves adverse movements in the price of raw materials or financial instruments, causing higher-than-planned costs and possible losses. These risks are managed using hedging instruments.

Comprehensive **enterprise risk management** (ERM) is intended to identify, prioritize and quantify the risks from all sources that threaten the strategic objectives of the corporation. The ERM approach views risk as pervasive in a company, and considers a coordinated approach through a formal organizational function to be essential. ERM reduces the volatility inherent in business activities and helps to achieve consistent earnings and manage costs.

Decision-Making Techniques and Payoffs

Certain decisions require a considerable amount of the manager's time and effort, and cannot be considered as routine. Other decisions involve **structured problems**, which are familiar, easily defined and subject to decision rules (often called **programmed decisions**). For example, our fast-food company about to do business in China has encountered various minor problems for which solutions are either taught or covered by written rules. A server who spills coffee on a customer must: 1.) apologize 2.) tell the manager; 3.) determine if medical attention is needed; 4.) offer to have the soiled clothes cleaned at store expense; and 5.) have the store provide a free meal.

An **unstructured problem** has ambiguous (unclear) information and there is no rule or standard procedure. The store location problem we discussed in the previous section is an example of an unstructured problem. Another problem of this type would be the introduction of a new sandwich and a forecast of a competitor's response. Will the sandwich cause little or no reaction from the competitor, a lower price policy, more advertising, a coupon offering with each meal (say, for a free sandwich on the next visit), or some other response? The results can be displayed in a profit payoff matrix, a decision analysis tool that summarizes pros and cons of decisions in a tabular format. In our situation, the matrix could be created as is shown in Figure 6-4.

Figure 6-4: Profit Payoff Matrix for Fast-Food Operation

($ in thousands)	Competitor's Reaction			
Our Strategy	No Reaction	Lower Price Policy	More Advertising	Coupon Offer
Introduce new sandwich	$100	$50	$65	$40
Do not introduce new sandwich	0	-$25	-$35	-$15

The matrix informs us that to maximize profits, we should introduce the sandwich and hope that there is no competitive response (+$100,000). If we are pessimists taking the "least-worst" solution, we would still introduce the sandwich but expect that competitors would counter with a coupon, reducing our payoff (to +$40,000). By studying the table, we would immediately see that we should introduce the sandwich because all outcomes provide positive results as long as we cover our costs. (If our costs exceed $40,000 but are less than $100,000, the action chosen will depend on the optimism or pessimism of the decision-maker.)

Other Advanced Decision-Making Techniques

There are various advanced techniques that quantify and improve decision-making, including those generically known as operations research, management science or decision sciences. These activities began to be used during World War Two to assist military planners, and are now focused on the development of mathematical models that can be used to analyze and optimize complex systems. Some of the problems addressed include project planning, factory layout and production scheduling, transportation routing, global supply chain management and pricing. However, any quantitative method is entirely dependent on the quality of the data that it analyzes; in information technology, we refer to this as GIGO (garbage in, garbage out).

Decision-Making in the 21st Century

The rapid pace and globalization of business make the decision process more difficult than ever while magnifying the potential loss from a bad choice. The actual costs incurred are bad enough; a worse outcome is that competitors may take away your customers and you may have to struggle to recover your previous share of the market. Companies often choose to introduce a new product, enter a new market or develop a new promotion because of the fear of competitors; unfortunately, no survival strategies could help Eastman Kodak, Montgomery Ward or countless other failed companies that made fatal decisions or failed to act.

Rules on Decision-Making

There are several rules in managerial decision-making that should be incorporated into the entire process.

- Understand cultural differences. Culture can change a rational decision in Country X to a poor choice in Country Y. A U.S. based corporate headquarters (think Disney) cannot possibly understand the attitudes, beliefs and value systems in another country. As EuroDisney was originally conceived – an American theme park with American themes and operational procedures but located in France – the project was doomed to failure. Involve the local managers in the decision and use research and marketing tools to determine if your plans are viable before investing any significant time and capital on the project.[66]
- Admit failure. Don't be afraid to admit failure and stop or at least delay further action until the situation becomes clearer. One of the more interesting recent developments in finance is **real options** (sometimes called "managerial options"), which allows the reconsideration of

---

66 This situation has been discussed by many articles, case writers and books. See, e.g., "Losing the Magic: How Euro Disney became a Nightmare," *The Independent*, November 13, 2010, at www.independent.co.uk/news/business/analysis-and-features/losing-the-magic-how-euro-disney-became-a-nightmare-2132892.html; or P. Nutt, Why *Decisions Fail*, Berrett-Koehler, 2002 (analyzing bad corporate and how the problem could have been approached differently).

capital investments at future pre-determined decision points. We may decide to expand or to abandon the project, or to wait by postponing activities scheduled for after the decision point until future unknowns become clearer.[67]

- Scan the environment. Instill in your organization the ability to notice unexpected but potentially damaging events and develop a quick-response mechanism. Smart companies are constantly scanning the environment for actions by competitors and for changes in government regulations that may interfere with plans. Never assume that you can extrapolate past experience into the future beyond a few months or perhaps a year, and constantly reevaluate assumptions that were made at the time of an important decision.

What are the Issues You Should Address?

In considering your organization's decision-making, here are some issues to review:

- Have we carefully considered critical problems in past situations of decision-making by our organization? Did we attempt to determine the essential factors or were we merely addressing symptoms of the underlying problem?
- Do we do an adequate job of analyzing facts and issues? Before considering alternative courses of action, do we make a reasonable attempt to determine if missing information is critical to the decision process?

---

67 A current example from Las Vegas: Echelon Place was a planned $4.8 billion Boyd Gaming Strip resort that remains uncompleted nearly three years after the company decided in August 2008 to halt the project. Echelon planned to open in 2010 with nearly 5,000 rooms spread over five hotels, along with a casino, convention space and theaters. Boyd found it tough to obtain the financing to complete construction. After the work stoppage, Boyd estimated it would delay Echelon's development for three to five years. Other abandoned projects in Las Vegas include several apartment developments and the Fontainebleau, an unfinished $2.9 billion planned Strip resort; one gaming analyst has said it could be at least 2015 before the 63-floor, 3,815-room hotel opens. See www.lasvegassun.com/news/2011/jun/24/abandoned-projects.

- Have we considered if doing nothing will result in a reasonable outcome at a low (or no) cost?
- Do we have a process that assigns points and weights to each criterion and do we reconsider our initial efforts at making choices by adding or changing these factors given other evidence?
- How have risk and uncertainty affected our decision-making? Have we considered using a payoff matrix or other tools to include these factors in our decisions?
- Have we considered the impact of cultural differences; do we consciously include the options to expand, abandon or postpone decisions; and have we instilled our organization's culture with a sense of awareness of changes in our business situation?

Discussion and Review Questions

1. What are the steps in a comprehensive decision-making process?
2. Once a decision is reached, what is a required document to assure that the decision will proceed successfully? What are the necessary components in this document?
3. How can a point and weight matrix can assist decision-makers in arriving at a thoughtful result?
4. How is risk management integrated into the decision-making process?
5. How can a profit payoff matrix support the decision-making process?
6. What are the essential rules to improve current-day decision-making?

CHAPTER 7

Organizing

After reading this chapter, you will be able to:

- Understand how companies organize for growth
- Appreciate classic concepts for the design of organizations and their current applicability
- Consider an organization's core competencies and options for other important activities
- Focus on the major determinants of the business structure including size, globalization and strategic positioning
- Be aware of newer, experimental organizational structures

How Should We Design the Organization's Structure?

Organizing involves a critical activity of management: to arrange the components and resources of the workplace to accomplish its missions and goals. This requirement was recognized at the time that the corporation began to become an important business form of ownership, beginning with the industrialization of Western economies in the mid-19th century. Corporations were necessary to accumulate capital from bondholders and stockholders to enable the construction and operation of large factories, and it was essential to organize the material and human resources needed for their efficient operation.

Ideas developed for the specialization or enrichment of work, the number of employees to manage (the span of control), the relationship between managers and employees at various levels of the organization (chain of command), the extent of centralization or decentralization, and other considerations. We will review some of these concepts and note those that continue to have relevance a century and a half after the industrial age began. For a brief description of relevant history, see Figure 7-1.[68]

Figure 7-1: Industrialization and the Development of Management

The Industrial Age transformed an agrarian society (one based on farming) to an industrial society (one based on mechanized production). The steam engine (usually credited to James Watt in 1775, although several inventors preceded Watt and others improved upon his work) is generally considered as the most important catalyst for this change. For the first time, a machine replaced animal power and the handwork of artisan (or craftsman) who laboriously fashioned each item required by nobility and peasants. As businesses grew, new inexperienced workers left subsistence farming for employment in the workshops that had been organized by craftsmen. This migration led to the division of labor, which was a way to employ these unskilled peasants. Each worker was assigned to a specific task, with several tasks eventually mechanized.

As workshops prospered, the accumulation of capital allowed investments in new technologies, enabling industrialization to continue. The wages paid to workers led to the demand for products previously unavailable while attracting more farm laborers to the cities where these industries were located. The industrial movement began in England, and it quickly spread to the rest of Western Europe and North America, particularly after the end of the American Civil War (1861 – 1865). The need for raw materials for these businesses, and for such consumer goods as tobacco and sugar, led to colonization and the exploitation of local populations.

68 For an excellent survey that focuses on industrialization in Great Britain, see E. J. Hobsbawm and C. Wrigley, *Industry and Empire: The Birth of the Industrial Revolution*, New Press, 1999.

Businesspeople realized that profits and borrowings from friends and family were insufficient to finance the plant, equipment and materials necessary to construct and operate a large machine-driven factory. As a result, the corporation developed and evolved into the primary form of ownership. However, these large companies required a formal type of organization to manage the hundreds (or even thousands) of employees, the supply chain, and the eventual distribution of product to markets. Engineers were used to analyze the processes of the business, and it is not a coincidence that the first acknowledged management analysts (Taylor, Gilbreth, Fayol) were from that discipline.

How Do Companies Structure Growth?

Despite decades of theory on the proper structure of organizations, companies and not-for-profits have determined designs based on their unique set of requirements. As Alfred Chandler so perceptively explained, the strategy of a company inevitably determines its structure. Chandler studied four companies,[69] analyzing how each evolved an organizational design appropriate to its mission. This work described very large companies that were horizontally or vertically integrated along the channels of distribution.[70]

Vertical integration involves a company's expansion by moving into either an earlier stage (backward integration) or into a later stage (forward integration) in the business system. An example of backward integration is the automobile industry, which acquired steel foundries early its history to assure a source of metal to stamp into automobile components. An example of forward integration is Apple, which manufactures computers and now retails them through more than 350 stores worldwide.

---

69 Chandler analyzed DuPont, General Motors, Standard Oil of NJ, and Sears Roebuck. *Strategy and Structure: Chapters in the History of the American Industrial Enterprise*, MIT Press 1969.

70 **Channel of distribution** is a marketing term that refers to the path products follow from raw material form to the final product form. The channel institutions in most frequent use are the manufacturer, who sells to the wholesaler, who sells to the retailer, who sells to the consumer.

Horizontal integration is growth through a merger or acquisition of a competitor at the same level in the business system. The recent acquisition of Anheuser-Busch (Budweiser) by Belgium beer brewer InBev is an illustration of this type of growth. While InBev could have created breweries to compete with Anheuser, it could never have duplicated its marketing reach and product recognition. There have been situations of both forms of integration occurring concurrently, and these are usually referred to as **conglomerates.** This type of growth has been generally difficult to manage, and past successes have generally not been duplicated in recent years. Conglomerates were popular in the 1960s due to low interest rates and the use of leveraged buyouts (LBOs), which use company profits to pay the interest on the borrowings ("the leverage") for the transaction.[71]

There is no one preferred way to structure the organization in response to the strategy that has been chosen. Companies like General Electric, an electrical and electronic manufacturing horizontal integration, largely defer management decisions to the specific operating segment (for GE: Energy, Technology Infrastructure, Capital Finance, and Consumer & Industrial), with the headquarters providing strategy, financing, accounting and legal services. Disney is a forwardly integrated company, and carefully controls the product sold or offered through its stores, theme parks and in theatrical release. Berkshire Hathaway, one of the few current day conglomerates, considers the holding company to be an investor rather than an active manager.

What are the Classic Concepts in Managing Work?

In Chapter 2 we noted certain classical management approaches to worker efficiency that developed about a century ago. Many of these concepts were in response to the industrialization of work and the need for efficiency. While scientific management and other early theories of organizing work have been largely discarded, certain concepts dating from that period continue and have applicability to companies in general.

---

71 Examples from that period included several companies that have disappeared: Ling-Temco-Vought (LTV), Litton Industries, ITT, Textron, Teledyne, Gulf+Western and Transamerica.

Line and Staff

The various functions of a company include sales (marketing), manufacturing (production), accounting, finance, information technology, legal affairs, product development (engineering), and other essential activities. As organizations expand and hopefully become profitable, these functions are assigned to specific areas of responsibility, often called departments. In fact, Max Weber, noted in Figure 2-1, was the first management figure to recognize the existence of these functions and to suggest an organizational format which he called "bureaucracy".[72] Within the organization, the **line** functions are directly focused on achieving the mission, and include sales and manufacturing. The **staff** functions provide assistance, advice and support.

Chain of Command and Related Principles

The **chain of command** is the path of authority from the senior managers to those at middle and supervisory management levels, clarifying who reports to which manager. The graphical description of the chain of command is the **organization chart** (see Figure 7-2), which visually represents these relationships. The concept of chain of command depends on the assignment of the **authority** or right for a manager to give direction and provide leadership, expecting that these requirements will be followed. (In certain organizations, these are orders or commands which must be obeyed. Failure to follow these orders can lead to fairly harsh consequences, as in the military or in a religious context.)

Figure 7-2 shows these relationships in a very simplistic manner, without indicating titles, names of incumbents, or layers of the organization below the second level of line and staff responsibilities. There are many variations of organization charts, and most public companies now have these graphic links on their websites. For examples, see General Electric's annual report at www.ge.com/pdf/company/ge_organization_chart.pdf.

---

72 A **bureaucracy** is usually defined as an organizational form that follows certain classical concepts in its structure. However, it also has the unfortunate connotation of a large, inefficient and direction-less organization without proper leadership or controls. Governmental agencies are often so-labeled.

Figure 7-2: Sample Organization Chart

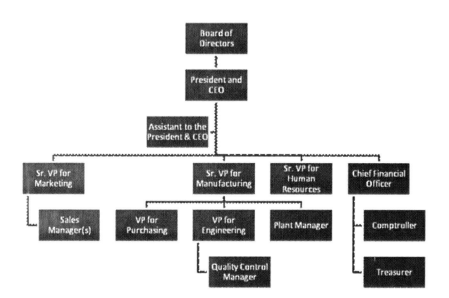

The requirements, once announced, imply two types of **responsibility**: 1.) on the manager to act in a responsible manner toward accomplishing the organization's mission; and 2.) on the worker, to accept and responsibly perform these assigned duties. These actions assume that the necessary training, equipment and other necessities of the work have been provided. **Unity of command**, which states that an employee should only report to one manager, is considered necessary for the work to be accomplished.

Centralization vs. Decentralization

The issue of centralization vs. decentralization is concerned with the degree to which decision-making occurs at the upper management levels, with **centralization** typically found in non-integrated single product line companies. An example of centralization is in the women's apparel industry, with dresses and other clothing designed, manufactured and marketed based on the decisions of a small team of senior managers. Medium-sized companies in that industry are not vertically or horizontally integrated as they buy fabric (known as "piece goods") from textile mills and sell through independent retailers such as department stores.

Decentralization is preferred where there is a large, integrated organization; the business environment is complex and uncertain; and mid-level managers and supervisors are capable of making decisions about specific business activities. Companies that are multi-country or global use decentralized managerial decision-making to address local concerns and issues, realizing that an executive in New York City cannot possibly understand a situation that has developed in Singapore.

An outstanding example of inappropriate centralization was the decisions on the features, rides, hiring practices and other theme park issues by senior management of Disney who were located in Burbank CA. EuroDisney was built outside of Paris, where the culture, climate and competition were largely unknown at corporate headquarters. The early years of the park's existence were a failure, and Disney has struggled to correct mistakes that have apparently doomed it to a break-even operation, at best.[73] The most egregious examples of decentralization perhaps have been in the securities industry, with such companies as Bear Stearns and Lehman Bros. failing because of a lack of oversight and control from senior management.

Other Classic Principles

Certain other principles have been used over the past century in developing organizational structures.

- **Span of control** addresses the number of employees that can be effectively managed. The traditional view was that no manager could have more than six to perhaps eight subordinates. The theory was that managers could not do their jobs and have a reasonable idea of the activities of the employees who were their direct reports.
- **Formalization** explains how much standardization and governance by rules exists in a company. Characteristics of formal organizations are organization charts, job descriptions and work procedures. In contrast, informal companies allow considerable discretion over job performance.

---

73 See, A. Lainsbury, *Once Upon an American Dream: The Story of Euro Disneyland*, University Press Of Kansas, 2000.

- **Work specialization** (also known as **division of labor**) is basic to the industrial age, when workers began to specialize in a limited task or set of tasks rather than produce a complete product. A classic example is a weapons armory where a worker would do only one job related to the manufacture of a rifle rather than assembly of the complete weapon, increasing his or her output multiple times.[74]
- **Departmentalization** refers to how jobs are grouped in an organization. Companies commonly use some variation of departmentalizing by function, by geography, by product line, by production process or by customer.

Do These Concepts Still Apply Today?

The classic concepts continue to be used by companies, although the application varies by the degree of standardization of the work flow, the need for speed vs. quality and various other factors specific to the organization.

- *Specialization* is critical in certain industries like fast-food due to the limited menu choices, the low prices offered, the customer expectation for the similarity of the product regardless of where purchased, and the low wages paid to workers. In other industries, like automobile retailing or real estate, salespeople must be able to "read" the customer and his or her needs and possible objections. A standard approach to selling a $30,000 car or a $300,000 house simply would not work.
- *Departmentalization* continues to be used, but the format often varies within a company to optimally meet goals. As an example, a large global insurance company organizes by function at U.S. headquarters (actuarial,[75] treasury, accounts payable, purchasing and so on), and by

---

74 The U.S. War Department sponsored the development of interchangeable parts for guns produced at the arsenals at Springfield MA and Harpers Ferry WVA in the early decades of the 19th century, finally achieving reliable interchangeability by about 1850.

75 Life, health, and pension actuaries analyze mortality risk, morbidity and consumer choice regarding the applicant's use of drugs and medical services.

country for customer coverage (for example, China, New Zealand and Canada). A consumer products company uses divisions organized by function, work process, geographic and customer depending on specific requirements.

- *Chains of command* have been replaced in many countries with formats that determine work assignments and likely problems such as groups and teams (discussed in Chapter 3). We noted that the focus on continuous improvement focus is often accomplished through "quality circles", workers who meet to discuss improvement, especially relating to quality of output to improve the performance of the organization. In addition, the use of computer technology has greatly reduced the requirement for the manager to gather and disseminate information to employees.
- *Span of control* has little relevance today, as companies rely on circumstances specific to job requirements to determine the number of employees who work for each manager. In a repetitive-task situation, a manager may have twenty employees, while a creative, nonstandard situation may minimize the role of the manager and utilize a group- or task force-type of arrangement.

Factors Affecting Decisions on Organizational Structure

In the present extremely competitive business environment, the most important factors appear to be the ability to react to changing market conditions and responsiveness to customer requirements. This largely explains the movement away from classic concepts by companies, and the orientation to flexibility, fewer management layers and the elimination of unnecessary organizational units. Current practice is for companies to focus on core competencies to the extent possible, and to outsource or offshore non-essential functions.

A **core competency** is an organization's value-creation capability determined by the products or services offered, unusual (or unique) features and support provided by the talents of employees. Companies often determine their core competencies by examining their position in their industry, and then deciding whether a leading role exists or is attainable. The important criteria of a core competency are:

- It would be difficult for competitors to emulate or match the competency.
- The competency can be used on a range of existing or planned products.
- Customers perceive the competency as a benefit worth buying, usually at a premium price.

Companies that have successfully developed core competencies include Apple (for its personal, state-of-the-art technologies), Best Buy (for its wide selection of electronics and customer service), Disney (for its story telling and efficient operation of theme parks), Celgene (for its pharmacological expertise for certain diseases) and e-Bay (for its auction marketplace and payment system). Many other companies have a niche or core competency that provides a lasting, profitable position in the market.

Outsourcing

There have been various results from the focus on core competencies. **Outsourcing** refers to the contracting of a business process to an independent vendor that was previously performed within an organization. The term "outsourcing" became popular in the 1990s when many businesses began to search for vendors to perform these activities. **Offshoring** extends this concept to performing these activities in another country. The reason that these concepts have become significant is the significantly lower cost experience in developing economies, where labor rates can be one-tenth of that in developed countries. Outsourcing offers flexibility, in that permanent expenses are avoided, such as equipment, buildings, permanent workers and management. In addition, regulations on workplace conditions tend to be significantly less restrictive in outsource sites.

While there are important cost advantages to outsourcing, businesses have found several disadvantages:

- Quality of service. As Dell and other companies have discovered, the responsiveness of customer service workers has been a serious issue with the outsourced service. Although production can be monitored using standard quality control routines, allowing inadequately trained foreign representatives to deal with previously loyal customers can result in alienation, even resulting in their loss to competitors.

- Confidentiality. Trade secrets can leak to competitors, and there is little that can be done to prevent these breaches of security.
- Public relations. Companies have experienced criticism for offshoring from news sources, lobbying groups and labor unions, and it was an important issue in the 2012 U.S. Presidential campaign.[76]

How Does Strategy Influence Organizational Structures?

While Chandler provided a landmark study of business structure, 21st century conditions require more adaptive forms to cope with a complex competitive environment.

Size

Large organizations tend to have considerable degrees of decentralization, with group vice-presidents and other lofty titles operating each business like an independent company. However, this structure may impede internal communications, so that a comprehensive view is only possible at the most senior levels. As a banker and consultant to about 300 companies, the author can attest that a large company is really a "forced marriage" of smaller firms, all presumably working toward the large company's mission and goals. As an example where this did not work, a large financial services company did not share customers and prospects among the various business units, and often competed for the same business opportunity as if the units were different companies! Needless to say, customers and prospects were confused and amazed.

---

76 See, e.g., G. Kessler, "Obama's New Attacks on Romney and Outsourcing," *The Washington Post*, July 2, 2012, at <u>www.washingtonpost.com/blogs/fact-checker/post/obamas-new-attacks-on-romney-and-outsourcing/2012/06/29/gJQA5FbbCW_blog.html</u>.

Extent of Globalization

The predominant characteristic of a business today may well be the requirement to design, manufacture and sell to international markets. Large
companies have known this for years, and now smaller businesses are either
learning how to participate or lose access to important customer segments.
There are various organizational structures that have been devised to deal
with the global component of their activities. Smaller companies may
use a freight forwarder, an export management company, a customhouse
broker, licensing, or any of various arrangements that simplify the process.
Larger companies have additional options, including operating their
own international departments or establishing subsidy or joint venture
operations.[77]

In addition, the structure of organizations also depends on inherent variations in global cultures. While there are significant similarities between developed economy companies, as globalization extends to developing countries
there may be the need to revert to certain of the classic concepts discussed earlier in this chapter. For example, a U.S. computer company using workers in a
Chinese factory may need to establish formal reporting relationships, chains of
command and other methods of what we once called "scientific management".
This is because many new factory workers in China have never held a produc-
tion-line job and previously were farm workers.

Strategic Positioning within an Industry

Companies must also choose *a* strategic position – multiple positions tend to
fail due to management's inability to focus on and execute successfully. The
basic strategic positions are as follows:

- To be innovative. The introduction of new products and services either as a continuous series of activities (3M and Apple) or a single (or
  a few) landmark changes that alter the business model for the industry
  (Dell, Best Buy and Facebook).
- To imitate: Copy the successful innovator often with a unique change
  or modification. Many companies today simply emulate a successful

---

77 For additional information, see J.S. Sagner, *Fast-Track International Business*, Fast-Track
Textbooks, due in 2013, particularly Chapter 9.

style or model, such as in the women's cosmetics industry where expensive designer perfumes and lipsticks are quickly matched by cheaper versions (called "knock-offs"); or frozen yogurt shops where the industry copied TCBY (which began in 1981).

• To minimize costs: Manufacturing and/or distributing at least cost, such as Wal-Mart in retailing or Teva Pharmaceutical in generic drugs (copying out-of-patent pharmaceuticals). Neither Wal-Mart nor Teva plans to devote its resources to product development or design.

What Are Recent, More Flexible Forms of Organization?

In the search for a structure that supports a dynamic strategy, companies have recently adopted more flexible forms of organization. In addition to the comments below, see the discussion of teams in Chapter 3.

Matrix

In a **matrix** organizational structure, workers representing various functions and disciplines are assigned to projects led by a manager (the project manager). This creates a dual command structure: the functional manager and the project manager, violating the unity of command concept of an employee having one manager. The project structure used by some companies requires this type of organization, with the controlling unit being the project team. Reports are provided by the project manager to the functional manager for purposes of personnel reviews and compensation decisions. Companies that provide specialized advisory services, such as architects, planners, consultants and attorneys, often use a matrix format.

Organizations without Formal Structures

Various attempts have been made to create organizations without formal structures. The term "boundaryless" was coined by former General Electric chairman Jack Welch to refer to an absence of boundaries or limits on how managers and employees use resources to perform their work. A "virtual" organization is often defined as a core of permanent employees supported by temporary workers brought on as needed for specific projects.

Flexible Arrangements

Flextime offers a variable work schedule usually built around a core of mandatory hours with other hours worked as a worker's schedule permits. Flexplace adds the component of allowing workers to decide where they will work. For many workers, the commuting time and cost to go to work have become intolerable. The situation is particularly difficult in Northern and Southern CA in the U.S., in the fast growing urban areas of China and India, in London and in Tokyo, but there are many other places around the globe when a one hour commute is a dream. **Telecommuting** is a work arrangement in which employers agree to allow workers to work at home and communicate through computer and the Internet.

The concern for supervision and control of hours worked has proven to be largely a non-issue, as companies report an increase in efficiency, less time wasted in idle conversation or worrying about family responsibilities, and even a greater number of hours actually worked (as the commute is one flight up to an in-home office). The company also benefits by not increasing office space, equipment, parking, office perks (such as a gym). The largest disadvantages are the security of confidential information (discussed in Chapter 9); and the loss of the organizational culture, although web-conferencing and a required attendance one or two days a week helps to overcome this problem. A further issue is resentment among employees who are not permitted this flexibility and must "cover" for co-workers who are on flextime/flexplace arrangements.[78]

---

78 See the discussion in H. Seligson, "When the Work-Life Scales Are Unequal," *New York Times*, September 2, 2012, Business Section, pages 1, 5.

Contingent Workers

Contingent workers are temporary workers, often freelancers, who do not have a fixed commitment to a company. The increasing popularity of this arrangement reflects the recent massive layoffs and need to manage costs by avoiding the fixed salary and benefit costs of permanent employees; see Chapter 10 for a discussion of these issues. The downsizing of the past several years and prospect for a continued weak economy has forced companies to rely on such workers at peak times.

A significant issue in using contingent workers is determining their employment status for purposes of reporting. Under government rules, contingent workers (also known as independent contractors) are not entitled to any of the usual benefits provided by companies, including Social Security or unemployment insurance. The definition relies on how much control a company has over the individual; the more say a company has over how a job is done, the more likely he or she will be considered an employee. For an analysis of the current status of the temporary worker in the current economic recession, see Figure 7-3:

Figure 7-3: The Contingent Worker during the Economic Recession

While there have always been part-time workers ... employers today rely on them far more than before as they seek to cut costs and align staffing to customer traffic. This trend has frustrated millions of Americans who want to work full-time, reducing their pay and benefits. "Over the past two decades, many major retailers went from a quotient of 70 to 80% full-time to at least 70% part-time across the industry," said Burt P. Flickinger III, managing director of the Strategic Resource Group, a retail consulting firm.

The Bureau of Labor Statistics has found that the retail and wholesale sector, with a total of 18.6 million jobs, has cut a million full-time jobs since 2006, while adding more than 500,000 part-time jobs. Technology is speeding this transformation. In the past, part-timers might work the same schedule of four- or five-hour shifts every week. But workers' schedules have become far less predictable and stable. Many retailers now use sophisticated software that tracks the flow of customers, allowing managers to assign just enough employees to handle the anticipated demand.

"Many employers now schedule shifts as short as two or three hours, while historically they may have scheduled eight-hour shifts," said David Ossip, founder of Dayforce, a producer of scheduling software used by chains like Aéropostale and Pier One Imports. Some employers even ask workers to come in at the last minute, and the workers risk losing their jobs or being assigned fewer hours in the future if they are unavailable. The widening use of part-timers has been a bane to many workers, pushing many into poverty and forcing some onto food stamps and Medicaid. And with work schedules that change week to week, workers can find it hard to arrange child care, attend college or hold a second job, according to interviews with more than 40 part-time workers. ..

But in two leading industries — retailing and hospitality — the number of part-timers who would prefer to work full-time has jumped to 3.1 million, or two-and-a-half times the 2006 level, according to the Bureau of Labor Statistics. In retailing alone, nearly 30% of part-timers want full-time jobs, up from 10.6% in 2006. The agency found that in the retail and wholesale sector, which includes hundreds of thousands of small stores that rely heavily on full-time workers, about 3 in 10 employees work part-time.

Retailers and restaurants use so many part-timers not only because it gives them more flexibility, but because it significantly cuts payroll costs. According to the Bureau of Labor Statistics, part-time workers in service jobs received average compensation of $10.92 an hour in June, which includes $8.90 in wages plus benefits of $2.02. Full-time workers in that sector averaged 57% more in total compensation — $17.18 an hour, made up of $12.25 in wages and $4.93 in benefits. Benefit costs are far lower for part-timers because, for example, just 21% of them are in employer-backed retirement plans, compared with 65% of full-timers.

Excerpted from Steven Greenhouse, "A Part-Time Life, as Hours Shrink and Shift," *New York Times*, Oct. 28, 2012, pages 1, 24, at www.nytimes.com/2012/10/28/business/a-part-time-life-as-hours-shrink-and-shift-for-american-workers.html?pagewanted=all.

What are the Issues You Should Address?

In considering your decisions on organizing, here are some issues to review.

- What forms of integration has your company used to organize for growth? Do these forms make economic sense, that is, do they logically extend the mission in a thoughtful vertical or horizontal manner?

- Does your company use classical concepts in its organizational structure? Assuming that some are used, is the application appropriate for the needs of the company as it faces 21st century challenges? Are these uses consistent with competitors and other companies that your management chooses to emulate?

- Have we identified our core competencies? Can we continue to depend on these competencies to sustain our competitive position?

- Do we outsource or offshore non-core activities? If so, are we satisfied with the quality and cost of the service provided? If not, should we outsource or offshore activities that are not essential to our position in the market?

- Have we considered size, globalization and/or our strategic positioning in our industry to determine our organizational structure?

- Should we consider using any of the flexible forms of organizational structure, including teams, a matrix format, not using a formal structure, flexible arrangements or contingency workers?

Discussion and Review Questions

1. Why did the corporate form of ownership develop?
2. What is classical management? Describe at least three of the principals from that management theory.
3. What is a core competency? How did a company (that you select) make its core competency an essential element in its strategy?
4. Why have outsourcing and offshoring become important concepts in managing a business? Is it likely that this will be a permanent trend? Explain.
5. What are the basic strategic approaches for a company to be positioned within its industry?
6. Why have classical management structures and principals become somewhat obsolete in the current economic and business climate?
7. What are some of the problems of contingent (temporary) workers during the current economic recession?

CHAPTER 8

Leadership

After reading this chapter, you will be able to:

- Understand theories and concepts of leadership
- Appreciate the difference between a leader and a manager
- Consider the behavioral, contingency and charismatic theories of leadership
- Be aware of current issues including global leadership variations and the importance of trust

What is Leadership?

Leadership is the ability of an individual to achieve the mission and goals of a group or an entire organization whether a business or a not-for-profit. For centuries, leaders have been formally chosen for this responsibility with an appropriate title, whether it be a church office (such as Pope or Cardinal), the military (such as general or admiral), or a business or government (such as president or chief executive officer [CEO]). The assignment of a title of leadership does not mean that the individual is in fact a leader, and there have been numerous situations where a leader reached his or her position without an impressive title.

Leaders in Fact and in Title

A very influential leader in the 20th century was Mother Teresa who founded the Missionaries of Charity, a Roman Catholic religious congregation, which in 2012 consisted of over 4,500 sisters and active in 133 countries. At the time of her death in 1997, the order had 610 missions in 123 countries including hospices and homes for people with HIV/AIDS, leprosy and tuberculosis, soup kitchens, children's and family counseling programs, orphanages and schools. The highest office that she held was Superior General of that order, yet her global influence and accomplishments were as important an example of leadership that we are likely to find.[79]

There are countless examples of leaders with titles of office that succeeded and of those who failed. Arguably the greatest leaders in the last century were Winston Churchill, Prime Minister (PM) of Great Britain, and Franklin Roosevelt, U.S. President. Yet the office is meaningless by itself; for example, most historians agree that James Buchanan, the 15th U.S. President, was the worst in the nation's history, and that Neville Chamberlain, Churchill's predecessor as PM, was one of Britain's greatest failures as its national leader. Similarly, U.S. Grant was the outstanding general of the Northern Armies during the American Civil War, but a disappointment as the 18th President.[80]

Even the great wartime leader Churchill was ineffective during a portion of his service as a member of Parliament (until the threat of World War Two), was out of appointed office in the1930s, and opposed both independence for India and the refusal of his government to allow Edward VIII's marriage to Mrs. Wallis Simpson (because of her divorce). The essence of a leader is to move constituencies toward a goal, but until the eve of the war, Churchill was somewhat of a failure.[81] Yet Churchill has been selected as the greatest British citizen

---

79 Other examples of leaders in fact were Martin Luther King, Jr., for the cause of ending racial segregation in the U.S., yet whose highest office was president of the Southern Christian Leadership Conference; and Mohandas Gandhi, prominent in the struggle for independence for India from the British, whose highest office was as the head of the Indian National Congress.

80 There are various published credible rankings of the Presidents. Grant generally is rated at about 25th to 30th of 43 (excluding Barrack Obama). Franklin Roosevelt is usually listed as second or third.

81 Other failed policies included his Gallipoli campaign during World War One when he was First Lord of the Admiralty, and returning Britain to the gold standard when he was Chancellor of the Exchecquer. The two biographies of Churchill that are considered as superior are: M. Gilbert, *Churchill: A Life*, Holt, 1992; and the three-volume series by W. Manchester (assisted by P. Reid), *The Last Lion*, Little, Brown, 1983, 1988, 2012.

of all time in various polls and was the winner of the Nobel Prize for Literature in 1953.

Leadership Qualities

Research on leadership is voluminous, and largely contradictory and inconclusive. Is it a matter of certain qualities, such as charisma,[82] intelligence, decisiveness, strength (although that appears to be less important in modern society), bravery and similar qualities? The great leaders should have similar qualities but no research has found such identities, and it is apparent that characteristics essential for leadership in a particular situation may be inappropriate in another situation. For example, would Abraham Lincoln have succeeded as a leader in the 1880s (a period of rapid industrialization), or would Mohandas K. Gandhi have led India to independence if it had been part of the Soviet Union and not Britain?

An important quality of leadership based on numerous studies consistently appears to be extroversion,[83] at least with regard to the emergence (but not the effectiveness) of a leader. **Extroversion** involves one's being predominantly concerned with and obtaining gratification from what is outside the self. Extroverts enjoy interpersonal contact, and derive pleasure from relationships with others. The complement of extroversion is introversion; those individuals tend to be reserved, quiet and somewhat uncomfortable in social settings.[84] Various attributes (including extroversion) are collectively known as the Big-Five Model[85] and include other leadership traits that more weakly correlate with leadership, as listed below:

---

82 Charisma is a term often used but not well understood. Most definitions include such descriptors as charm, compelling attractiveness or a certain appearance that inspires others to follow. Charisma can be a positive force, as with President John F. Kennedy, or an evil force, as with Adolf Hitler. The essential trait is an individual's ability through speech, demeanor or ideas that people follow without fully considering the rationale for their behavior.

83 The term was coined by the psychiatrist Carl Jung, a contemporary of Sigmund Freud. We examine extraversion in the Edward Gilmore case in Appendix B.

84 Although it is not usual, introverts can be great leaders. An example is Mother Teresa, who was discussed at the start of Chapter 8.

85 There are numerous references to the Big Five model in the literature. See, for example, R.R. McCrae, "The Five-Factor Model: Issues and Application," *Journal of Personality*, June 1992 (special issue); P.J. Howard and J.M. Howard, *The Owner's Manual for Personality at Work: How the Big Five Personality Traits Affect Your Performance, Communication, Teamwork, Leadership, and Sales*, Bard Press, 2000.

- Agreeableness: The individual's tendency to defer to others, with leaders likely to be highly agreeable. However, Churchill did not defer to the opinion of others, nor did U.S. President Lyndon B. Johnson, particularly on controversial social issues.
- Conscientiousness: The individual's tendency to be reliable, responsible, well organized and dependable. This trait is somewhat irrelevant in leaders today (at least in top management positions) as they tend to have aides, assistants and secretaries to keep them on schedule.
- Emotional stability: The individual's ability to withstand stress and remain calm and confident. However, leaders have to be able to adjust to changing circumstances, and a confident (or over-confident) leader may refuse to adjust to unexpected results (as happened to Robert Nardelli, CEO of Home Depot; see Chapter 1).[86]
- Openness to experience. The individual's range of interests and creativity. While Steve Jobs is an outstanding example of this trait, many leaders of companies continue much of successes of the past while trying to be cognizant of opportunities for innovation and new techniques.

Leaders vs. Managers

Throughout this book we have been discussing management. In this chapter we focus on leadership, which is a quite different organizational function. Managers are expected to maintain the equilibrium that has been established by others, albeit it with incremental changes to improve efficiency and effectiveness. Leaders take companies to the next generation of performance; in effect, they try to accomplish change. We contrast leadership and management in Figure 8-1.

---

86 A great wartime leader who quickly adjusted to an unforeseen event was U.S. General George S. Patton, who was able to move the U.S. Third Army to repel the last major German offensive at the Battle of the Bulge (December 1944). However, observers questioned Patton's emotional stability based on the anger and impatience he displayed at various times.

Figure 8-1: Leadership vs. Management

Leaders	Managers
Is visionary and not bound by established policies or procedures	Is formalistic, relying on planning, organizing and other foundation skills
Must influence actions of a large number of individuals	Works with a limited number of employees
Has a vision and the enthusiasm to achieve high performance	Works to accomplish goals and objectives that have been defined
Uses creativity and imagination to overcome obstacles	Uses well-established procedures to solve problems
Works with stakeholders to accomplish the mission	Primarily deals with senior and first level managers and employees

What Do Behavioral Theories Contribute to Understanding Leadership?

The research of behaviorists has explored factors of leadership that would allow leadership to be taught (as opposed to trait theories which assume that leaders are born with that quality). There have been several groups of studies that pursued this understanding, which we discuss below.

Ohio State Studies

After World War Two, researchers at Ohio State University attempted to examine specific aspects of leadership.[87] After reviewing more than one

---

87 See R.M. Stoghill and A,E.Coons, eds., *Leader Behavior: Its Description and Measurement,* Research Monograph No. 88, Ohio State University, 1951.

thousand such dimensions, it was determined that the two important aspects are *initiating structure* and *consideration*.

- Initiating structure: How the leader structures organizational roles to achieve goals. The successful leader on this dimension would be characterized as assigning subordinates to specific tasks, requiring standards of performance, and meeting time constraints.
- Consideration: How the leader develops respect, trust in and feelings for his or her subordinates. This dimension closely reflects the research of Maslow and Herzberg on the satisfaction of individual needs; see Chapter 2.

A leader high in both characteristics tended to achieve better performance than those ranked low on these attributes. However, the research indicated situations where this was not the result; for example, an initiating structure leader could alienate workers with unreasonable performance demands, and a considerate leader could create an overly unstructured work environment. These findings indicate that the situation can dominate the dimensions. The Cran Fan Stan case in Appendix B in part speaks to this situation.

University of Michigan Studies

The studies at the University of Michigan essentially replicated those at Ohio State with similar findings, that leaders are either production-oriented or employee-oriented.[88] To no surprise, the latter type of leaders was considered more successful.

Managerial Grid

These dimensions of leadership were applied to a graphic presentation by Robert Blake and Jane Mouton; see Figure 8-2. The grid has nine positions on each axis. The research concluded that leaders performing in a 9,9 style (team

---

88 R. Kahn and D. Katz, "Leadership Practices in Relation to Productivity and Morale," in D. Cartwright and A. Zander (eds.), *Group Dynamics: Research and Theory*, 2nd ed., Row, Peterson, 1960.

focused) were superior to other combinations (such as 9,1, task-oriented). There is scant evidence that a 9,9 style is generally effective.[89]

Figure 8-2: Managerial Grid

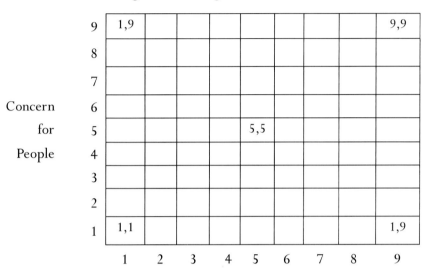

Concern for Production

Note: Blake and Mouton characterized the five leadership positions as follows-

5,5: Middle-of-the-road management

1,9: Country-club management (meaning concern for people but not for production)

9,1: Task-oriented management

1,1: Impoverished management (meaning concern neither for people or for production)

9,9: Team management

To summarize, these theories focus on behaviors without taking account of situations and whether or not a crisis exists, if employees are intelligent and motivated, or if the work is mostly routine. The obvious situation of a military leader who fails in peacetime (think U.S. Grant) or a peaceful civilian who

---

89 R.R. Blake and J. S. Mouton, *The Managerial Grid*, Gulf, 1964. The findings of Blake and Mouton have been criticized by other researchers; see, e.g., P.C. Nystrom, "Managers and the Hi-Hi Leader Myth," *Academy of Management Journal,* June 1978, pages 125-131.

excels in wartime (think Lincoln) strongly support the importance of the circumstances influencing the success or failure of the leader.

What are the Contingency and Charismatic Theories of Leadership?

When researchers failed to find a consistent explanation of leadership based on behavioral theories, attention began to be paid to appropriate styles under varying situations. The leading contingency models include Fiedler, LMX, Path-Goal and Leader-Participation, which are explained in this section. In addition, charismatic models are discussed.

The Fiedler Leadership Model

Fred Fiedler developed a measurement instrument purporting to determine whether an individual is task or people in orientation.[90] By ranking least-preferred co-workers the respondent supposedly reveals whether he or she focuses on personal relations or productivity. The logic of the model is murky and applying it in real-world situations is difficult as leaders typically encounter various situations that require focus on task, on people and on both concurrently.

Leader-Member Exchange Theory (LMX)

The LMX suggests that leaders establish a special sub-group of subordinates as the "in-group": they are trusted, are with the leader for a disproportionate amount of the leader's time, and receive overly generous rewards.[91] These subordinates tend to be stable in this relationship over time, understand their "in" (or possibly their "out") status, and make their career decisions

---

90 F.E. Fiedler, *A Theory of Leadership Effectiveness*, McGraw-Hill, 1967.
91 There are several research papers on the LMX theory. See, e.g., C.C. Cogliser and C.A. Schriesheim, "Exploring Work Unit Context and Leader-Member Exchange: A Multi-Level Perspective, *Journal of Organizational Behavior*, August 2000, pages 487-511.

accordingly.[92] While this theory has predictive capability, it does little to assist in training or selecting leaders who can accomplish the company's mission and goals.

Path-Goal Theory

The Path-Goal Theory suggests that the leader must support followers to attain their objectives (MBOs), and by so doing, to achieve the goals of the organization.[93] Accomplishment requires an understanding of those objectives by the leader and the followers, providing resources required and reducing obstacles that hinder this "path-goal". A strength of this approach is the assumption that leaders are flexible, and it proposes four types of leadership styles contingent on the situation: directive (provides direction and guidance), supportive, participative and achievement-oriented. Figure 8-3 provides several path-goal outcomes. Path-goal may be effective when the leader compensates for worker deficiencies, but may be counterproductive when the result is an unnecessary (or pointless) repetition of methodology or process.

Figure 8-3: Path-Goal Outcomes

Leadership Behavior	Outcome
Directive	Best when tasks are ambiguous or stressful
	Not effective when employees are intelligent and/or experienced
	Useful when there is work group conflict
Supportive	Effective when structured tasks are performed
	Helpful with bureaucratic or formal authority organizations

92 The author worked for such a leader and quickly became aware of who the "in's" and "out's" were. As the model predicted, the "in's" stayed with the leader for lengthy sections of their careers, received large rewards and supported the leader without questioning the appropriateness or wisdom of that person's behavior. The "out's" usually chose to move to other job opportunities.

93 R.J. House, "A Path-Goal Theory of Leader Effectiveness," *Administrative Sciences Quarterly*, September 1971, pages 321-338; updated 25 years later in "Path-Goal Theory of Leadership: Lessons, Legacy and a Reformulated Theory," *Leadership Quarterly*, Fall 1996, pages 323-352.

Participative	Successful with self-motivated workers
Achievement-oriented	Functions with workers that effort leads to job performance

Leader-Participation Model

One of the few theories to recognize the varying situations faced by leaders is the leader-participation model of Victor Vroom.[94] Leaders must adjust to the situations faced, and Vroom provided a series of rules to be followed based on a decision matrix. This analysis may be useful but is considered as too complex to be practicable for the typical manager.

Charisma

We previously defined charisma (see footnote 82) although leaders possessing this characteristic seldom are similar to each other. Furthermore, who has charisma? Most people would consider Prime Minister Churchill, President Kennedy and Dr. King as charismatic, but there is little agreement as to whether Prime Minister Margaret Thatcher of Great Britain or Governor Chris Christie of NJ would qualify. Clearly, Churchill, Kennedy and King could influence their audiences into action by speech and by personal example, but could Thatcher or Christie, or most other persons who might be so-labeled.

If you worked for a charismatic leader, you might be inspired to walk through a minefield if he or she asked. Since few of us ever have that kind of inspired manager (including the author), the research may be useful to cite but is unlikely to be encountered in our working lives. Studies indicate that such leaders have specific traits, as noted in Figure 8-4.

---

94 V.H. Vroom and P.W. Yetton, *Leadership and Decision Making,* University of Pittsburgh Press, 1973.

Figure 8-4: Characteristics of Charismatic Leaders

Characteristic	Application	Selected Examples
Vision	Has a clear vision or goal of a better future; is able to make others understand that the vision is attainable	Gandhi: Independence for India King: Ending segregation in the American South and throughout the U.S.
Personal risk	Is impervious to personal risk and actually demonstrates fearlessness through actions	Kennedy: Led crew of PT boat to safety during World War Two at great personal risk King: Attacks by segregationists (including the Ku Klux Klan) during civil rights marches
Unconventional	Behaves in an unusual manner to achieve vision	Gandhi and King: The adoption of non-violent civil disobedience as a strategy for changing government policy
External constraints	Assesses the external constraints faced in achieving the vision and the resources required	Gandhi and King: Assessed the likely response of the governments in power to non-violent civil disobedience
Considerate of followers	Perceives the needs of followers and is responsive to their issues	Kennedy: Cared for and saved PT crew after a collusion with a Japanese destroyer King: Arranged for some protection and basic needs during marches

Charismatic leaders may be effective in certain situations involving public policy; they are less successful in the business world and may do real harm. In fact, a charismatic business leader probably developed that reputation from public relations efforts with investment bankers, security analysts and the financial press, and not necessarily because he or she is in fact a leader who manifests the qualities described in Figure 8-4. There have several such situations in recent years, particularly in the financial services industries, such as

Angelo Mozilo of Countrywide Financial (now Bank of America Home Loans) who hyped residential mortgage loans.[95] Other examples that could be cited include Kenneth Lay of Enron,[96] Dennis Kozlowski of Tyco International[97] and Bernie Ebbers of WorldCom.[98]

Current Issues in Leadership

Current leadership insights have focused on appropriate style, global issues and trust in the organization's leader.

Leadership Style in the Current Environment

Leadership approaches vary across the spectrum of styles discussed in this chapter, including charismatic, intelligent, decisive, extroverted, agreeable, emotionally stable, open to experiences, have an initiating structure, considerate, unethical and supported by an "in-group". Six brief profiles and several shorter comments of global business leaders are provided in Appendix A, including:

95 In 2010, Mozilo reached a settlement with the Securities and Exchange Commission (SEC), over securities fraud and insider trading charges. Mozilo agreed to pay $67.5 million in fines and accepted a lifetime ban from serving as an officer or director of any public company; it is the largest settlement by an individual involved with the 2008 housing collapse.

96 Kenneth "Ken" Lay was known for his role in the corruption scandal that led to the downfall of Enron Corporation. Lay, his CEO Jeffrey Skilling and Enron became synonymous with corporate abuse and accounting fraud when the scandal broke in 2001, leading to the Sarbanes-Oxley Act of 2002 (containing various provisions regarding corporate governance of American publicly-traded companies). Lay was the chairman of Enron until his resignation on January 23, 2002. In 2004, Lay was indicted by a grand jury on 11 counts of securities fraud and related charges. Lay was found guilty in May 2006, of 10 counts against him and could have faced 20 to 30 years in prison. However, he died while vacationing in July 2006.

97 Dennis Kozlowski, a former chief executive officer of Tyco International, was convicted in 2005 of crimes related to his receipt of $81 million in purportedly unauthorized bonuses, the purchase of art for $14.7 million and the payment by Tyco of a $20 million investment banking fee to Frank Walsh, a former Tyco director. He is currently serving 8⅓ to 25 years in prison.

98 . Bernard "Bernie" Ebbers co-founded and a former CEO of the telecommunications company WorldCom. In 2005, he was convicted of fraud and conspiracy as a result of WorldCom's false financial reporting and subsequent loss of $100 billion to investors. The WorldCom scandal was (until Bernie Madoff's Ponzi scheme) the largest accounting scandal in U.S. history. He is currently serving a 25-year prison term.

- Jack Welch (General Electric): attentive to detail; personally knew many company managers; informal in his relationships with employees; frank in the evaluation of managers and employees; impatient with mediocre results
- Rattan Tata (Tata Group): cohesive in structuring companies; integrative in developing a comprehensive strategy; concerned for social responsibility and sustainability; humble; grateful to his employees for their contributions; tacit approval of antisocial company actions
- Carl Hahn (Volkwagen): consensus builder; communicative; open to the discussion of new ideas; not commanding or sufficiently focused on cost efficiencies and profits
- Howard Stringer (SONY): conciliatory at first, later a tough leader; attempted to be a cultural transformer; complacent in the face of declining company results; had the responsibility at the time of various company scandals
- Percy Barnevik (ABB): energetic; driven; overtly conciliatory but covertly unwilling to compromise; preferred speedy decisions to thoughtful action; something of a gambler with the resources of a publicly-traded company and its stakeholders; not disposed to follow normal rules of business
- Al Dunlap (Sunbeam): unethical; unscrupulous; unconcerned for potential impact of his actions on stakeholders; possibly sociopathic[99]

While the selection of these business leaders is admittedly somewhat arbitrary, the intent is to provide a representative selection of leadership styles including those with successful and those with disastrous results. A danger in attempting to define an appropriate style is the time and context of the leader's regime, as we noted at the beginning of this chapter in referring to Lincoln and Gandhi (in the section "Leadership Qualities"). As a result, considering the style of any of these business leaders in the current weak global economy is probably only marginally relevant.

However, the profiles and available experiential evidence indicates that many leaders have been driven by one of two concerns:

---

99 A "sociopath" is a person whose behavior is antisocial, possibly criminal, who lacks a sense of moral responsibility, ethics or social conscience. Sociopaths (unlike psychopaths) typically do not use violence to achieve their goals.

I.   Profits and the stock price of the companies they led, at the sacrifice of long-term success or manager or stakeholder satisfaction. In fact, certain of these leaders ignored established ethical and legal behaviors in their efforts to meet their goals.

II. Compromise and conciliation in an effort to build a consensus for change and the pursuit of game-changing strategies.

Can past management leadership styles function in the 21st century organization? Other styles of leading that involve the interests of all affected constituents are likely necessary.

Global Leadership

Understanding leadership is difficult in Western civilization; it is nearly impossible in the cultures of the Orient and other areas of the world. What works in Canada is not likely to succeed in China. Cultural differences are likely more reflective of the follower than of the leader; review the discussion in Chapter 2 regarding differences in cultural attitudes. As an example, Asian managers appear to prefer competence, communications and support from their leaders, which is consistent with their cultural attitude of teamwork (as opposed to individualism).

The study of leadership style continues to have a Western orientation, focusing on U.S. and European leaders and organizations, and often conducted by U.S. researchers. The most significant international study to date has been the GLOBE program, which has determined that there are universal traits of leaders,[100] including those noted in Figure 8-3. The unknown factor is whether leadership actually is consistent on character traits across cultures, or whether the globalization of business has forced this result. Certain cultural differences in leadership are noted below.

- Some Asian cultures prefer humble, paternalistic leadership.
- Middle Eastern leaders are expected to be strong and to refrain from showing concern for employees.

---

100 GLOBE (Global Leadership and Organizational Behavior Effectiveness) has examined data from 18,000 managers including desired and expected leadership traits. There are several GLOBE reports on leadership; see for example, R.J. House *et. al., Culture, Leadership and Organizations: The GLOBE Study of 62 Societies*, Sage Publications, 2004.

- Northern Europe leaders should not praise individual employees to avoid embarrassing them.
- German leaders are oriented to high achievement with slight regard for issues of individual employees.
- Russian leaders are expected to be fairly ruthless in their pursuit of business success.

Trust

Trust is the sense of followers that the leader has integrity, character and ability. These attributes are essential for followers to believe in the leader and his or her actions. The most important dimension is considered to be integrity, which involves honesty and truthfulness, particularly in an environment of social networking and Internet communications. If the leader is dishonest or untruthful, the facts of a situation cannot long be held secret from employees, stockholders, regulators and those legally injured. In addition to integrity, a very important quality is credibility, measured by competence and inspirational vision.

The former employees of Enron have been quite vocal in their dismay over the behavior of Lay, Skilling and other senior executives, which is evidence of the fragility of this trust relationship. While some undoubtedly have been understandably venting over the loss of jobs and pensions, the depth of the feeling of betrayal cannot be overstated.[101] While the Enron situation was an extreme, trust of business leaders has generally declined for various reasons:

- The spread of compensation between senior managers and employees has grown steadily, particularly in the U.S., with a CEO often earning in the millions of dollars and the production worker around $50 - $60,000 a year, a multiple of more than 100 times.
- The pain of a weak economy often does not feed into the executive suite, where top management seems to continue to receive huge pay packages.

---

101 See, M. Swartz and S. Watkins, *Power Failure: The Inside Story of the Collapse of Enron,* Crown Business, 2004 (Watkins was a Vice-President in Auditing at Enron); and L. Brewer and M. Hansen, *Confessions of an Enron Executive: A Whistleblower's Story,* AuthorHouse, 2004 (Brewer was an Executive for Risk Management in Energy Operations). For an account by a senior manager at WorldCom, see C. Cooper, *Extraordinary Circumstances: The Journey of a Corporate Whistleblower,* Wiley, 2009 (Cooper was WorldCom's Chief Audit Executive).

- Company pensions are underfunded and employees have no assurance that they will be able to retire with the company's and their contribution intact.
- Trust is severely tested when companies exploit child labor in global manufacturing facilities or violate other norms or laws regarding fair labor practice. Similarly, companies use bribes to win contracts in violation of U.S. law (the Federal Corrupt Practices Act of 1977 as amended). Banks have been particularly egregious in their violation of appropriate corporate behavior.

Trust is particularly important in today's economic climate, given the reduction in employee headcount and the greater use of work teams. Employees have to believe that their organization will endure, that the leader knows what he or she are doing, and that the leader trusts employees to act responsibly in the absence of formal structures and relationships. Job performance and commitment to the organization are notably enhanced by such trust. Figure 8-5 lists specific trust characteristics of a leader.

Figure 8-5: Characteristics and Examples of a Trustworthy Leader

States intentions for a particular action, and delivers.
— Liars and those who break the law or violates the policies of the organization will be terminated.
Is thought of as reliable, truthful and a person of integrity.
— Does nothing to cause suspicion and keeps word regarding actions.
Delivers the news accurately even if there has been (or expects future) difficulties.
— Downsizing may be necessary or other budget cuts may be required.
Expects all employees to participate in the pain of cost cutting.
— Cuts his (her) pay and that of senior managers proportionally.
Delivers messages consistently regardless of the audience.
— Tells employees, stockholders and the press the same account of recent and expected future results.
Does not engage in questionable behaviors.

— Refrains from excessive drinking or other unacceptable activities.

Pays attention to others who speak in meetings or in other venues.

— Maintains eye contact with the speaker and does not seem bored or upset.

Extends personal complements for individual, group or sub-organizational performance.

— Appears to have reviewed a situation and can thoughtfully and positively comment.

Listens and promises to consider reasonable suggestions.

— Responds to statements and comments in a timely manner by memo or e-mail.

What are the Issues You Should Address?

In considering your organization's leadership, here are some issues to review.

- What type of leadership style is used by senior managers? Is this style appropriate to accomplish our organization's mission and goals, or is the actual intention to satisfy external constituencies such as stock analysts, banks and the financial press?

- Do we understand the actions of our leaders based on behavioral, contingency or charismatic theories of leadership?

- Are we aware of differences in leadership qualities in other countries where we do business? Have we selected the appropriate leader for those situations (or are we home country "culture bound")?

- Do our leaders inspire the trust of our employees? Are there situations where trust is being compromised by inappropriate actions of those leaders or by their acquiescence to policies that compromise the reputation of the company?

Discussion and Review Questions

1. What are essential characteristics of leaders? Can a person be a leader without those qualities?
2. Do behavioral theories of leadership succeed in explaining how leaders function?
3. What is the general point of view of contingency theories of leadership?
4. Do you believe that a charismatic person will be successful in any leadership position? Can you name a respected leader who clearly was (is) not charismatic?
5. How does cultural bias affect research into leadership?
6. Does the characteristic of trust have a significant or a minor role in the current economic environment?

CHAPTER 9

Controlling

After reading this chapter, you will be able to:

- Understand the two elements of control: procedures and a monitoring process, and safeguarding the assets of the organization
- Appreciate the problem of delays throughout the working capital timeline and their impact on the company
- Be aware of the issues in measuring performance and developing alternative actions
- Evaluate sources of primary and secondary data to use in developing controls
- Consider safeguards for information (and other company assets)

What is Controlling?

Controlling is the examination of work performance to assure that standards are being met. The process typically involves comparing results and making corrections as deviations are uncovered. The word *standards* is critical: the observer must derive (or be given) standards from established requirements for the organization, and/or from industry norms when available. The standards must tie back to the MBOs we discussed at the beginning of the book, which in turn are based on the mission and goals of the company and should be consistent with industry practice.

Here's an example: In the insurance industry, agency written coverage (that is, an agent writes the policy rather than direct writing through the company) requires the agent to send the initial premium notice to the insured. (Practice varies as to subsequent bills: some companies have the agent do the billing and some use a company-prepared billing system). The insureds' payments are sent to the agent who then remits the payments to the company less the commission earned. A major insurance company allowed its agents to postpone billing the insured and to delay remitting the amount due to the company for periods up to ten weeks beyond the contractual date required in the agency contract.

An analysis determined that the value of the loss of revenue to the company amounted to nearly $8 million annually. The solution was to design and implement accelerated billing procedures and a monitoring process. This was a situation of poor or non-existent controls on billing and collection procedures despite a contract specifying the obligations of the agent and the company, and was in contradiction to established industry practice.

Critical Elements in Controlling

This situation illustrates two critical elements of controlling:

1. Essential components are procedures and a monitoring process, the traditional role of controlling, to:

    -   Provide a link back to planning and then through the other management functions.
    -   Allow employees to become empowered to broaden their job responsibilities, as controls can provide data on job performance.

2. The control function has expanded from the first role to the 21st century requirement to include the safeguarding of the organization's assets. These assets involve all of the vital resources that are owned or employed, such as cash, proprietary information and systems, and security for employees and customers. This is a tall order! Furthermore, these necessary activities are not well understood or managed in

organizations. In fact, we would argue that of the five management functions (planning, decision-making, organizing, leadership and controlling), controlling is the most weakly enforced. In the insurance company incident, management simply had no idea that this (or several other lapses) were occurring; when all of the control opportunities were totaled, they amounted to about $25 million a year! The protection of company information (another concern at this insurance company) is discussed toward the end of this chapter.[102]

Organizational Delays

The working capital[103] timeline is a graphic presentation of the events along the continuum of events from the first activity in the sales cycle until the final disbursement of funds for accounts payable, payroll or other outflow requirements; see Figure 9-1. Every organization we have observed (*i.e.*, some 200 of the Fortune 500) has significant timeline delays. These may be attributable to billing lags due to systems "priorities" or incomplete data, inefficiencies in receiving and depositing cash receipts, delayed posting to accounts receivable, archaic financial systems or other factors.

Figure 9-1: Working Capital Time Line

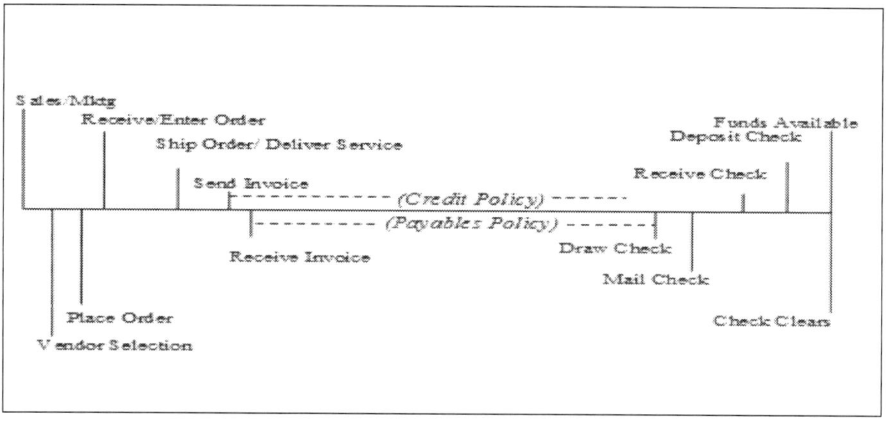

---

102 The protection and management of cash is a specialized field administered by the treasurer of a company. For specific concepts, see J.S. Sagner, *Essentials of Working Capital Management*, Wiley, 2010, Chapters 1-4.

103 **Working capital** is defined as current assets less current liabilities, which are accounts on the balance sheet.

The horizon axis represents time, and each activity along the timeline – and note how many there are – requires the commitment of days for completion. A typical transaction cycle in business can involve 90 or 120 days from the purchase of raw materials through the receipt of funds from the customer.

The time segments in a transaction cycle have a financial value or cost, identified as float,[104] as measured by the transaction dollars being managed times the cost of capital[105] times the time period (measured as the percentage of a year). For example, assume a $50,000 transaction requiring 3½ months. If the cost of capital is 10%, there is nearly $1,500 in the cost of float, calculated as $50,000 times 3.5/12 times 10%. And this is just one transaction cycle of possibly thousands in a year of activity! Cash and information are the critical elements in examining and improving the timeline because each step in the operation of a business involves decisions that impact both resources.

How Companies Muddle Through

The aggregated impact of unrealistic working capital assumptions as to time may be to convert a profitable business activity to one with marginal returns or even losses. Let's examine how that can occur. Assume that our target return-on-sales (ROS) is 10% to make a 15% return-on-equity (ROE),[106] and we sell widgets for $100 at a target cost of $90 in a processing cycle of 90 days. However, it actually takes 60 days to produce, ship and invoice, and another 42 days for the customer to pay. By the time we receive funds in our bank, another 6 days have passed, for a total of 108 days.

The 18 days we did not forecast is 20% greater than the target (90 days), which would drive the ROS to 8% and the ROE to 12%. An ROE of 12% is just above our cost of capital of 10%. Our research with clients indicates that the average delay is about five days (vs. the 18 days in this example). With the working capital component of the U.S. industrial economy at more than

104 **Float** is defined as funds in the process of movement from one place to another, such as accounts receivable owed to a company by its customer, or accounts payable that are owed by a company to its vendors.
105 **Cost of capital** is the weighted average cost of a company's after-tax cost of debt capital and cost of equity capital (including common stock and retained earnings), expressed as a percentage.
106 ROS (return-on-sales) is measured as net profits (after taxes) divided by sales. ROE (return-on-equity) is measured as net profits (after taxes) divided by equity (stockholders equity and retained earnings).

$1 trillion, a rough forecast measure of the inefficiency of the U.S. business economy is greater than $50 billion annually![107] (Of course, this assumes that all U.S. businesses are equally inefficient, which we sincerely hope is not the case.)

In fact, many businesses have long accepted these lapses as a cost of doing business. They experience discontinuous intervals of mediocre results, but use such outcomes to trigger adjustments to delays and inefficiencies. Modifications may be at any point in the business timeline, and can involve a production process, the terms of sale, the financial arrangements for the transaction, or any of a nearly limitless number of variables. Managers may not be able to quantify the days or costs of delay, but they eventually discover that the profitability targets (usually measured as returns-on-sales and returns-on-equity) are not being met. In this way, corrective action is taken to return close to expected profitability.[108]

When Muddling Through Doesn't Work

Serious problems obviously arise where corrective action is not taken. Unfortunately, this happens all too often in organizations for several reasons.

- B − I − G Business. The modern corporation has become so large and diversified that no one individual can oversee all of its activities. While the CEO may be briefed on sales, profits and product developments by sector or market, a large company may simply be too complex to manage in any sense of controlling the company's use of scarce resources. We often find that managers do not understand their own businesses, do not adequate calculate profitability, and cannot relate the activities in one business unit to those in another unit.
- Inadequate Measures of Profitability. It is nearly impossible to match costs to sales in order to accurately determine profits. Generally accepted accounting principles ("GAAP") used in the U.S. allow

---

107 This is calculated assuming a five day delay on a 90 day processing cycle, or 6%, times $1 trillion.

108 A popular concept beginning in 1960s management literature was "management-by-exception", which advocated establishing control limits for production processes. Any result outside of those limits should be examined to initiate corrective action. See, i.e., P.E. Torgersen and I.T. Weinstock, *Management: An Integrated Approach*, Prentice-Hall, 1972, Chapter 20.

considerable leeway in the statement of business income. "Accrual accounting" assigns costs to the timing of the sale of product rather than to the time that the cost was incurred, and recognizes sales at the time of invoicing rather than at the time that funds are received.[109] Both the nature of accrual accounting and the permitted leeway in the interpretation of the recording of business events allow companies to report earnings which may not accurately reflect economic results.

- The Wrong Performance Measures. Managers are often motivated through objectives or measures which emphasize their own business unit needs but are not entirely consistent with the goals of the company.

  o A sales function is motivated and tasked to sell without regard to the profitability of the transaction; the impact of promises made to customers on manufacturing, quality control and shipping; or whether the customer will pay on time (or ever!).

  o An information systems function protects its computing resources and may be oblivious to the optimal timing of invoicing, upgrading systems serving customer service functions, or the needs of management to access management information it can use.

  o A manufacturing function is concerned with production and delivery dates, with limited motivation for quality issues, customer complaints (see the Balto/Nectis case in Appendix B), or the impact of increased materials costs on company profitability.

Few businesses tie manufacturing, sales and administrative costs to specific sales, and even fewer have any idea if a particular sale, product or market generates appropriate profits. Accounting treatment of unit costs has historically been oriented to production and not to marke-

---

109 "Cash accounting", which recognizes sales and costs at the time when cash is received or spent, is used primarily by small businesses.

ting, and the job of the cost accountant is to tell us to the tenth of a penny the cost to manufacture.

Profits are critical to the enterprise, but the concept has little meaning because of the difficulty in calculating the appropriate allocation of non-direct organizational costs to specific business units. The manager often has very imprecise data on which to judge the profitability of his/her product, service or business line, and little input to the process of assigning costs against revenues.

Furthermore, although certain cost elements are variable in the long-run and therefore subject to some control, nearly all costs are fixed in the short-run. For example, labor is usually considered as a variable direct cost, yet hiring, transfer and termination decisions are subject to various contractual and legislated restrictions (to be discussed in Chapter 10).

What are the Procedures Used in Controlling?

Companies often fail to establish a baseline of current performance, and have no idea whether that baseline is being exceeded or not achieved. If the question is asked of a manager regarding the cost to perform a certain activity, he or she will probably not know the answer. Here are some examples:

- What does it cost to completely verify and disburse an accounts payable amount due to a vendor?
- What is the length of time to complete an accounts receivable cycle including invoicing, receiving funds and posting to the customer's account?
- What is our complete cost for a manufacturing cycle of product X?
- What is our defect rate and related cost to manufacture product Y?

Float and Processing Expenses

Managing working capital involves the organization of a company's short-term resources to sustain ongoing activities, mobilize funds, and optimize liquidity. The two most critical cost efficiencies are float and processing expenses.

- Float was defined in footnote 104. Although we cannot eliminate float, we can examine every step of the cash-flow timeline to search for savings opportunities.
- Processing expenses are similarly important, as each transaction along the timeline — whether performed internally or outsourced — has a cost that directly impacts profitability.

Managing the float cost throughout the timeline can significantly impact the bottom line. For example, a business experiencing $1 billion a year in revenue will receive $4 million in sales each business day (assuming 250 business days a year). At an assumed cost of capital of 10%, each day of delay in receiving, processing, and banking funds is equal to $400,000. On the disbursement side of the timeline, each day probably involves two-thirds or so of the revenue received in salaries and wages, materials, and other accounts payable. That same $1 billion a year business will have about $2.7 million in daily outflows ($667,000,000 ÷ 250 days), valued at about $270,000.

Any activity in the working capital timeline can cause a variation from the baseline; see Figure 9-2. Here is an example: A large paper-products company allowed customers to delay payments while disputes were investigated on monthly invoices. Some of these statements included hundreds of transactions, but even a few disputes caused a remittance delay during the investigation period, which could last weeks. The time wasted involved, on average one week, translates to $2 million a year for our $1 billion company!

Figure 9-2: Working Capital Time Line - What Can Go Wrong?

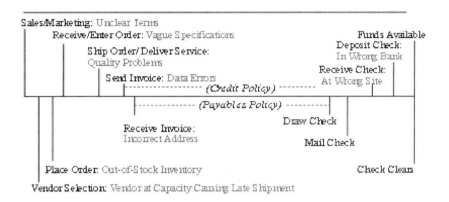

Measuring Performance

We measure performance by observation, the analysis of existing reports using statistics and financial analysis, and other primary data. Primary data is data observed or collected from direct experience. In contrast, secondary data is collected and published by another, unrelated source. Some of these data are regularly collected by businesses, such as financial results required for accounting statements, budgets and employee turnover or absenteeism. Other data may have to be created for the explicit purpose of establishing a baseline of performance. A useful rule is to measure the cost of an activity whenever possible. An example of a baseline cost for the operations of a company's processing centers (along with outsourcing) is provided in Figure 9-3.

A large U.S. corporation had three such centers that had been established in suburban locations due to historic reasons that were no longer relevant. However, the company continued to support these operations due to a lack of appreciation for the cost of these operations and due to attention to other business matters. Activities performed at the centers included preparing and sending bills to customers, receiving and banking payments received, responding to and resolving customer inquiries, reconciling local bank accounts, reviewing vendor invoices, and preparing and mailing check disbursements. The total number of documents processed throughout the U.S. was 250,000 each year, managed by 60 employees.

This situation had not received a management review until the current lease on one of the centers was submitted for approval by legal counsel prior to renewal. As part of its procedures, weekly cabinet meetings of senior management were held, at which time counsel submitted contracts in the amount of $50,000 or more for cabinet discussion. The lease was for an additional five years at $10,000 a year, which was the minimum for such consideration. While most decisions were routinely approved, the chief financial officer (CFO) realized that her responsibilities included the financial analysis of these types of expenses. The suggestion was then made to evaluate the entire situation, develop an economic analysis, and prepare a recommendation for future action.

Figure 9-3: Processing Centers Alternatives, Cost per Document (in cents)
(I.I. = internal improvements)

		Site A (75,000 documents)	Site B (100,000 documents)	Site C (75,000 documents)	Total Company (250,000 documents)
1	Baseline (current system)	85.0	75.0	77.0	"78.0"
2	Baseline with 15% I.I.	72.3	63.8	65.5	"66.3"
3	Baseline with 25% I.I.	63.8	56.3	57.8	"58.5"
4	Outsource ½ of processing functions	60.0	54.7	60.0	"60.0"
5	Outsource and merge ⅔rds of processing functions	55.0		60.0	"56.5"
6	Outsource all functions	50.0*			
7	Outsource most functions and merge all sites**	54.5			

Notes: " " indicates a company-wide average, not an actual configuration.
*Bid price from outsource vendor.
**Company would continue to prepare invoices and payments; all other activities would be outsourced.

How Should We Analyze Working Capital Alternatives?

Once the baseline is established, the analysis becomes a multi-step process as outlined in this section.

1. Establish alternatives. There are various operational alternatives for a significant portion of the timeline that utilize three processing choices within these segments: 1) internal processing, 2) outsourcing, and 3) a combination of internal processing and outsourcing.

   - With *internal processing,* the organization performs timeline activities. Internal processing of processing center activities would include the functions noted earlier.
   - *Outsourcing* involves bank or vendor processing. Corporate initiatives to reduce headcount and internal operating costs have spurred the use of outsourcing, particularly as outsourcing vendors use benchmarking, total quality management and other programs to assure outsource service quality.
   - *A combination of internal processing and outsourcing* would choose the optimal mix of each approach; for example, the CFO could envision having a bank handle all payment activities while the processing center staff prepared customer bills and managed accounts payable.

2. Quantify each alternative. Each segment of the timeline must be quantified, including relevant cost and float elements. Float is significant because nearly all business elements have inherent delays that increase costs. Although float cannot be eliminated, every step of the timeline should be examined in the search for savings opportunities. Processing costs are important because each transaction has an expense and an impact on profitability.

3. Create an "impact table" to compare alternatives. The amount of data developed in the previous step can be overwhelming. A graph of the quantified results, called an impact table, helps organize the critical

summary data for clearer review and analysis. Normally there will be several components to the table: in Figure 9-3, the vertical axis contains the alternatives and the horizontal axis contains the site combinations. Additional alternatives can be developed by visualizing different table combinations.

4. Select the optimal alternative. The alternative that is chosen is not necessarily the most cost-effective because of political, quality, or other factors. Are there concerns for service quality? Are there unique processes that would be disrupted? Are customers accustomed to dealing with certain service personnel? Can a vendor provide an equivalent level of service to what is currently being provided? Will the company lose control over the outsourced processes? In making a decision, the company may not wish to terminate employees by eliminating a site, or may conclude that a potential customer may be impressed if a site is located close to their offices.

In this situation, the company selected alternative 7 to retain internal supervision over certain critical functions including customer inquiries and the management of payables. The annual savings were $58,750 (250,000 documents times [78.0¢ - 54.5¢]). In addition, better control was attained, equivalent to $50,000 annually. The total savings were estimated at nearly $110,000 a year.

Actions other than the Alternative Selected

The process we have described led to changes in a process. It will work equally well should the decision be made to improve rather than change that process; see alternatives 2 and 3. The manager must initiative whatever corrective action is considered as appropriate, keeping in mind the reality of short-term "fixes" and the possibility of longer term "heroic" changes.

Sources of Data for the Analysis

The concept we have described obviously needs data, some of which will have to be collected as primary data. Secondary data, particularly for making internal improvements and for outsourcing, can be obtained by contacting vendors and consulting trade associations and websites. For example, if the analysis requires new mail handling equipment, the company should contact vendors in that business for ideas, products, references and pricing.[110] If you are considering new banking services, contact several commercial banks for their input. Many trade associations provide industry statistics and information on baseline performance.[111]

Websites

Websites can provide two types of data: evaluative data for company and industry comparisons, and ranking data to determine how a company compares to its peers.

- Evaluative data. Financial websites provide a thorough presentation of various information sources that allow comparisons with peer companies and the industry. See Figure 9-4 for topics from MSN.com, which is representative of what is available on the web.

---

110 A Google search on mail handling equipment resulted in 2½ million "hits", from the largest companies like Pitney-Bowes to small, local businesses.
111 For a list of U.S. trade associations with their website links, see en.wikipedia.org/wiki/List_of_industry_trade_groups_in_the_United_States.

Figure 9-4: Topics Available on Publicly-Held Companies on the Web
(MSN.com)

Stock Quote
Stock Options (puts and calls)
Historical Stock Prices
Interactive Chart of Stock Prices
News Headlines
Key Company Developments
Financial Highlights
Profile of the Company and its Activities
Key Financial Ratios
10-Year Summary of Financial Results
Earnings
SEC Regulatory Filings
Stock Reports
Analyst Ratings
Trades by Company Insiders
Ownership
Financials:
Income Statement
Balance Sheet
Cash Flow

- Ranking data. For larger organizations, publications with web-sites provide rankings that can be used to match a company to its peers. A list of selected rankings is provided in Figure 9-5.

Figure 9-5: Selected Rankings Available from Websites

Fortune Magazine
Fortune 500 and Global 500 Companies
Top MBA Employers
Most Admired Companies
Best Companies to Work For
Fastest Growing Companies

BusinessWeek
Most Innovative Companies
Best Customer Service Companies

Forbes
Forbes 2000
Best Small Companies
Largest Private Companies

Feedback Controls

Feedback controls are measures that determine how work is being performed, and may be used before, concurrently with or after the work.[112] There are any number of feedback activities that occur before the work is begun, such as preventive maintenance on machinery, mandatory airline checks on critical airplane metrics prior to take-off, fast food operations that report on food quality before preparation to prevent any possibility of contamination (such as days in transit to the restaurant and degree of refrigeration), and similar situations where failure could result in serious illness or even loss of life.

Most companies do not face that situation, and are more concerned with concurrent feedback through supervision by first-line managers or after the fact feedback.

- Concurrent feedback: Nearly all manufacturing has a supervisory activity to observe and make corrections to production line work. In the

---

112 The term "feedback" literally refers to the situation after the work, but is generally used in management to refer to any of the three situational "times".

service industries, two examples include nurse supervisors in hospitals and pit bosses (floor managers) in casinos, who observe the actions of nurses and dealers to make certain that rules are being followed (and in the casino example, that no cheating is allowed!).

• After the fact feedback: Management-by-exception sampling of completed work is a frequently used after the fact feedback control. Variance between standard and actual performance is observed and remedial actions are initiated when the percentage of errors exceeds an acceptable level.

Financial results are fairly useful indicators of company results for investors and bankers, but are not particularly helpful in controlling performance except at the senior management level. As we discussed earlier in this chapter, profit reporting is impacted by accrual accounting conventions and other problems make financial ratios and other measures in general use fairly meaningless at the supervisory level of management.

How Do We Safeguard Information?

In too many organizations, inadequate attention is given to safeguarding a most critical corporate asset: information. This is due to the widespread responsibilities for information and systems throughout most companies. Auditors, information or computer specialists, operations managers, security personnel – there are many and yet no one accountable – and all are assumed to have this assignment. For this reason, senior managers should consider assigning responsibility for information control.

The loss of proprietary information through carelessness, theft or corporate espionage costs tens of billions of dollars each year with intrusions by and into U.S. and international organizations and companies. Although data are sketchy, only about 10% of all intrusions are detected (according to the FBI), and even fewer are ever solved and prosecuted. To combat this threat, some billions of dollars are spent each year on computer and communications security measures.

The Value of Information

Most management experts agree that <u>the</u> resource of value in the 21st century organization will be information more than any physical asset, and it is essential to formalize the responsibility for protecting this asset. In order to create the necessary defenses, a comprehensive plan should be developed to identify organizational information vulnerabilities and to prepare specific strategies to combat those risks. Information can have value to the organization in various forms:

- Proprietary knowledge, involving secret marketing, production, personnel and financial data.
- Computer software and hardware, including programs, computers, input/output devices, storage media, telephone lines and other components of a computer system.
- Hardcopy documents, both draft and final, such as plans, status reports, manufacturing specifications, working papers, internal correspondence, minutes of meetings and similar files and papers.

The integrity of information may be compromised by various internal deficiencies.

- Failure to document systems. Although systems engineers and programmers are supposed to flowchart and describe the systems they design, it is unusual to find intact, comprehensive documentation including changes and fixes to the original programs. This is a particular problem when an outside party has participated in the systems installation and then departed, leaving you with the technology but no in-depth explanation of the workings.
- Employees. Employees represent a significant threat to information. They are inside of the organization, know the layout and security measures utilized in most areas of your premises, can be difficult to detect in any wrongdoing, and may perceive that a negative job review, company downsizing or other adverse job action is legitimate grounds for sabotage or theft. Employees may take hostile actions for a variety of reasons, including revenge for injustices against themselves or their colleagues, monetary gain, "the challenge" or simply boredom. Despite the popular media's portrayal of professional criminals as the enemy, the real threat is often the trusted employee.

- Vendors and customers. Organizations tend to establish special relationships with their vendors and certain important customers, allowing casual entry to sensitive areas of a company. While the requirement for visitor badges is common, individuals who frequent your premises may be taken for granted and not observed with the same care as strangers. During periods when meetings or other contact activities are on break, vendors and customers routinely have access to telephones, restrooms and food vending, which may permit them to observe and eavesdrop on information and computer systems. On company visits we frequently challenge client security, and are often allowed to pass security barriers, eavesdrop, or talk our way into protected areas!

Criminals and Competitors

Corporate espionage attempts to compromise security measures while eluding detection in the search for information with potential value. This may involve professionals who steal information for clients (often competitors) through breaking ("hacking") into information systems. Espionage may take the form of masquerading or social engineering.

- "Masquerading" is the impersonation of a legitimate employee to gain access to a secure area.
- "Social engineering" is a more circuitous approach, involving subterfuges to manipulate employees into revealing confidential information.

Attacks on systems and communications are intended to steal, alter or disrupt information, or to destroy data and computer systems. There are numerous approaches to attacking an organization's systems and communications, and most of these are difficult to detect and prevent.

- Trap doors. The trap door is a back way into a computer program, written by programmers to quickly enter software to update or modify program instructions. Trap doors are often based on a keyword recognized by the program and known "only" to the programmer. If the intruder can discover the trap door, he or she can gain entry to the computer and can probably access to your entire system.

- Session hijacking. A legitimate system user may temporarily leave a workstation to gather files, use the restroom, attend a meeting, or for other activities. While procedures normally require users to log off, they may fail to do so, expecting to return to their computer shortly or not wanting to be bothered with logging off and logging back on. During this period, any individual could read and/or change files, copy information, or commit acts of sabotage.
- Viruses and Trojan Horses. A virus involves lines of computer code which are inserted into legitimate computer programs to modify and possibly destroy data and software, often replicating the virus so that it spreads through a computer system. If data are sent to other computers through the Internet or by copying a file, other computers can become infected. A Trojan horse involves the planting of unauthorized computer instructions inside of a legitimate function, such as commands to enable fraudulent transactions.
- Illegal listening. The communications intrusions of wiretapping and eavesdropping involve illegal listening on voice or data transmissions. A wiretap uses an electrical tap or connection, usually attached to a junction box, to listen to communications. Eavesdropping uses wireless electronic listening devices for the same purpose.
- Falsification of data. Data may be altered or falsified at the time it is first recorded. Information such as payroll, sales results, or manufacturing or sales costs may also be changed as it is entered into a computer system. Any alternations that occur during keying or data entry are information systems concerns, and require programs to monitor.

What Are Other Protections for Information?

Auditors may suggest various "traditional" barriers to entry, including security personnel and guard dogs, and surveillance devices such as cameras and television monitors. These forms of protection assume that an attack will be physical and *overt*. However, current breaches of physical security are usually *covert*, comprising such activities as searching through discarded trash and the disruption to company facilities by utility interruptions and other vandalism.

Employees

The principal defense against people hazards is to hire responsible, trustworthy employees. It is common practice to conduct "new hire" reviews with detail appropriate to the responsibility of the position being filled and the commensurate access to company data. Clerical workers who may be hired with minimal background checks often have access to most information systems and can cause extensive damage in that role.

Workers who are hired are seldom subject to subsequent monitoring or review other than for job performance and promotion. Unfortunately, financial problems, family strain, addictions or other psychological illnesses, or other stresses may lead to undesirable behaviors. Organizations should develop monitoring routines, from simple observation or more formalized programs, such as periodic medical examinations and mandatory personal financial statements.

Observation should focus on conspicuous spending, an unusual number of incoming telephone calls, extensive intraday absences from the workplace, changes in physical appearance, and deterioration in job performance. Electronic surveillance or monitoring procedures now exist to eavesdrop on telephone calls and such computer activity as keystroke production and e-mail messages.

Electronic Devices and Barriers

Organizations no longer find that locks, alarms and guard dogs protect their most valuable assets. Current technology and the proliferation of information and systems make it difficult to merely enclose a facility to adequately safeguard technology. Information is on nearly every desk, in every file and on laptops and other computing devices. Therefore, security begins with prohibiting entry to these areas using electronic devices and barriers.

Entry to computer systems should require positive identification of the individual, using a password, a special key or badge, or an eye or fingerprint scan. Surrounding this secure area should be various types of physical barriers to obstruct intruders, including locked doors and windows, guards and watch dogs, alarmed entries and exits, and surveillance cameras. The barriers should be periodically tested using personnel from outside of the area to determine if established procedures are being followed.

Communications Protections

Because of the complexity of communications networks, any exchange of information between computers potentially involves multiple telecommunications connections. The resulting vulnerability from these possible points of intrusion may not be obvious to the computer user, but has resulted in countless incidents of eavesdropping, hacking and theft. Communications must pass through a firewall barrier to protect internal communications from outsiders (or portions of internal systems from other internal networks). All traffic is reviewed and entry is refused to any message not meeting predetermined criteria.

Telecommunications cables can be wiretapped at nearly any point, inside or outside of your premises, allowing the display and recording of any information being exchanged. Taps can be placed at panels, in walls, at junction boxes, and in tubing placed in dropped ceilings and raised floors prepared for electronic equipment installations. Such cables should be encased in steel or pressure-sensitive conduits; the latter safeguard signals when there has been an intrusion on the line.

Computer Back-Up Procedures

The regular backing-up of computer files was standard procedure when systems were based on mainframe systems and personnel were assigned the task of creating a replacement copy on magnetic tape or other media. Back-up procedures typically included retaining logs of back-up responsibilities and the offsite storage of such files. The dissemination of computer systems throughout the modern organization has substantially reduced the ability of management to control the timing and procedures for the backing-up of files.

Many companies deal with this difficult problem by issuing policies (e.g., employees *will* back-up every night) and hoping that computer users obey. Unfortunately, there have been numerous instances where personal computers crash or laptops are stolen, and data is irretrievable lost or the cost and time to recreate it is exorbitant. An on-going audit function should be established to monitor back-up procedures on an unannounced basis. A control officer should construct an appropriate back-up plan for each program and system, including timing, media, and procedures for file reconstruction. The storage of backup files and records at an auxiliary site should be established in the event of a system crash or other disaster.

Protection of Other Documents

Important information may also exist in non-computer form. These include evidence of the organization's structure (e.g., incorporation papers, Board of Directors minutes, lists of stockholders, copies of tax returns, titles to real estate); documents relating to customers, vendors and employees (e.g., contracts, correspondence, orders, invoices sent/received, payroll data); and documents relating to the protection of intellectual property (e.g., copyrights and patents, licenses, engineering drawings, key employee contracts).

Unfortunately, practice in the safeguarding of these documents is often somewhat haphazard, with papers in desks and filing cabinets, vaults, safe deposit boxes, permanent off-site storage, and elsewhere. All important documents should be cataloged and microfilm/fiche copied or scanned, and a conscious decision made as to appropriate storage location and custodian.

What are the Issues You Should Address?

In considering your organization's control activities, here are some issues to review.

- Do we have data on the baseline (current) situation with regard to our operational activities? Does this include float and processing costs? Are we about equivalent to, better than or worse than our peer companies?
- What data are we using to control performance? What was the source of that data and is it still relevant?

- Have we considered (or should we consider) alternatives to our current procedures?
- Do we use feedback to monitor operating performance? Are the results attained adequate to meet our quality and other standards?
- Do we adequately safeguard our proprietary information? Do we rely too much on the honesty of employees and company visitors, and on physical barriers rather than electronic protections?
- Would we know if our information were attacked or stolen?
- What is our policy on backing up our computers (including PCs and laptops)? Is that policy enforced?

Discussion and Review Questions

1. What is the purpose of and the two elements of control in organizations?
2. Why are organizational delays tolerated and how do they impact the organization's successful pursuit of its mission?
3. What procedures are used in control?
4. What are the sources of information for control?
5. What procedures are used in evaluating working capital alternatives?
6. How is feedback used in control?
7. Why is information of high importance in the modern organization?
8. What procedures are used to protect this resource?

CHAPTER 10

Human Resources Practices

After reading this chapter, you will be able to:

- Understand various issues in hiring, including interviews, personality testing and other procedures
- Consider current hiring practices, including legal considerations and the use of job descriptions
- Recognize important training issues, including employee orientation, regular training including on-the-job, and mandated job skills
- Appreciate the difficulties and concerns in the employee appraisal process
- Be aware of the current emphasis on managing employee costs, particularly healthcare

What are the Issues in Hiring Decisions?

In a hiring situation, organizations have come to accept the fact that a prospective employee may be "performing" for the interview (or series of interviews), or may simply not be responding to cues and openings for interesting responses. Unfortunately, the "performers" too often are chosen only to disappoint, while the quiet applicants are not hired and may have proven to be loyal and hard-working. Most research finds that interviewing is a poor selection technique.[113] When the process works, it is because intelligence, motivation and interpersonal skills are evaluated.[114]

Interviews

The author conducted dozens of interviews for the bank where he was employed, and the outstanding impression is that the most positive conversations produced the least effective employees. This was made worse by the many interviews each candidate would have to endure, usually eight in a day, including the bank's recruiter, numerous managers and staff, and a senior executive. The process becomes more of an endurance test than an indication of competence.

Furthermore, many companies use an unstructured interview process (as did the author's employer), allowing the questioner to ask anything that he or she wants (within certain limits as proscribed by law). This can lead to a lack of objectivity, with the applicant being approved perhaps based on an attractive appearance, past sports prowess, or an ability to discuss the latest political, international or local news; or rejected because of age, race, religion or some other factor.

The interviewer is usually required to submit a brief evaluation of the candidate, with responses on such matters as maturity, subject-area knowledge and interpersonal skills. The process may be made easier by using a form that has a forced rating system on these and other criteria. The personnel department will normally require an employee application, university transcripts, letters of recommendation and references, all of which will be verified. For specific interviewing topics, see Figure 10-1; for questions to avoid for legal reasons, see Figure 10-2.

---

113 M.A. McDaniel et. al., "The Validity of Employment Interviews: A Comprehensive Review and Meta-Analysis," *Journal of Applied Psychology*, August 1994, pages 599-616.
114 W. F. Cascio, *Applied Psychology in Personnel Management*, Prentice-Hall, 4th ed., 1991, page 271.

Figure 10-1: Interview Topics

Topic	Possible Candidate Responses
Why is the individual applying for this position?	If the answer is "I need a job," the interviewer will probably not be very impressed. A good answer might discuss how the applicant's education and work experience matches the employer's needs.
What do you know about our company?	When a candidate was asked this question, the response was "what do you do in a bank all day?" The interviewer was not amused; the expectation was that the candidate would have done at least some research on the industry he or she hoped to enter.
Tell me about your work experience	Resumes are necessarily succinct; asking this question can open a discussion about how a candidate has learned from work experiences.
Tell me about your leisure activities	Resumes often do not reveal whether a candidate has outside interests; it is important to know that a candidate has a life outside of work.
How would you handle an emergency?	Pose a situation such as a 5 p.m. telephone call from a client requiring an answer by the next morning. The candidate should be able to indicate how he or she would organize a response, including recruiting other company staff, determining essential data and other logical tasks.
Does the candidate have any questions?	The candidate should be able to sustain a dialogue with the interviewer; as an indication of this characteristic, being prepared with a few questions is a positive indicator.

Figure 10-2: Interview Topics to Avoid for Legal Reasons

Age
Arrest/conviction records
Significant debts
Disabilities
Height/weight
Marital status and children
National origin
Race/ethnicity
Religion
Sex/sexual orientation

How is Psychological (Personality) Testing used in Hiring?

Psychological testing uses a series of objective questions that require an applicant to agree or disagree in an attempt to analyze the extent of personality in certain generally accepted areas:

- agreeableness
- conscientiousness
- extroversion (that is, an outgoing, friendly person)
- openness to experiences
- stability

There is no right or wrong personality; rather, the profile of the applicant is matched to the job's requirements. As an example, an extrovert may become a good salesperson, while an introvert (a more withdrawn, colder person) may be more suited to an administrative assignment. Of course, other skill sets and personality attributes need to be analyzed in making a hiring decision.

As companies face increasing cost pressures, testing has become computerized and now even offered to applicants on-line. A major global food retailer uses about three dozen on-line questions that attempt to determine the applicant's compatibility with the company's customer service orientation. Of course, no applicant is likely to admit that unpleasant situations (such as an angry patron) result in hostile reactions, so the value of these tests is debatable. Furthermore, there are any number of books and Internet sites that assist the job seeker to cheat on the tests, especially when the company will not be observing the process. Finally, there is no substitute for in-person testing, and hearing and observing the applicant's responses.[115] The most widely used tests are listed in Figure 10-3.

Figure 10-3: Personality Tests Used in Hiring Decisions

Myers-Briggs Type Indicator: Most widely used test; uses 100 questions that ask how applicants would feel about or act in specific situations. The test taker is ranked as extroverted or introverted, sensing or intuitive, thinking or feeling, and judging (controlling and structured) or perceiving (flexible and spontaneous). Rankings are combined into various personality types.

Sixteen Personality Factors: Measures a number of personality traits, classified as normal-range and global.

Dominance, Influence, Steadiness, Conscientiousness: Based on a four-quadrant behavioral model; behavior is grouped into personality styles, each of which exhibits specific characteristics.

Caliper Profile: Measures 25 personality traits related to job performance based on a person's strengths, limitations, motivation and potential.

---

115 Concern that the applicant may use a surrogate (a substitute) to take the test can be overcome through various required proofs, such as fingerprinting, a question and answer known only to the applicant (such as his/her mother's maiden name), or other identity verification techniques.

California Psychological Inventory: Uses 18 scales to measure social skills, intellectual flexibility and interests; supposedly determines what the applicant will do under specific circumstances.

Minnesota Multiphasic Personality Inventory: A psychopathology test that is generally used in clinical psychology to reveal mental health disorders. (Psychopathology is the study of mental disorder or distress, and of abnormal behavior.)

Performance simulation tests have been used in the past to observe how a job applicant will perform in a mock-up of a real situation. This can take various forms, such as responding to a series of memos within a set time, having a welder or truck driver actually perform a weld or drive a vehicle, or role-playing. A **role-play** is an enactment of a work situation involving interactions among employees and/or customers. For example, an applicant may be given a short statement regarding a typical issue encountered in business, such as a conflict between a manager and a worker or a dissatisfied customer. The interviewer will play one role, and the interviewee the other role, with the intention of observing how effectively the situation is resolved.

What are the Current Practices in Hiring?

There is no generally accepted approach to the hiring decision. As with many aspects of management, practices go in and out of fashion, and companies generally rely on the least costly method available, which is the interview. Personnel staff realizes that mistakes are made, and some have implemented a probationary period, usually about three months, during which the new employee is observed and can be terminated without cause.

Companies continue to use testing to select employees, but with the understanding that there is limited predictive power and some legal problems in their use. Estimates vary on companies using testing, with probably one-third of all hiring decisions relying to some extent on their outcome. Tests have been found to be only vaguely correlated with job performance, and are costly to construct and score. When testing is used, it is largely for job-specific skills, such as intelligence, spatial perception, motor skills, reading comprehension, writing ability and ethical values.

Governing Law

Companies are limited in their use of testing by various legal cases, including Griggs v. Duke Power Co. that found that the employer must be able to demonstrate the relationship of the test to the job.[116] The central issue of this case is that a test given indiscriminately to all job applicants may not be reasonable should the matter be heard in a court of law. For example, a company using a math test for every applicant would probably not be able to show that certain customer service representatives, receptionists and file clerks need such skills for employment. Employers cannot probe into mental health or stability issues (as could be determined in the Minnesota Inventory noted in Figure 10-1) unless such factors are essential to job performance; e.g., for police officers and security personnel who carry weapons.

Job Descriptions

Larger companies develop databases of employees, including personal information; job skills on past and current assignments (including former employers); education, seminars and certifications; language skills; and previous global assignments. As positions become available, it is relatively simple to determine if a current employee has the necessary skills to meet the requirements of the position.

The components of a job are specified in a **job description**, which is a written statement that explains the responsibilities of the position, the job grade, the educational or other skill requirements, the specific tasks that must be performed and the managerial reporting relationship. Job descriptions are important to maintain control of employee activities and to assure that situations are avoided where there is an inherent conflict of tasks. For example, a cashiering function should not be accounting for cash received to prevent the possibility of fraud. Unfortunately, the current economic recession has forced the consolidation of job responsibilities, sometimes resulting is these control

---

116 Decided by the U.S. Supreme Court and reported at 401 U.S. 424 (1971).

conflicts. A properly designed job description can protect a company against a claim of discrimination or unfair hiring practices, or the possible conflict if a current employee is not considered for a new position. For an example of a job description, see Figure 10-4.

Figure 10-4: Job Description Format

Job Title:	Office Manager	Job Category:	
Department/ Group:		Job Code No.:	
Location:		Travel Required:	
Level/Salary Range:		Position Type:	[i.e.: full-time, part-time, etc.]
HR Contact:		Date posted:	
Co. Will Train?		Posting Expires:	
Applications Accepted By:			
Fax or E-mail: (999) 555-0123 or someone@ example.com Subject Line: Attention: [Recruiting or HR Department RE: Job Code No. and Title]		Mail: [Recruiting Contact or Hiring Manager] [Department, Company Name] [P.O. Box] [Street or Mailing Address with ZIP Code]	

174

Job Description			

Job Purpose: Supports company operations by maintaining office systems and supervising staff.

Duties:

- Organizes office operations and procedures: preparing payroll; controlling correspondence; designing filing systems; reviewing and approving supply requisitions; assigning and monitoring clerical functions.
- Defines procedures for retention, protection, retrieval, transfer, and disposal of records.
- Plans and implements office systems, layouts, and equipment procurement.
- Establishes standards and procedures; measuring results against standards; making necessary adjustments.
- Schedules and assigns employees; follows up on work results.
- Participates in the recruiting, selecting, orienting, and training employees.
- Prepares an annual budget; scheduling expenditures; analyzing variances; and initiating corrective actions.

Skills/Qualifications:

- Supply Management, Tracking Budget Expenses, Delegation, Staffing, Managing Processes, Employee Supervision, Developing Standards, Inventory Control.

Reviewed By:		Date:	
Approved By:		Date:	
Last Updated By:		Date:	

Revised from the template at: office.microsoft.com/en-us/templates/office-manager-job-description-TC010356795.aspx?AxInstalled=1&c=0.

What are the Issues in Employee Training?

Employee training includes new employee orientation, regular training and mandatory training to comply with legal requirements.

Orientation

An orientation program is designed to familiarize the new employee with the company's policies and procedures, and to begin the process of teaching the organizational culture. The process can quite specific; for example, Microsoft has a formal new employee orientation (NEO) process for new hires, including basic personnel information and meetings with the employee's work team. An early requirement at the company is to prepare specific objectives (MBOs) and an execution plan to complete each one.

In other organizations, the new hire may simply be assigned to an experienced employee who explains necessary job-specific matters. Nearly all companies require a personnel briefing to cover such matters as pay options (check or direct deposit), health insurance, the company identification card or badge, the pension and savings plans, and other issues.

Regular Employee Training

In current economic conditions, companies have reduced or eliminated most discretionary spending, including training not mandated by regulation or concern for safety (discussed in the next section). Basic educational skills require the ability to read, write, do math calculations and use a computer, and when employees need assistance (as when English or the language in use is not the employee's first language) such training may be offered. For example, most workplaces require the ability to read at a high school level, but about one-fifth of U.S. adults cannot read at even a middle school level.[117]

Extensive training programs still occur in some organizations for company-specific systems, but the time when educational workshops were generally

---

117 Reported by the Educational Testing Service (ETS), *From School to Work*, 1990.

available for nearly any relevant skill, whether job-related or not, has largely ended. Arguably the most famous company-specific program is McDonald's Hamburger University near Chicago IL, which offers a two-week course for store managers to learn operations, equipment and employee management, computer systems for inventory and reporting sales, and customer contact skills.[118]

Since new and transferred employees do not necessarily have appropriate skills, companies are forced to use on-the-job training (OJT), which usually involves supervision of the trainee by experienced employees who have the necessary skills. There are various disadvantages to OJT:

- Due to the time required to explain procedures, the organizational unit inevitably experiences lower production and a higher error rate
- The training is casual, as the experienced worker may not be motivated to help the trainee at the expense of his or her productivity
- There is a lack of an objective evaluative procedure to determine if the trainee is making adequate progress

Mandated Training: Sexual Harassment

Sexual harassment is intimidation, bullying or coercion of a romantic, lustful or lascivious nature, or the unwelcome or inappropriate promise of rewards in exchange for sexual favors. In most modern legal contexts, sexual harassment is illegal. As defined by the Equal Employment Opportunity Commission (EEOC), "It is unlawful to harass a person (an applicant or employee) because of that person's sex. Harassment can include 'sexual harassment' or unwelcome sexual advances, requests for sexual favors, and other verbal or physical harassment of a sexual nature."[119]

In the U.S., the Civil Rights Act of 1964 prohibits employment discrimination based on race, sex, color, national origin or religion. Initially only intended to combat sexual harassment of women, the prohibition of sex discrimination now covers both females and males. Barnes v. Train is commonly viewed as the first sexual harassment case in America, even though the term

---

118 See a description on the website, at www.aboutmcdonalds.com/mcd/corporate_careers/training_and_development/hamburger_university.html.
119 "Sexual Harassment," at www.eeoc.gov/laws/types/sexual_harassment.cfm.

"sexual harassment" was not explicitly used.[120] Companies generally require training on sexual harassment because of prevailing state law or from fear of a legal action by an employee which can lead to substantial fines by the EEOC and civil awards of millions of dollars. Two companies that experienced these penalties are Philip Morris and UPS. In addition, such behavior can cause:

- Reduced productivity, decreased job satisfaction and increased conflict
- Possible lowered self esteem of the person who is harassed
- Increased healthcare costs and sick pay costs because of the consequences of harassment and/or retaliation
- The undermining of ethical standards and discipline in the organization

Mandated Training: Occupational Safety

The U.S. Congress determined that occupational health and safety risks required a federal supervisory organization, and created the Occupational Safety and Health Administration (OSHA) in 1970. Standards were developed to protect employees from dangerous hazards and toxic substances in the workplace, and training was mandated for employees in hazardous job situations. The agency requires that employers provide training to employees in safe handling and use of hazardous chemicals, spill containment, cleanup, and emergency procedures and evacuation.[121] Safety training must be provided for workers in construction, shipyards, general industry, agriculture, hospitals and healthcare, and any field where employees face dangers to health or safety.

---

120 Reported at 561 F.2d 983, 1974; decided on appeal in 1977.
121 See Training Requirements in OSHA Standards and Training Guidelines, at www.osha.gov/Publications/osha2254.pdf.

What are the Issues in Appraising Employee Performance?

The MBO system was discussed in Chapter 1. While there are problems with this process, it does provide a reasonably objective approach, particularly as the employee being evaluated must agree in advance to the measures being used.

Difficulties in Doing Appraisals

MBOs are only the first part of the appraisal process. It is often more troubling for managers to provide appraisals and honest feedback because of several factors:

- Fear of confrontation and arguments regarding negative comments. Employees have difficulty being objective about their own performance, and tend to excuse a mediocre year by blaming anyone and everyone else.
- Concern for retaliation by the reviewed employee and/or appeals through the company's personnel system.
- Forced distribution of ratings, often implemented as a small percent of superior and unsatisfactory ratings and a higher percent of other, more mid-range ratings. This requires the manager to somewhat arbitrarily choose those who receive the ratings in the highest and lowest categories.

There is no simple method to perform a review for an average or poor performance. When the author was a banker he faced this situation with his subordinates; emotions and hard feelings are probably inevitable no matter how the review is conducted. Academicians generally assume that the problem can be managed by conducting fair, constructive reviews, and that the employee will leave the discussion with an upbeat attitude, ready to improve. This is unrealistic and ignores human nature. As a result, the manager should provide as much documentation and objective evidence as can be gathered to support the outcome, and to this end a personnel file should be maintained on each employee and regularly updated.

Coaching and Counseling

Why should a manager help his or her employees? The textbook answer typically is "it's the manager's job". However, we tend to do whatever provides a payoff and to ignore other tasks. The real answer requires some faith in the eventual recognition of good work by the manager's manager in the form of a promotion or salary increase. Employees have various needs, and failing to fulfill those needs cannot be in the interest of the organization. These include:

- New information that is important in getting a job successfully completed
- Preparing a replacement for you (the manager) or for employees likely to be promoted or transferred
- Challenging and stimulating employees
- Developing employee plans for career development
    - Courses and seminars to increase the knowledge base
    - Shadowing another employee who is considered competent (as on sales calls, during presentations or in meetings with senior managers)
    - Assignment to a multi-discipline team
- Making time for advisement

Termination

The U.S. generally follows **employment-at-will** law, which allows employers to end an employee's position at any time for no reason.[122] The only exceptions are if an employment contract exists or if the employee is a member of a collective bargaining group (a union). In practice, many large organizations have detailed procedures for termination after the probationary period ends, requiring fairly extensive documentation to protect the company and the employee. This can include:

---

122 The U.S. is one of only a few countries where employment is predominantly at-will, with most allowing employers to dismiss employees only for cause. Note that civil law countries, particularly in Europe, have strong social contract arrangements between employers and employees, and dismissal requires following protocols established by individual governments. For a review on international practices, see R. Blanpain, S. Bison-Rapp, W. R. Corbett, H. K. Josephs and M, J. Zimmer, *The Global Workplace: International and Comparative Employment Law – Cases and Materials*, Cambridge University Press, 2007.

- meetings to discuss problems and their possible resolution
- copies of reports of counseling including the signature of the manager and the employee
- a statement of actions required to restore the good standing of the employee
- evidence of unsatisfactory performance such as excessive absences or sick days; unacceptable written work (such as reports or letters) or recorded conversations with customers or vendors where unprofessional conduct was present (assuming employees have been previously informed that their conversations are recorded); or complaints from customers, vendors or other employees
- repeated failure to achieve job objectives (such as an MBO contract)

Part-time employees and independent contractors are not entitled to any job security and may be terminated at any time.[123]

What are the Issues in Personnel Management?

While salaries and wages continue as the most significant portion of the cost of an employee, the skyrocketing out-of-pocket expense of non-salary/wage compensation has become an important factor as companies consider hiring decisions. Fringe benefit costs are approximately 30% of salaries paid, a significant portion of which are healthcare costs. This latter group of costs have risen in excess of 10% annually during this past decade, and certain behaviors, including smoking, obesity, alcohol and drug addictions and lack of exercise add even more to this expense, perhaps another 25% for those employees. As a result, two actions have been recently initiated to manage the problem of non-salary/wage costs.

---

123 An **independent contractor** is not employed by a company, but retains control over his or her schedule and number of hours worked, jobs accepted, and performance. The company compensates them as services are rendered, such as legal, accounting or courier services. This is in contrast with a regular employee, who usually works at the schedule required by the employer and whose performance is directly supervised by the employer.

Healthy Lifestyle Programs

Nearly half of companies now encourage healthy behaviors, including changing fast-food to healthy menus, encouraging walking and health club participation at a subsidized rate, banning smoking from company facilities, and even paying people to lose weight (if they keep it off for a minimum period). As an example, CalPERS (California Public Employees' Retirement System for public employees), working in conjunction with its health insurer Blue Shield of CA, offers a wellness assessment payment to employees of $50, and $50 additional for each 12-week period (up to three periods) for which the results are reported to the company in such areas as:

- Exercise: creating a workout program
- Nutrition: learning the basics of good nutrition and developing a workable eating plan
- Stress: understanding stress and its causes
- Tobacco use: finding ways of thinking and new techniques for quitting smoking
- Weight management: learning the facts about determining a healthy weight

Pensions

Pensions are payments to retirees and others unable to work on a full-time basis. The original form of pensions in the U.S. were defined benefit (DB) plans, which specified the amount each person would receive based on years of service, the average of the most recent years of base salary and a percentage of that salary for each year worked. As an example, an employee retiring at 65 years might be entitled to 2% for each year worked, times an assumed 30 years of employment, or 60%, times the average salary of say, $60,000, or $36,000. This would continue until death, with some companies providing cost-of-living adjustments.

There have been three significant problems with DB plans: 1.) the cost to companies became unmanageable, particularly as improved healthcare extended life expectancies; 2.) many plans were not completely funded, so there was no assurance that the pensions would be paid; and 3.) the plans inherently made it difficult to change employers, although DB plans generally began vesting[124] after five years of service.

Many plans today are defined contribution (DC), where amounts are paid into an individual account owned and managed by the employee.[125] The contributions are invested and the returns are credited to the individual's account. On retirement, the member's account is used to provide retirement benefits. DC plans have become widespread all over the world in recent years. This conversion to DC has greatly reduced company costs, while requiring employees to take a more informed and active interest in their savings and investment positions.

Federally-Mandated Health Coverage

The Patient Protection and Affordable Care Act of 2010 (PPACA or informally "Obamacare") requires most adults not covered by an employer or government-sponsored insurance plan to maintain health insurance coverage or pay a penalty, a provision referred to as the individual mandate. People earning less than four times the poverty line will receive tax credits to subsidize their purchase of insurance. Medicaid eligibility is expanded to include those earning up to 133% of the poverty line although individual states may opt out of the Medicaid expansion.

PPACA was enacted by Congress in the effort to partially manage the rapidly escalating cost of healthcare, and it is now estimated that the number of uninsured Americans will decline by 30 million.[126] The U.S. has lagged many countries in providing universal health coverage, and this law, found Constitutional by the Supreme Court in June 2012, is an attempt to provide preventive medical care for the poor and to prevent the use of hospital

---

124 Vesting is the ownership of the employee in a portion of his or her pension. Typically, vesting starts at 25% of ownership and increases an additional 5% a year until becoming fully vested.

125 About one-half of all companies offer DC plans, while only about one-third offer DB. "Employee Participation in Defined Benefit and Defined Contribution Plans, 1985-2000," at www.bls.gov/opub/cwc/cm20030325tb01.htm.

126 Cost Estimate for Pending Health Care Legislation". Congressional Budget Office. March 20, 2010, at /cboblog.cbo.gov/?p=546; "The Effects of the Affordable Care Act on Employment-Based Health Insurance," Congressional Budget Office. March 15, 2012, at www.cbo.gov/publication/43090. "Highlights and Key Findings," CBO and JCT's Estimates of the Effects of the Affordable Care Act on the Number of People Obtaining Employment-Based Health Insurance, March 23, 2012.

emergency rooms for people without access to regular physician services. It remains unclear whether a future Congress will attempt to change the law.

The "Disappearing" Personnel Department

This chapter has attempted to note some issues faced by companies in managing personnel.[127] The various laws and regulations that govern employment practices strongly suggest that most companies create a personnel (or human resources) department. Specialists can determine the policies and practices required to meet legal and other requirements while assuring the equitable treatment of employees. However, recent cost management initiatives have been particularly difficult for staff departments (such as finance, personnel, and information technology), and many companies have outsourced major portions of these activities.

As recently reported in the media, employees who previously could discuss issues human resources specialists are now often directed to a toll-free telephone number or a website, with the worker forced to deal with various firms who may handle anything from payroll to training to performance appraisals. The complexities of Obamacare will have a significant impact on employers who will likely turn to external benefits advisors and insurers for advice and worker assistance.[128]

What are the Issues You Should Address?

In considering your organization's human resources practices, here are some issues to review:

- What process do we use to find, interview and select new employees? Do we have an established interview process, or can interviewers ask any question they choose? How are interviews scored?

127 There is a large body of literature available on such topics as industrial and labor relations, employment practices, coaching and counseling, and other related topics.

128 See, Phyllis Korkki, "When the H.R. Office Leaves the Building," *New York Times*, Dec. 2, 2012, page BUS 8.

- Are we aware of questions that should not be asked in job applications and interviews?
- Do we use psychological (personality) tests in our hiring decisions?
- Is there any true predictive capability in using these tests?
- Are we aware of current practices in hiring and are we in compliance with laws and court decisions?
- Are we current on our job descriptions, and are we matching hires to those descriptions? Are there any situations of inappropriate assignment of duties that could compromise our company?
- How are we providing orientations for new employees and regular company training? Are we conducting sexual harassment or job safety training (or any other training required by regulation)?
- Do we have a formal system of employee appraisal? Do employees receive coaching and counseling to help them prior to the appraisal? Do we have a termination policy?
- Are we taking appropriate actions to reduce personnel costs? Do we have a healthy lifestyle program? How is our pension plan managed? Are we taking appropriate steps to comply with PPACA?

Discussion and Review Questions

1. What are the problems in the use of interviewing in the selection of new employees? How can organizations refine the interview process to overcome these difficulties?
2. Why is psychological testing a flawed process? If properly used, can it overcome the problems in interviewing?
3. How do job descriptions assist organizations in hiring and placing new employees?
4. What types of training programs are used today by organizations? How does this vary from the period before the start of the current recession?
5. How do organizations handle the employee appraisal process?
6. What are current practices in managing personnel costs?

CHAPTER 11

Interpersonal Dynamics

After reading this chapter, you will be able to:

- Review the significance of and methods to improve communications in organizations
- Appreciate the role of conflict and its contribution to change and defeating groupthink
- Consider how individuals perceive situations and people, and the danger of stereotyping
- Be aware of issues in negotiation particularly in global business situations
- Understand the role of politics in organizations and possible negative outcomes of political behavior

What is the Role of Communications in Interpersonal Dynamics?

Interpersonal dynamics include communications, conflict, information processing, perception and political behavior. Organizations face a changing, difficult business environment managing these factors that some researchers have recently combined into this sub-field of management theory.[129] The effectiveness of a manager is often determined by his or her understanding and response to the interpersonal dynamics of employees, other managers, customers, vendors and other constituents. Various concerns are addressed:

- Which employees are likely to work together to achieve the goals of the organization?
- How can the potential of interpersonal conflict be harnessed in a work group context?
- Are there any disadvantages to having a high quality relationship between managers and employees?
- Do differences in perception arise from the ways employees take in information and use it to communicate?
- Would our results be enhanced if we better understood collaboration?
- Are barriers to communication negatively impacting our performance?

To summarize, how can our understanding of the individual worker, and his or her emotional traits, perceptual processes and personal motivations contribute to both individual and organizational performance? Our appreciation and utilization of the processing mechanisms of communications can assist employees to work together to achieve desired outcomes.

Communications

Communications involves transferring and understanding the meaning of an idea or a thought between the sender and the receiver. The exchange of information is far more than writing or speaking, although these actions are the most common methods of communicating. People also exchange message by gestures (usually of the face or hands), body movement[130] and even by not sending a message (such as not extending an invitation to a meeting or a party). **Noise** is interference in communications, as it is a barrier that can distort

---

129 See the survey of recent studies in T.A. Beauregard, "Introduction: The Import of Intrapersonal and Interpersonal Dynamics in Work Performance," *British Journal of Management,* Vol. 21 (2010), pages 255-261.

130 A variation of body movement is **body language,** which is a form of human non-verbal communication, which consists of body posture, gestures, facial expressions, and eye movements. Humans send and interpret such signals almost entirely subconsciously. The reading of body language has become a somewhat over-used pastime, and has been applied in business venues in sales situations and employment interviews.

the message's clarity and lead to misunderstandings. Noise can result from problems in translation, in perception and in cultural differences.

Verbal and Nonverbal Communications

Body movement takes many forms, including winking, shrugging our shoulders, clasping our hands, folding our arms, giving a "thumbs up" or "thumbs down" sign, furrowing our brow, stomping our feet, and smiling or frowning. The impact of such signs is to indicate agreement or disapproval, and to show the superior-subordinate relationship between the parties. Certain cultures (i.e., the Japanese) are somewhat stiff and formal, and do not touch or even get close to another person during communications. In contrast, U.S. President Lyndon Johnson liked to intimidate others by bringing his face as close as he could to another person.

Intonation (a variation in pitch or sound), facial expressions and physical distance contribute to subtle differences in communications. Soft, smooth tones are less likely to be threatening than a louder, harsher statement. The teacher who stands behind a podium during a lecture is much less likely to engage students than one who moves around the classroom, while a seminar room arrangement (seating around a large table) encourages visual and verbal communication. The manager who has an open door policy but folds his or her arms, looks at a wristwatch and taps on a desk is not likely to be too interested or willing to engage an issue, and the visiting employee usually can "read" this disinterest.

What are the Problems in Communicating?

There are various problems in communications, several of which are reviewed in this section.

Barriers to Information Exchange

The loss to business by communications waste is most certainly in the tens of billions of dollars, from selective filtering to e-mail disclosures of confidential information (discussed in Chapter 9) to personal activities.

- Filtering. This is the deliberate alteration of information to recipients, usually managers in a business setting. As an example, a call on a prospect does not produce any results, so the salesperson reports on the visit but not the lack of interest by the prospect. The manager believes that the contact may result in a sale, but there is no actual movement toward that result. The more hierarchal the organization (see Chapter 7), the more likely that filtering will occur.
- Overload. How many of us went on a trip (possibly a vacation) and found hundreds of e-mails on our return? Information overload occurs when our processing capacity is exceeded by the stimuli we regularly encounter. E-mails are not the only culprit: we regularly receive faxes, letters, FedEx's, telephone calls, "invitations" to meetings (in quotes because you had better be there) and other communications. If the limit of information is exceeded, we forget, ignore, or stop our communications.
- Personal Activities. Employees may use their computers and telephones for activities that have nothing to with a business purpose, such as messaging to friends, Internet surfing, computer game playing, and similar inefficient pastimes.
- Other Barriers. Various psychologists and linguists report that communications can be affected by emotions, including defensiveness; the use of language; and cultural differences.

There are several procedures that managers can use in overcoming communications barriers.

- Feedback: verification by the receiver of the content and an understanding of the message
- Language: use of simple words that are unlikely to cause confusion or require clarification

- Encourage listening: simply paying attention to the sender rather than allowing your mind to wander (as in "I think I'd like pizza for lunch"); in many respects, listening is a discipline
- Remaining calm: do not allow personal feelings to interfere with sending the message or with the listener's understanding the content being conveyed
- Body cues: the previous section noted body movement (body language), which can be more effective (or more of a hindrance) than the actual message
- Monitoring of employee communications: courts have held that company computers and communications devices, and the resulting input and output, are the property of the employer, and that most monitoring is reasonable and protected by law[131]

Communications and Conflict

Conflict may be defined as one person negatively impacting another or something that a second person cares about. Attempts at communications may lead to conflict, either by accident or by design. Accidental offense can occur by content (as in "I didn't mean to offend you by calling you stupid") or by intonation (as in "what do you want" said in a condescending, hostile manner rather than calmly and politely). The traditional view of conflict was that it resulted from poor communications and should be avoided as mutual feelings may be negatively affected.

A current view of conflict is that it is inevitable as a result of human interaction, whether in a family, at work or in a social setting. Conflict has the potential to improve performance in an organization by breaking the mold of harmony and cooperation, and encouraging creativity and self-criticism. Conflict can be constructive when the quality of decisions is improved, and when interaction among employees is increased. If properly used, conflict is a remedy for groupthink (see Chapter 3), possibly preventing organizational decisions that can do serious harm. Recall General Motors (discussed in Chapter 1), the securities industry collapses in 2008 (e.g., Bear Stearns and Lehman Bros.), or any of countless failed companies.

---

131 A statement on acceptable practice can be found in FindLaw, "Monitoring Employees," at http://smallbusiness.findlaw.com/employment-law-and-human-resources/monitoring-employees.html.

Developing a Culture of "Positive" Conflict

Reread the previous paragraph. The outstanding factor (other than failure) is conflict-avoidance by senior managers. Executives attained their positions by avoiding conflict and going along with company policy. It is the unusual manager who becomes an executive through conflict – and then he or she often cannot keep that position. An interesting example is Lee Iacocca, who participated in the design of several successful Ford automobiles, most notably the Ford Mustang. Eventually, he became the president of the Ford Motor Company, but clashed with Henry Ford II and was fired in 1978 (a year that the company had a $2 billion profit!). Iacocca later became the CEO of Chrysler Corp.

The anti-conflict culture is something of a global characteristic: North Americans, Western Europeans and Asians all generally avoid conflict. However, global competition compels positive conflict to end the groupthink cycle and allow creative ideas to emerge. Several major companies (e.g., IBM, General Electric) have institutionalized conflict through various methods; some of the more popular include:

- Regular offsite meetings to encourage discussion, with arguments encouraged for and against possible corporate planning decisions[132]
- Reward systems to promote positive dissent
- A decision process that requires an advocate for the contrary position to that being considered
- Training sessions on interpersonal dynamics and change

What are Issues in Perception?

Perception is how we derive meaning from our environment by organizing our impressions and interpreting their meanings. Two people can observe the same stimulus and perceive it quite differently. In business, we can go on a sales call, make a presentation, listen to objections and conclude the meeting with a

---

132 See the discussion of team building in Chapter 3. Since managers and employees often resist this type of activity by not volunteering or speaking up, facilitators may be used to create and run exercises where situations require disagreement and conflict to solve a problem.

promise to follow-up in a week. Salesperson A may take this as a positive and expect a deal once the idea is studied. Salesperson B may take this as a negative and assume that the delay is a polite rejection (or a stall so that the client can be entertained at lunch to talk things over). No one truly knows reality unless it is subject to scientific proof; instead reality is our perception of events (or in the words of one manager, "perception is reality").

Influences on Perception

The characteristics a person brings to a situation are a strong influence on perception. These factors include inherited and taught traits, involving experiences, prejudices, motives and personality. Of course, the thing being perceived (the "target") affects perception. How the salesperson presents him- or herself influences our receptivity to the selling effort. If the salesperson is well groomed, attractive and punctual, we are likely to be favorably impressed; if sloppy, unattractive and tardy, we are less likely to respond positively.

These impressions are further influenced by light, heat, color and various other contextual factors, many of which are controllable by the person attempting to influence the outcome of a situation. If you have shopped for a car, you may have noticed that the car was clean (probably recently washed), that the lighting was bright but not glaring, that the showroom was maintained at a comfortable temperature, and the salesperson was well groomed and cheerful. However, some retailers work at the "bare", no-frills look to reinforce their low price philosophy; examples include Wal-Mart and Sam's Club, Dollar Stores and Motel 6 or similar hotel chains.

Attribution Theory

To this point we have been discussing perception as regarding objects (e.g., a car, the auto showroom) and people (i.e., the car salesmen). **Attribution theory** focuses on people, as it attempts to discuss how we judge others based on meanings attributed to specific behaviors. We attempt to determine if behavior is caused by factors that are internal (that is, under the control of the person) or external (that is, caused by the situation). The theory has various complex levels of evaluation, but an important finding is that we underweight the external situation and overweight internal factors (the "fundamental attribution error"). This is significant because managers too often blame poor performance on an employee's personal traits (e.g., laziness, sloppiness, a lack of motivation) rather than on such external factors as the competition, the mood of the sales prospect or the economy.

How We Sometimes Judge Others

Attribution theory is more of an effort than most of us care to do or have time to do. As a result, we look for similarities or differences, place the person we are judging in one or more groups with which we have had experience, and assume that our previous dealings with that group are valid for the person in question. Most of us do this without causing too much harm; for example, if a job applicant has an MBA from a good university, the interviewer is likely to believe that he or she is well educated and intelligent. If that same applicant has an unexplained gap in employment history, we may wonder if the applicant was in prison, unemployed or having a similarly "down" period.

Stereotyping is forming an opinion about someone based on our perceived attitudes toward the person's group, be it race, religion, nationality, age, gender, education, physical appearance, or any of several other attributes. "People who are older than 35 years are more mature than those in their twenties." While this may be true, it may not be valid for a specific individual and can erroneously help (if over 35) or hurt (if 25 years old) that person.

An unfortunate form of stereotyping is of a protected class (see Chapter 4, particularly Figure 4-1), because of legal rights afforded that person due to a past history of discrimination. In an ideal world these actions would be eliminated; in the real world, a conscious effort must be made to evaluate a person based on objective criteria (such as MBOs) and to avoid overcompensating for past prejudice or undercompensating due to factors that do not reflect the person's current job performance.

What are the Issues in Negotiation?

In a strictly economic sense, a **negotiation** involves an attempt to exchange goods or services for an agreed-upon price. The global differences in negotiating style are reflective of those in national cultures. Some cultures (i.e., Americans) want to resolve issues quickly in the name of getting to a conclusion and using time efficiently. Other cultures (e.g., Chinese) are long-term relationship oriented and tend to draw out discussions even past the point when there appears to be agreement. The cultures involved influence the length and necessary preparation for bargaining, the extent of socializing expected, the tactics used, and the location of the negotiation.

When parties are from similar cultures, negotiation tends to be much like any business activity. However, in an era of global business, certain protocols seem to help to keep the discussions on point without necessarily favoring either party; see Figure 11-1.

Figure 11-1: Protocols for Negotiating Global Business

Location for the Meeting. Choose an office setting, not a restaurant or place of entertainment. This is especially relevant for international travelers who may find themselves jetlagged and unable to endure five-hour meals and alcoholic drinks. A good rule of thumb is to try to meet in a neutral location, such as Hawaii for North Americans negotiating with Asians. The office is a neutral choice but may favor the host with regard to supporting staff and necessary information.

Negotiating Teams. Have equal numbers present with similar skills. Too many Americans expect a single person to negotiate with a team from another country. The individual cannot be expected to cope with perhaps five or six experts from the opposite side.

Punctuality. Americans, Canadians and Northern Europeans operate on **monochronic time** (often called "M-time"), focusing on one activity at a time and keeping on schedule. The perceived value of time is so high for some companies that quick decisions are required as to whether a conversation with a prospect is worth pursuing. **Polychronic cultures** ("P-time") act on multiple activities concurrently, including business and personal matters, and are predominant in the Middle East and Latin America. Time has a much less specific meaning, and being made to wait for an appointment past the designated hour may mean that the visitor is considered as so important that all other lesser activities will be completed and interruptions will be avoided.

Tactical Positions. Maintain a bargaining position, and do not change negotiating tactics. In some cultures changing positions may be interpreted as a sign of weakness or uncertainty, and could cause a loss of credibility with the other party.

Conversational Tone and Style. Avoid clichés, idioms and jokes. There is an extensive history of unintended insults, slights and offenses made by one of the parties in a negotiation; sadly, too often the Americans seem to be the most frequent offenders. To avoid this possibility, keep the discussion on business and the issues being negotiated.

Preparing for Negotiations

While we may briefly rehearse and prepare for a domestic business meeting (and all too often we don't bother!), it is advisable to do extensive preparation for any serious international business exploration. Pre-negotiation steps should include the following:

- The Choice of the Participants. When choosing managers who will be involved in negotiations with a foreign company or government, consideration should be given to gender, age, technical knowledge, linguistic ability, previous international experience, social skills, and other factors. An advisor or language specialist may be necessary, and many companies are now using consultants with specific knowledge of the country or region and/or of the industry.

- Identification of Business Objectives. What is the purpose of an international visit? Is the focus on gathering information, building trust, or on striking a deal? One trip cannot accomplish all three objectives. The American goal of pragmatic results may be at odds with developing a long-term relationship, a focus more typical in Latin America and Asia.
- Protocol Negotiations. The visiting team must have a fairly specific idea as to the time that will be committed to its efforts and the concessions that it can reasonably make. There must be some willingness to compromise on price and non-price issues, and to attempt to understand the negotiating style of the other party.

An International Negotiation

Here's an example from a U.S.-China negotiation. A shoe company in Texas has sales of $100 million mostly through discount retailers in the U.S. and Canada, and requires quality but a less costly product. Global competition and high labor costs have reduced profits and have focused attention to possible sourcing in China due to lower labor costs and a huge potential market. After reviewing possible Chinese partners, a company is selected in Shanghai and contacts were initiated with the general manager. A business proposal was developed and after carefully considering many issues, a trip to China was arranged for the president, the operations manager and the marketing manager.

The three Americans arrived at the Shanghai airport at 9 a.m. and had their first appointment with Chinese senior staff at 3 p.m. that day. The Chinese provided an interpreter for the meetings. Social conversation was conducted until 5 p.m., followed by dinner from 7 to 11:30 p.m. The business discussions began the next day at 9 a.m. with presentations until noon. There was no resolution of any significant issues during the visit and so a second trip had to be scheduled. What went wrong?

The negotiations had no possibility of success at the initial meetings, because the Chinese simply do not conclude business with strangers that quickly. Planning should have assumed that a second and even a third trip would be necessary. Furthermore, the Americans would have been exhausted after a 22 hour trip from Texas and would need at least one day to recover. To convene so quickly on arrival and be subjected to more than six hours of socializing is ridiculous and could not succeed. The Americans should have been prepared for lengthy negotiations or not bothered to consider an arrangement. Other mistakes included the location at the restaurant for the first contacts, not having an interpreter who was employed by the Americans, and not clarifying the expectations for the outcome of the first visit.

Is Politics a Significant Organizational Issue?

Politics (or political behavior) uses persuasion and power to affect decision-making by organizations and by sub-units within organizations. In any managerial or political science discussion of politics, the terms "influence" (or the attempt to influence) and "persuasion" are often used. There is of course no job description that includes political behavior in the tasks of an employee. However, many workers use politics to gain some perceived advantage, to influence goals and objectives, or to improve their position.

Politics can be a positive activity, as when a manager wants some performance outcome and uses a small reward to accomplish it, such as a pizza party or a group or team outing. The connotation is often negative, as when a worker spreads stories about a colleague to discredit that person from a promotion or simply to make mischief. Negative activities cast a wide net, and may include rumors, complaining about management within the organization or to the press, withholding essential work information, verbal and/or physical threats or abuse, and similar behaviors.

Do you remember Lloyd, our college student in Chapter 3 who takes a summer job in a low-level, menial job, and is excluded from the group of full-time employees? Lloyd wants to do his work but would also like to be accepted by the group, whose members feel defeated and pretty much hopeless in terms of their expectations for the future. In addition to the previously discussed issue of groups and norms of work performance, Lloyd is a victim of politics.

Organizational Politics

Nearly every organization experiences some political activity and as it appears to be an inherent human personality trait, there is simply nothing that can or should be done unless negative politicking goes beyond normal interpersonal communications. Situations that appear most susceptible to the promotion of politics are when change is occurring and zero-sum becomes the general assumption. In a zero-sum game, some people win and some lose,[133] and most members of an organization (and of society) prefer to be among the winners. The usual situations causing political responses are when a company:

- Believes its competitive situation to be deteriorating and workers fear retrenchment
- Is redeploying its resources to respond to opportunities or threats
- Has a vacancy and may be promoting to that position (see the Chris Farr case in Appendix B)
- Fails to develop equitable reward systems and instead uses a process subject to manipulation

When he was a banker, the author worked for a senior manager who used an annual trip to reward the top performers. The problem was – and everyone knew what was going on – that individual objectives that set the "par" for the reward were manipulated by the closest friends of the senior manager. As a result, some bankers won the trip every year, and others never received that award. Politics in action!

A similar problem is fairly endemic in managing companies today, in that day-to-day manipulation occurs to thwart overtly democratic or participative decision-making and priority setting. Managers may be encouraged to bring employees into the discussion but often do not really want their input. Political maneuvering may be used to attain the manager's desired outcome and he or she can truthfully state that all opinions were heard. In the current

---

133 The concept of the **zero-sum game** is derived from game theory and economics, and refers to the outcome that when the total gains of the participants are added up, and the total losses are subtracted, they will sum to zero. When all parties have a positive outcome, the result is a positive-sum game (as in global trade due to each participating country's comparative advantage). When all parties have a negative outcome (as in crime and its prosecution due to the costs to the victim, society and the criminal justice system), the result is a negative-sum game. Most situations are zero-sum. The concept is attributed to John von Neumann and Oskar Morgenstern, *Theory of Games and Economic Behavior*, Princeton University Press, 1944.

environment, politics presents a dual impact: the change factors noted above are prevalent and active, and employees unwilling to "play" the political game are not as likely to have many job choices given the economic recession.

What are the Issues You Should Address?

In considering your organization's interpersonal dynamics, here are some issues to review.

- Is our organization aware of issues of interpersonal dynamics? Do we consciously attempt to improve communications, perception, conflict, information processing, perception and political behavior?
- Are communications reliably initiated and then understood by the recipients? Have there been situations when misunderstood or misinterpreted directions led to critical mistakes? Have we taken appropriate corrective action to prevent a recurrence?
- Are we aware of conflicts that occur in our organization? Do we encourage positive conflict as a mechanism for change?
- Do we understand how our managers and employees perceive situations and people? Do we have programs to prevent stereotyping for fairness and so as to be in compliance with federal regulations?
- Have we considered negotiation successes and failures? Have there been global (or domestic) negotiating situations that either ended badly or required substantial additional time to complete? Have we gained any knowledge about other cultures from those situations so that we will be better prepared in the future?
- Are we aware of political problems in our organization? Do these politics unfairly distort such outcomes as rewards systems, decisions about resources and other mission critical concerns? Have we initiated remedial actions to moderate the impact of such political activity?

Discussion and Review Questions

1. How does the concept of interpersonal dynamics affect the manager's responsibilities? What are the reasons for its recent emergence?
2. What role does communication have in managing an organization? What are the more significant barriers to communicating in organizations?
3. How can conflict assist an organization in coping with a changing, difficult environment for businesses and not-for-profit organizations?
4. What is the concept of perception? What are important influences on perception?
5. What actions can managers take to improve their global negotiating position?
6. What is the role of politics in the management of organizations?

CHAPTER 12

Managing In A Time Of Change

After reading this chapter, you will be able to:

- Review the significance of management during difficult economic times
- Be aware of laws that impact management decisions
- Appreciate the role of technology in business strategies
- Understand how sustainability and corporate governance affect managerial behavior
- Consider other challenges of global management

Manager Attitudes during Economic Recession

The rapid pace of management today requires close attention to the business environment, competitors, government and many other factors that affect our success. While we briefly mentioned concerns of managers in earlier chapters, in this final text material we devote our attention to a more in-depth look at several of these challenges.

Coping with Difficult Economic Conditions

The stock market concept of "blue chip" meant a corporation with a national reputation for quality, reliability and the ability to operate profitably in good times and bad.[134] The problem with this concept is that companies – even those considered "blue chip" – unable to respond to changes in their environment, cease to exist or are bought by stronger competitors. See Figure 12-1 for the status of the blue chip companies of more than a century ago.

Figure 12-1: Blue Chip Stock Market (in Dow-Jones Stocks
(Dow Jones Industrial Average, 1896)

American Cotton Oil Company, a predecessor company to Bestfoods, now part of Unilever.

American Sugar Company, became Domino Sugar in 1900, now Domino Foods, Inc.

American Tobacco Company, disbanded into separate companies in a 1911 antitrust action.

Chicago Gas Company, bought by Peoples Gas Light in 1897, now an operating subsidiary of Integrys Energy Group.

Distilling & Cattle Feeding Company, now Millennium Chemicals, formerly a division of LyondellBasell, the latter of which recently emerged from Chapter 11 bankruptcy.

Laclede Gas Company, still in operation as the Laclede Group, Inc., removed from the DJIA in 1899.

National Lead Company, now NL Industries, removed from the DJIA in 1916.

North American Company, an electric utility holding company, disbanded into separate companies by the U.S. Securities and Exchange Commission in 1946.

Tennessee Coal, Iron and Railroad Company in Birmingham, Alabama, bought by U.S. Steel in 1907; U.S. Steel was removed from the DJIA in 1991.

---

134 In "Frequently Asked Questions," a page of NYSE Group, Inc. at www.nyse.com/content/faqs/1042235995602.html?cat=Listed_Company_General.

U.S. Leather Company, dissolved in 1952.

United States Rubber Company, changed its name to Uniroyal in 1961, merged with the private company B.F. Goodrich in 1986, bought by Michelin in 1990.

The current economic downturn has caused companies to become risk averse and limit whatever innovation, product development and expansion that would normally occur in times of prosperity. We can see such conservative behavior in lower debt (financial leverage) ratios in the financing of companies, reluctance to hire (the unemployment rate in early 2013 was about 8%), and only limited spending on research and development. These situations have been experienced in past cycles, and it is interesting to note that some of the most enduring companies were founded during recessions: Disney (in the early 1930s during the Depression), and General Motors and J.C. Penney (both during the recession that began in 1907) are examples.

Troubled economic times tend to speed up creative destruction (which was introduced in Chapter 5), as clever businesspeople see opportunities to be more efficient or less-costly than competitors. Unsuccessful job seekers may seize the opportunity to establish businesses that may not have been attempted in more prosperous times.[135] Entrepreneurship and intrapreneurship may face difficulty in starting or in getting the attention of their companies, but there will always be opportunities to create, change and be successful.

Throughout this textbook, we have made repeated references to change and the problems of managing change. Previous generations had it relatively easy (when they weren't fighting wars or an economic Depression), because the strategies, workforce profile, competitors, profit expectations and other business factors were relatively stable year after year.

---

135 An interesting analysis is provided in "Economic Focus: Downturn Start Up," *The Economist,* January 7, 2012, page 70.

Which Laws and Regulations Challenge Today's Managers?

The requirements and limitations imposed by governments, regional economies and international organizations limit the independence of companies to deploy their assets as many companies did at the start of the industrial age; see the discussion in Chapter 7. In those days, sovereign governments had little or no concern for antitrust, consumer protection, corporate governance, the environment, the rights of workers or any of several other areas of current law and regulation.

Traditional Business Law Applications

Business laws traditionally largely focused on contracts and deciding business disputes through a judicial resolution.

- Historic contract law traces back to its origin in Roman and Napoleonic civil (statutory) law; and the *lex mercatoria*, the body of commercial law relied on by merchants throughout Europe during the medieval times.
- Modern contract law in Britain and the U.S. is composed primarily of common (case) law decided by courts, following the Judicature Acts passed by the British Parliament beginning in the late 19th century. Common law is used in Australia, Great Britain, India, Singapore, Hong Kong, the U.S., Canada, Pakistan and Malaysia.
- Modern contract law in civil law countries, which uses written law or statutes to decide disputes. Civil law is used throughout the European countries (except Great Britain), and in such countries as Brazil, China, Japan, Mexico, Russia, Switzerland and Turkey.

There are other applications of business law as noted below:

- Forms of business organization as reviewed in Chapter 5. In addition, business law includes the field of agency, the relationship when one party (the principal) engages another person (the agent) to represent him; and bankruptcy, when a debtor company (or individual) is unable to pay outstanding debts and the process is handled by a judicial proceeding.

- Specialized commercial transactions, such as mergers and acquisitions, leasing, sales and secured transactions, mortgages, real estate transactions, debtor and creditor, and negotiable instruments.
- Admiralty law, which deals with loss sharing in the event of a sinking at sea or other disaster, liability for injuries or death to passengers, loss of cargo and vessel, and rights to salvage. This field of law was later supplemented by insurance agreements to pay claims against such losses.

Business law has been made consistent through the Uniform Commercial Code (UCC), adapted by all states, which provides standard legal applications throughout the U.S.[136] Other countries use federal jurisdiction to determine the applicable law of business.

U.S. Federal Law on Business

The first significant national laws that provided specific business regulation did not appear until the period of the Civil War. Banking regulation – the National Currency Act of 1863 and the National Bank Act of 1864 – established a system of government regulation and established the Office of the Comptroller of the Currency. The legislation was required to assist in the financing of the Civil War and to standardize a system of federally supervised national banks.

The Reconstruction period following the War began a period of industrialization that was to continue until nearly the end of the 20th century. However, at the time of the passage of the first laws regulating business (other than banking), the U.S. was largely agrarian. Nearly two-thirds of the population lived in rural America and over 40% of all employment was still based on farming.[137] The first significant federal business regulation was the Sherman Antitrust Act of 1890 restricting the power of monopolies and trusts to control markets.[138] Figure 12-2 lists the important federal business laws on antitrust (of a total of

---

136 For Constitutional reasons, business law has been under the jurisdiction of the states and not the U.S. government. See the discussion which follows.

137 U.S. Dept. of Commerce, *Historical Statistics of the United States*, 1989. Population data is from series A57-72; employment data is from series D11-25.

138 A **monopoly** is a single company operating in an industry; a **trust** is a combination of companies acting to restrain trade in an industry.

seven laws), consumer protection (of a total of 16 laws), and environmental protection (of a total of eight laws) passed in the U.S.

Figure 12-2: Selected Antitrust, Consumer Protection and Environmental Protection Laws (U.S.)

Legislation and Purpose	Purpose
Sherman Act (1890): antitrust	Sets a competitive business system as national policy, specifically banning monopolies and restraints of trade
Clayton Act (1914): antitrust	Places restrictions on price discrimination, exclusive dealing, tying contracts, and interlocking boards of directors that reduce competition or might lead to a monopoly
Pure Food and Drug Act (1906): consumer protection	Protects against the adulteration and misbranding of foods and drugs sold in interstate commerce
Food, Drug, and Cosmetic Act (1938): consumer protection	Protects against the adulteration and sale of foods, drugs, cosmetics, or therapeutic devices; allows the Food and Drug Administration (FDA) to set minimum standards and guidelines for food products
Fair Packaging and Labeling Act (1966): consumer protection	Makes unfair or deceptive packaging or labeling of certain consumer commodities illegal
Consumer Product Safety Act (1972): consumer protection	Creates an independent agency to protect consumers from unreasonable risk of injury arising from consumer products and to set safety standards
Truth-in-Lending Act (1968): consumer protection	Requires full disclosure of all finance charges on consumer credit agreements and in advertisements of credit plans
National Environmental Policy Act (1969): environmental protection	Establishes protections for the environment by establishing policy, setting goals, and requiring environmental impact statements for major construction projects

Clean Air Act (1970): environmental protection	Regulates air emissions from area, stationary, and mobile sources, and authorizes the Environmental Protection Agency (EPA) to establish National Ambient Air Quality Standards to protect public health and the environment
Clean Water Act (1977): environmental protection	Establishes a structure for regulating discharges of pollutants into U.S. waters; gives EPA the authority to implement pollution control programs; sets water quality standards for contaminants in surface waters

Other countries and international organizations have instituted similar legislation and rules, and have become aggressive about limiting the power of corporations. Some observers suggest that the European Union (EU) – to be noted in a later part of this chapter – has more aggressive policies than the U.S. on antitrust and the environment. The result of these legislated mandates and such other areas of law as labor relations and specific industry regulation (e.g., the airlines, banking and financial services) have been to limit the power of management to conduct its affairs and freely use the private property of business.[139]

What are the Technology Challenges to Today's Managers?

The changing technological capabilities of manufacturing, marketing and information systems have occurred at an astonishing rate in recent years. Consider Eastman Kodak as a recent example of an industry leader unable to respond to changing technology.[140] In contrast, Apple is a company that has

---

139 For a more complete discussion, see J. Sagner, *Is U.S. Business Overregulated?* York House Press, 2008.

140 Eastman Kodak Company had been a leader in photography products, and in 1976 had a 90% market share of photographic film sales in the U.S. Kodak began to struggle financially in the late-1990s as a result of the decline in sales of photographic film and its hesitancy to transition to digital photography. In 2012, Kodak filed for bankruptcy protection and announced that it would cease making digital cameras, pocket video cameras and digital picture frames, and focus on digital imaging.

built its strategy on a continuing stream of new product development concepts. Selected technology that managers should consider using are discussed below.[141]

Robotization

Robotization is replacing production workers at a rapid pace in newly emerging industrialized countries like China and India, and the only real impediment is resistance by organized labor in the fear of a massive loss of jobs. The newest models of robots allow multiple functions without changes to the configuration of the equipment; in a automobile factory, that could include welding, riveting, bonding and installation of a component. Distribution systems are being "robotized" particularly in warehouse applications such as inventory picking and packing boxes for shipment. With robots doing the heavy work, humans are providing less physical ancillary services resulting in fewer injuries. Some activities cannot easily be automated, like construction jobs and certain assembly work that does not lend itself to lengthy production lines.[142]

Mass Customization

The concept of **mass customization** refers to the use of computer-aided manufacturing to produce specific products based on customer orders. These systems use low unit cost production modules and flexible manufacturing to meet customer requirements. This concept has been used by several businesses, including L.L. Bean (clothing), BMW and Toyota (automobiles), Mattel (toys) and firms that produce builders' suppliers based on architectural specifications. A company offering mass customization assists the customer in selecting among various product features such as size and color that are housed on a standard basic product. An ongoing dialogue with customers is necessary to learn about and respond to product design preferences.

---

141 The interested reader should review "Technology Quarterly" published by *The Economist* that provides brief explanations of advances in technology; see, for example, the special issue "The Third Industrial Revolution," April 21, 2012.

142 For recent global applications to industry, see J. Markoff, "Skilled Work, Without the Worker," *New York Times*, August 19, 2012, pages 1, 17.

Mobile Connectivity

Manager-employee communications through handheld devices and **mobile connectivity** allow organizations to be productive through the real-time exchange of information, customer orders and inquiries, price changes notifications and other critical information. The concern for security is largely alleviated by the encryption of data using key fobs with codes that change periodically, safely allowing employees to access company databases.

Value Chain Management (VCM)

The **value chain management** concept involves coordinating all aspects of work activities to enhance value from vendors to receiving raw materials through manufacturing and distribution to customers. The technology requirement is the necessary collaboration among the VCM participants to optimize order quantities and improve quality control, automate purchasing procedures, create logistic efficiencies, enhance product development and customer order management through data scanning systems, and other innovative technologies. Companies that have been particularly successful at VCM include Wal-Mart and Dell.

Renewable Energy Technologies

A discussion of **renewable energy technologies** (that is, other than fossil fuels) could fill another entire book. Managers should be aware of renewable energy sources, which now comprise about one-sixth of global final energy consumption. Available sources include wind (forecast to increase at a 20% annual rate), photovoltaics (the generation of electrical power by converting solar radiation into direct current electricity), thermal power and ethanol fuel To select one interesting development in photovoltaic technology, there are innovative applications in solar panels, which have been previously considered too expensive and inefficient for industrial applications. The new concept uses a polymer gel to change the light absorption capability to include infrared solar energy.

Memory Chips

Technology development is critical in consumer and business computer applications. Microchip manufacturers have been able to squeeze more computing power onto their **memory chip** products with one of the most important innovations being the introduction of "multi-core" processors, microchips with two or more processors, or "cores", on them. Smartphones often are used only for simple tasks such as calls and e-mail, which do not use all of their computing potential. By using multi-core chips and smart software, one or more of the phone's processors can be shut down, reducing the drain on batteries. Many industrial applications use memory chips to store data and instructions in computer-based applications. A new class of such chips – phase-change memory – is capable of changing states from solid to liquid and back. These chips are smaller, faster and considerably more durable than traditional chips.

What are the Sustainability and Governance Challenges to Today's Managers?

Sustainability and stakeholders were defined in Chapter 1, and corporate governance was mentioned in Chapter 4 in our discussion of organizational culture. Both of these concerns are relatively new developments for managers who are being forced to consider their actions and those of their company on the external world. Companies today are under the microscope of public opinion and cannot take the attitude of William Henry Vanderbilt (son of "The Commodore" Cornelius Vanderbilt) who said: "The public be damned! ... I don't take any stock in this silly nonsense about working for anybody but our own."[143]

The current interest in sustainability requires a careful balancing of the interests of stakeholders, and may reduce the obsession with stockholder expectations in deference to other obligations of a business. Managers are aware that resources are finite, and that sustainability provides an opportunity to be efficient and ecology-friendly. This includes developing products that require

---

143 Interview, Chicago *Daily News*, October 9, 1882.

smaller portions (such as concentrated detergent), innovative manufacturing techniques and the redesign of existing products.

A recent analysis prepared for Ernst & Young, an accounting firm, outlined steps to encourage efforts at corporate sustainability; see Figure 12-3. The emphasis must be on developing financial motivation through customer demand for the products and services of businesses that support these initiatives. This is the strategy used by several large companies, including UPS, Coca-Cola, Publix (a supermarket chain), McDonald's, Dell and others that are leaders in their industries.

Figure 12-3: Action Steps toward Corporate Sustainability

- Actively pursue a sustainability and reporting system that is similar to the transparency and rigor to the system used for financial reporting.
- Engage senior managers in sustainability efforts, such as choosing appropriate tools to measure, monitor and report on environmental and sustainability issues in a way that can measure progress, create value and enhance investor confidence.
- Recognize that employees are a key stakeholder and a vital source of sustainability engagement and ideas to enhance the company's sustainability journey.
- Understand that greenhouse gas disclosure has value outside of the regulatory arena due to its utility for stakeholders, investors, customers and suppliers.
- Assess the availability and reliability of strategic business materials and resources from a sustainability perspective. Develop a risk management plan addressing contingencies for disruptions in access to key resources, and integrate risk assessments and plans in sustainability reporting.
- Understand the value of sustainability reporting to ranking and ratings organizations, particularly those of interest to investors.

Source: Edited from "Six Growing Trends in Corporate Sustainability," at www.ey.com/US/en/Services/Specialty-Services/Climate-Change-and-Sustainability-Services/Six-growing-trends-in-corporate-sustainability_Trend-7

Governance and Ethics

As noted, ethical behavior has been an embedded element in the cultures of certain organizations but without regulatory oversight. This situation began to change about 25 years ago due to several situations of corporate scandals both in financial institutions and some industrial companies. The principles contained in four critical documents have focused global attention on the problem.[144] Two European reports contain general principles for various constituencies in support of proper corporate governance:

- Rights and equitable treatment of shareholders
- Interests of other stakeholders
- Role and responsibilities of the board of directors
- Integrity and ethical behavior
- Disclosure and transparency

For a recent U.K. situation, consider the aggressive response of the British government to action by Rupert Murdoch's publishing business,[145] which may lead to civil and criminal charges under existing statutes. The approach of the U.S. was to enact specific laws in 2002 and 2010 to force appropriate management behavior.

The Sarbanes-Oxley Act of 2002 broke new ground by mandating that U.S. publicly-traded corporations regularly assess their processes to ensure transparency and protect shareholder value. The law was enacted to restore investor confidence by requiring actions concerning financial reporting, conflicts of interest, corporate ethics and accounting oversight. Heavy fines for senior managers and their corporations, and even imprisonment, are available remedies; the idea was to construct a strong enough incentive for business executives to obey the law. Selected provisions include the following:

---

144 The Cadbury Report (*Report of the Committee on the Financial Aspects of Corporate Governance*, Great Britain, 1992); the Principles of Corporate Governance (OECD, 1998 and 2004), at www.oecd.org/corporate/corporateaffairs/corporategovernanceprinciples/31557724.pdf; and the Sarbanes-Oxley Act of 2002 (US, 2002) and the Dodd-Frank Act of 2010 (which significantly restrict and control the activities of public companies and financial institutions).

145 Murdoch faces allegations that his publishing companies, including the *News of the World* had been regularly hacking the phones of celebrities, royalty and public citizens. Police and government investigations have been launched into bribery and corruption by the British government and by FBI investigations in the U.S.

- Certification. Senior managers are now required to certify that a periodic financial report "fairly represents, in all material respects, the financial condition and results of operation of the issuer." A knowingly false certification can result in a fine of up to $5 million and imprisonment of up to 20 years.
- Audit Committee Independence. The act requires an independent audit committee (of the board of directors) with authority over external auditors, and requires disclosure of whether an audit committee includes a financial expert. Financial reporting has now effectively become the responsibility of the audit committee, and that body is a potential antagonist of and separate from senior management. The audit committee and its members must be independent and cannot be compensated for other services provided to the company.
- Regulation of the Accounting Profession. The failure of the accounting firm Arthur Andersen in 2002 was caused by its participation in several fraud cases, the most critical of which undoubtedly was Enron. Congress feared a general loss of investor and business community confidence in auditors and the independence of their opinions in financial reports. In addition, lawmakers were not convinced that the accountants' self regulatory organization, the Financial Accounting Standards Board (FASB), would have adequate power to restore credibility. As the result, the Public Company Accounting Oversight Board (PCAOB) was created in the act to be the federal regulator over the profession.

What are Other Challenges of Global Management?

It is impossible to list or do justice to the myriad challenges faced by managers in global business. This final section lists a few additional challenges that were unknown back when the Dow-Jones Average was constructed (noted at the start of this chapter) or when mid-20th century was reached.

Terrorism and Political Risk

Managers face the risk of terrorism as they invest, find vendors and customers, and hire employees in countries as promising and yet as threatening as the Philippines, Egypt, Russia, Indonesia and nearly any of the more than 200 global countries and territories. Religious fanatics and nationalistic splinter groups can destroy property, threaten lives and generally make doing business a very risky proposition. There is no perfect solution. However, evaluation of country (or sovereign) risk (**country risk assessment** [CRA]) is a measure of the possibility that a foreign government or insurgents will interfere with normal business transactions between counterparties due to an economic or political crisis.

Examples of such actions include the debt moratoria declared by the Brazilian and Mexican governments in the early 1980s, the economic problems of various Asian countries in the late 1990s (discussed below), and the financial and political crisis of Greece in 2011. Various types of political risk are listed in Figure 12-4. Country stability can be monitored through evaluation models published by *The Economist, Euromoney,* Business Monitor International and other sources.

Figure 12-4: Leading Sources of Political Risk

Type of Political Risk	Explanation
Expropriation (seizure by a national government)	Legitimate private owners are denied access to and use of property, with either no or slight compensation. Flagrant examples of this behavior have been in Cuba, Chile and Iran. International repudiation of these actions has largely ended recent incidents of expropriation (although claims against some governments continue).
War or civil strife	Various international or local military conflicts, such as those in Afghanistan and Iraq, result in the destruction of assets and the loss of life. In past decades, India experienced civil unrest over the actions of global businesses.

Political unrest	Countries experiencing a period of socio-political transition may experience civil unrest that could interfere with the normal functioning of the economic system. In recent times, France has held strikes and demonstrations in opposition to former President Sarkozy's efforts at modernizing the economy, and Greece has experienced violence as the government attempts to comply with European Union requirements for austerity.
Breach of contract	A government may repudiate or breach a contract previously negotiated with an international company. A current example is Venezuela, which has threatened to change contracts with global energy companies to increase local participation in profits.
Administrative actions	Rather than imposing tariffs, a country may delay time sensitive approvals, require local vendor and/or labor participation, or demand bribes as payment for permission to proceed.
Criminal actions against people or property	Crimes may occur against employees or their families, including kidnapping, extortion, piracy[146] or other offenses. Recent cases involved the kidnapping of workers in Colombia and piracy against ships operating in Western African waters.
Restrictions on funds repatriation	Limits may be set on the movement of funds to the home country derived from the operations in a host country. The former Soviet Union established these controls when it began allowing capitalistic enterprises in the country.

CRA metrics rank countries on the basis of political and economic hazards. The various CRA systems quantify the possibility that transactions with international counterparties may be interrupted by the interference of the foreign government or due to adverse local conditions. In addition to political risks, such disruptions may take the form of economic restrictions.

---

146   Piracy is defined in this chapter

Economic Interdependence

From an economic view, the world no longer consists of independent countries. There are two major regional economies: **NAFTA** (North American Free Trade Agreement), which consists of the U.S., Canada and Mexico;[147] and the **European Union** (EU), which is comprised of 27 countries (and six applicants for membership).[148] See Figure 12-5 for a listing of important international and regional organizations. In addition, there are aspiring regional groups, including ASEAN[149] and CAFTA-DR.[150] Today's manager must learn the protocols for doing business within these economies and in the situation of much of the EU, deal with the euro currency and the various difficulties it is now experiencing.

Figure 12-5: International and Regional Organizations

Name	Date Created	Purpose
International Organizations		
Bank for International Settlements (BIS)	1930	Fosters cooperation among central banks, international financial institutions and governments
International Monetary Fund (IMF)	1944	Fosters stable foreign exchange arrangements; support balance-of-payments equilibria; assist countries experiencing financial crises

---

147 For additional information, see the official website, www.nafta-sec-alena.org/en/view.aspx.

148 For additional information, see the official website, europa.eu.

149 The Association of Southeast Asian Nations (ASEAN) was conceived to allow freer trade among its various member nations, a region that totals nearly 600 million people. However, there has only been limited progress as certain nations have refused to reduce tariffs in an attempt to protect local industry. Should China, Japan and/or Korea join, or execute separate free trade agreements, the impact on the region and on global trade would undoubtedly be significant. See www.aseansec.org.

150 The Central America Free Trade Agreement originally included the U.S. and the Central American countries of Costa Rica, El Salvador, Guatemala, Honduras, and Nicaragua, and was called CAFTA. In 2004, the Dominican Republic joined the negotiations, and the agreement was renamed DR-CAFTA. As the name implies, the intention is to move toward free trade within the member nations. See www.caftaintelligencecenter.com.

World Bank	1944	Provides loans and grants to developing countries to enable development of infrastructure
Organization for Economic Cooperation and Development (OECD)	1961	Promotes economic development among member nations; develops model legislation on international trade
World Trade Organization (WTO)	1995	Negotiates reduction and elimination of tariffs and other trade barriers; mediates trade disputes
Regional Economies		
European Union (EU)	1993	Establishes economic policy for member nations; abolished trade barriers between members; operates central bank and euro currency (except for non-euro countries)
North American Free Trade Agreement (NAFTA)	1994	Operates free trade area among member nations; no common central bank or currency

Piracy and Counterfeiting

Piracy traditionally is an act of robbery and/or criminal violence at sea. The term has been popularly extended to include stealing licensed intellectual property such as computer software and proprietary knowledge of engineering and manufacturing processes. Certain countries have only provided a weak response to requirements for enforcement of anti-piracy rules. China has been in regular violation of licensing agreements, and patent and copyright ownership, and the protection of global companies has been lax. Leading situations have been the copyright violations by Chinese businesses that pirate Western software, DVDs, music and other material, and sell it without the payment of any royalties.

Improved protection of intellectual property is essential for any company considering locating in China because of the weak enforcement of protections available in most of the industrialized world. As an example, Microsoft has claimed that to 90% of its software used in China is counterfeit.[151] Part of the explanation is cultural, in that during the Communist era, property was owned collectively by the Chinese government and people, and not by individuals or companies. The WTO and Western governments have international protocols in place that prohibit this practice, and have exerted enormous pressure on the Chinese and others to end piracy. Reports indicate that some progress has occurred.[152]

India has been through the experience of ignoring piracy, but the country has come to accept the global repudiation of the practice. Many of India's more innovative businesses are welcoming the possibility of intellectual property protections. As these companies began to consider establishing investment in other countries ("foreign direct investment"), enforceable safeguards for processes and discoveries have become necessary.

Global Cultural Differences

Competition from global companies long ago ended the total domination of markets by American and Western European companies. Responding to the intense struggle for customers in nearly every market requires knowledge of markets, demands for access to products, market pricing, excellent service, implementation of methods toward efficiency and constant innovation. Senior managers must be on-site to meet customers, see problems first-hand, and quickly implement solutions to hold and expand market share.

Global cultures encompass differences in religions, history, values, traditions and attitudes toward manager-employees relationships. For example, South Koreans focuses on *inhwa*, or harmony, respect for hierarchy and authority. In contrast, Chinese emphasize *guanxi* or personal connections and relationships. Culture is a determinative factor in business; the influence of collectivism (versus individualism) can lead to conflict with the essential management characteristic of entrepreneurship. Achieving success in this environment is an extremely complex problem, particularly given the speed of

151 "Hu Pledges to Protect U.S. Intellectual Property in China: Political Rhetoric or Valid Promise?" *Wake Forest University Journal of Business and Intellectual Property Law*, February 16, 2011, at ipjournal.law.wfu.edu/2011/02/ hu-pledges-to-protect-u-s-intellectual-property-in-china-political-rhetoric-or-valid-promise.

152 See, "Doing Business in China: 850,000 Lawsuits in the Making," *The Economist*, April 10, 2008, page 76, for a comment on recent responses to piracy; and A.C. Mertha, *The Politics of Piracy: Intellectual Property in Contemporary China* (2007), for an in-depth discussion of civil, criminal and geopolitical responses.

communications and misunderstandings that naturally occur in a highly competitive and weak economic climate. As a result, managers must constantly monitor the various issues discussed throughout this book and make adjustments as conditions require.

What are the Issues You Should Address?

In considering your organization's management in a time of change, here are some issues to review.

- Are we becoming too conservative in our management style due to the weak economy and avoided appropriate levels of risk-taking necessary for continued prosperity?
- Are we adequately prepared for legal restrictions and the regulations that affect our business activities? Do we understand the laws in those countries in which we operate?
- Do we have a current understanding of technological developments that may affect our industry?
- Are we aware of sustainability and corporate governance issues?
- Do we appreciate other challenges of global management, including terrorism and political risk, economic interdependence of countries and regions, piracy and counterfeiting, and global cultural differences?

Discussion and Review Questions

1. How have organizations reacted to the difficult conditions resulting from the current economic downturn?
2. What is the traditional approach to regulating businesses through the law? What are specific types of laws that have extensive histories in addressing business issues?

3. What has been the philosophy of the U.S. federal and state governments toward business regulation? How this has evolved as economic and social conditions have required adjustment?

4. What are three current technological challenges to managers? Briefly describe these challenges.

5. What are the sustainability and governance challenges to today's managers? How have attitudes changed in the past 125 years?

6. What are other challenges to global managers? Explain at least one of these situations and possible responses.

Appendix A: Profiles Of Management Leaders

The profiles that follow describe selected management leaders from various countries to illustrate both successes and failures. The group does not include a founder-leader, such as Walt Disney, Bill Gates, Rupert Murdoch, Sam Walton, Li Ka-Shing[153] or Steve Jobs, in attempting to show paths of management after the founder's unique form of stewardship. The company affiliations that are noted relate to the period described in the profile; as of the publication date of this text, a number of these leaders have gone on to other positions or have retired. In addition to the six profiles provided in this section of the book, the interested reader is referred to various sources on more recent experiences, including the eight women global leaders who are briefly profiled in the *Financial Times*; see Figure A-1. Lengthier profiles are available in a variety of sources; see, for example, those of David Simon[154] and John Browne[155] of British Petroleum; Cheong Choong Kong[156] of Singapore Airlines; and Jamie Dimon[157] of J.P.Morgan Chase.

Jack Welch, General Electric (home country: U.S.)

John "Jack" Welch, Jr., who was trained as a chemical engineer, was Chairman and CEO of General Electric (GE) between 1981 and 2001. During that period, the company's value rose 4,000%, from just $12 billion to about $280 billion. No organizational leader has created more shareholder value than Jack Welch. His approach can be summarized into a few critical attributes: close attention to detail in every phase of GE's dozen businesses; personal

---

153 Chairman of Hutchison Whampoa Limited (HWL) and Cheung Kong Holdings and the richest person of Asian descent in the world.

154 Manfred F.R. Kets de Vries (with Elizabeth Florent-Treacy), *The New Global Leaders*, Jossey-Bass, 1999, pages 109 – 172.

155 Michael J. Marquardt and Nancy O. Berger, *Global Leaders for the 21ˢᵗ Century*, State University of New York Press, 2000, pages 71 – 84.

156 See footnote 152, Mertha, pages 133 – 144.

157 Patricia Crisafulli, *The House of Dimon: How JPMorgan's Jamie Dimon Rose to the Top of the Financial World*, Wiley, 2011.

knowledge of thousands of company managers through visits to their locations and attendance at various company meetings; informality in his relationships with GE employees (everyone called him "Jack"); frankness in the evaluation of managers and employees; and impatience with results that did not meet expectations (MBOs in the language of this book).

Welch enjoyed confrontation and criticism from his managers, but made his own decisions and insisted on his priorities and goals. At one internal meeting a complaint was voiced about the difficulty of accomplishing objectives that were short-term (profits) as well as long-term (building an industry-leading business). ''You can't grow long-term if you can't eat short-term," he stated. ''Anybody can manage short. Anybody can manage long. Balancing those two things is what management is."[158]

GE's extraordinary growth during the Welch years was attributable to several factors: a bureaucratic organization that he took over from predecessor Reginald Jones (who organized around nine management layers!) and largely dismantled; an unusually favorable economic climate in which to operate (he retired just as the 2001 recession started); an extremely competent group of senior managers; and a relentless drive to succeed. He was ruthless in eliminating inefficiencies by reducing inventories, closing factories, reducing payrolls and cutting low-performing traditional business units.

Welch believed that a company should be either first or second in a particular industry or else leave it completely. Each year, Welch would fire the bottom 10% of his managers, earning a reputation for brutal candor in his meetings with GE managers. "Each person, each piece of equipment, each division, and each manager had to contribute to the bottom line in a positive manner. Those that could not or would not were summarily relieved of their duties."[159]

Welch's leadership culture was continually emphasized throughout GE, particularly in the use of rewards for top performers. He required that compensation be non-standard; for example, one year (1997) the company's salary increase averaged 4%, but base salaries could rise by as much as 25%. Other rewards greatly expanded under his leadership, including cash

158 John A. Byrne, "How Jack Welch Runs GE," *BusinessWeek,* June 8, 1998, www.business-week.com/1998/23/b3581001.htm.
159 "Famous CEOs: Jack Welch (GE)," at www.famousceos.com/profile-jack-welch-GE.php.

bonuses and stock options. His senior manager promotions were similarly unconventional. For example, he passed over several candidates in line for the position of chief financial officer (CFO) in choosing then 38-year-old Dennis D. Dammerman, who was two management layers below the logical candidates because Welch was taken with how Dammerman handled previous tasks.

GE's Six Sigma program illustrates Welch's attention to details that can add up to billions of dollars for the company when properly implemented.[160] The gap between GE's performance and Six Sigma increased costs between $8 billion and $12 billion a year in productivity losses and inefficiencies. It was a major initiative to begin a quality program, as it required a huge investment in training employees in the necessary methodology. Welch began GE's Six Sigma effort in 1995 with 200 projects, increased the scope to 3,000 projects in 1996, and then to 6,000 projects in 1997. The program was a huge success, delivering greater benefits than expected by Welch and producing hundreds of millions of dollars in benefits.

Welch transformed an old-line American industrial giant that primarily was in electrical and electronics manufacturing into a competitive global company.[161] Welch changed GE through more than 600 acquisitions and entry into newly emerging markets. At the same time, he exported thousands of jobs, terminated many managers, exercised unrelenting pressure on his managers for success (his nickname inside of GE was "Neutron Jack" in reference to the neutron bomb), and caused employees to cut corners to succeed and sometimes fail (as in the Kidder, Peabody bond trading and defense contracting scandals). After his departure, GE's stock price fell from about $50 a share to its current price of about $23 a share (although it recovered temporarily before the 2008 recession to $40 a share).

---

160 A Six Sigma quality level generates fewer than 3.4 defects per million operations in a manufacturing or service process based on the number of standard deviations (a statistical measure) from the mean. During the time of Welch's leadership, GE was running at a Six Sigma level of three to four.

161 GE is currently a diversified technology and financial services corporation. The products and services of the company range from aircraft engines, power generation, water processing, and household appliances to medical imaging, business and consumer financing, industrial products, and television and entertainment.

Ratan Tata, Tata Group (home country: India)

The Tata family of India founded and controls the Tata Group of companies. Headquartered in Mumbai, the conglomerate encompasses seven business sectors: communications and information technology, engineering, materials, services, energy, consumer products and chemicals. The Tata Group operates in more than 80 countries across six continents and its companies export products and services to 80 nations through about 100 operating companies, including steel, motor vehicles, consulting, power generation, chemicals, beverages, telecommunications and hotels. The combined market value is in the hundreds of billions of dollars; measurement is difficult as only about one-third of the Tata companies are publicly-traded.

Ratan Tata, the current chairman, worked in various positions in the Tata steel mill (including shoveling limestone and operating the blast furnace), the communications company, the textile mill (since closed) and other assignments. In 1981, his father retired as chairman and named Ratan to be his successor (later to become group chairman). Ratan's most significant contribution has been to create an interconnected, cohesive company from what was a portfolio investment in very different businesses.

He has been responsible for the acquisition of three British companies: Tetley Tea, Jaguar Land Rover (automobiles) and Corus (steel), in addition to the Plaza Hotel in New York City, which with other acquisitions have transformed Tata into a global business with 65% revenues coming from outside India. In addition, he has established joint ventures with various international companies and has attacked "vested interests" (or the crony capitalism endemic that is in India), by which companies profit by providing rewards for politicians and officials. These practices and reports of corruption have contributed to the slump in economic growth to about half that of the recent past.

Rattan has publicly avowed concern for social responsibility, sustainability, philanthropy and environmental integrity. He is particularly adamant about water and agricultural conservation. He has received various honors during his career, including the Indian prizes Padma Bhushan, (in 2000) and Padma Vibhushan (in 2008). He is a Lifetime Achievement Award winner from the Rockefeller Foundation (in 2012).

The 2009 annual survey by the Reputation Institute ranked Tata Group as the 11th most reputable company of 600 global companies. The Tata Group has helped establish and finance numerous educational, research and cultural institutes in India. The group was awarded the Carnegie Medal of Philanthropy in 2007 in recognition of its long history of philanthropic activities. Despite the commitment to philanthropy, the Tata has attracted several controversies:

- In 2006, policemen opened fire at a crowd of tribal villagers who were protesting the construction of a compound wall for a Tata steel plant on land that had historically been owned by them. Some of the corpses were returned to the families in a mutilated condition. Tata officials said the incident was unfortunate but that it would continue with its plans for the plant.
- Later in 2006, survivors of the Bhopal gas disaster were outraged by Ratan Tata's offer to support Union Carbide (the plant owner) and facilitate investments by Carbide's new owner Dow Chemical. Survivor's groups felt that Tata's offer was aimed at frustrating legal efforts to hold the company liable, and motivated by a desire to facilitate Dow's investments in India.
- In 2009, Tata Motors announced plans to manufacture trucks in Myanmar despite that country's oppressive and anti-democratic military junta. As a result, Tata has been criticized by from human rights and democracy activists.
- Other negative reactions have resulted from a port project that threatens a maritime sanctuary and national park; and a soda ash plant in Tanzania due to the possible effects on a nearby lake and its ecosystem.

At the occasion of his Rockefeller Award, Rattan noted that he followed a leader "…who had very large shoes… Mr. J.R.D. Tata [Rattan's father]. He was a legend in the Indian business community. He had been at the helm of the Tata organization for 50 years… You feel suddenly that you've been thrown into the deep end of the swimming pool, trying to follow him. I think the greatest dilemma in mind was how to mimic him and follow in his footsteps. And I realized that I could never be him and I should try to be whoever I was… I realized fairly soon it was not you but the entire workforce that you count on. I think I have only achieved what that force of 400,000 people has been able to support me to do."[162]

Carl Hahn, Volkswagen (home country: Germany)

Carl Hahn is the chairman emeritus of Volkswagen (VW), the German automotive company that includes Volkswagen and various smaller car manufacturers, including the Spanish brand SEAT and the Czech car maker Škoda. The acquisitions during Hahn's tenure as chairman (1982 – 1993) made VW a global competitor with 1985 earnings of $225 million on sales of more than $20 billion. Three VW group vehicles are in the top ten listing of all time best-sellers: the VW Golf, the VW Beetle and the VW Passat.

While he is credited with expanding the company to international markets, Hahn failed to understand and control the enormous fixed costs of his operation, particularly the production facility in Wolfsburg, Germany, which at five square kilometers (nearly two square miles) is one of the biggest and most advanced car factories in the world. Among other distinctions, it has the largest state-of-the-art paint shop in Europe. Among the problems faced by Hahn were:

- German labor unions that actively participate in management decisions and cause among the highest labor costs in the world. These issues were not addressed by management and the unions until a dozen years after Hahn's tenure at VW ended when global competition began to change the 50 years of privileges won by German workers. In 2005, the unions reached three wage deals with VW with the company demanding and receiving significant concessions, partly by threatening to move the production to Portugal where hourly wages are less than a third of those in Germany.[163]

- Due to aggressive pricing, VW achieved a very low profit per vehicle, about $1\frac{1}{8}\%$ per dollar of sales in the mid-1980s but losses in the hun-

---

162 Interview excerpt reported in "Ratan Tata Looks Back," *Fortune Magazine*, June 27, 2012, at tech.fortune.cnn.com/2012/06/27/ratan-tata-looks-back.

163 In 2005, the average hourly cost of an auto worker in western Germany was the highest in the automobile industry, at $40.80. That compared with $35.40 in Japan, $34.80 in the U.S., $27.60 in France and $5.40 in Slovakia, where Volkswagen has an assembly plant. Statistics are quoted in Mark Landler, "German Labor's New Reality," *New York Times*, October 26, 2005, www.Nytimes.Com/2005/10/26/Business/Worldbusiness/26labor.Html?_R=1&Pagewanted=All.

dreds of millions of marks (400 million euro or $500 million) a few years later. Hahn expected to maximize company profits outside of North America (primarily in Europe) at a time when cars from Japan and other countries were achieving market penetration in the U.S.

- A loss of interest in the North American market which had produced annual sales in the hundreds of thousands of cars through the early 1980s. VW was the breakthrough vehicle in the U.S. and Canada in terms of large volume foreign car sales at the expense of General Motors, Ford and Chrysler. However, sales dropped to about 75,000 units due to a resuscitated American marketing and design effort, and because of competition from the Japanese.

- Quality problems with products for North America, particularly with such later models as the Super Beetle and the Rabbit. In an effort to improve VW products for this market, Hahn fired the VW of America president (James McLernon) and brought in new management although significant improvement did not result.

Hahn attempted to manage a large organization that could only be successful through large production runs and careful attention to cost efficiencies. The Japanese proved to be more adaptable through the use of better manufacturing, quality circles, just-in-time inventory management[164] and producing on-site for American and other markets.[165] VW profit margins could not be significantly increased given the car's market position and long history of low pricing (about $2,000 in the U.S. in about 1970); the requirement for long production runs in the Wolfsburg operation (estimates were that the operations had to run at 90% of capacity to break-even); and Germany's high labor costs.

The solution would have been to emulate the Japanese in globalizing manufacturing but Hahn did not sufficiently pursue that strategy. In fact, he envisioned the European market as VW's most lucrative opportunity and the primary stra-

---

164 Just-in-time (JIT) is described in footnote 61.

165 For example, the Toyota Motor Corporation has factories in most parts of the world, manufacturing or assembling vehicles for local markets, including Australia, India, Sri Lanka, Canada, Indonesia, Poland, South Africa, Turkey, Colombia, the United Kingdom, the U.S. (in AL, KY, IN, TX, WV and MI), France, Brazil and Portugal. Recently opened facilities are in Argentina, Czech Republic, Mexico, Malaysia, Thailand, Pakistan, Egypt, China, Vietnam, Venezuela, the Philippines, and Russia.

tegic emphasis.[166] Hahn did expand into China, and during his tenure, was the only foreign automobile manufacturer in that country.

At a time when VW required a strong, dominant leader, Hahn was perceived to be a consensus builder, a communicative manager and open to the discussion of new ideas. He was (and is) brilliant, analytical and perceptive, but unable to come to terms with the realities of costs and market share. VW's board of directors decided that Hahn had entrenched ideas that were not working, and he was replaced by Ferdinand Piëch in 1993.

Howard Stringer, Sony (home countries: Great Britain by birth and a naturalized U.S. citizen)

In the media and consumer electronics business, innovation and creativity are critical components of a long-term strategy. Industry leaders of yesterday (think of the old Hollywood movie studios like RKO or Republic) have disappeared, as have the traditional legitimate theaters and newspapers in many cities. The company that led analog innovation for several decades after World War Two – Sony Corporation – started to lose market share and customer acceptance in many of its business lines by about 1995, as competitors began to produce and market exciting digital and home entertainment products.

Howard Stringer had a successful career at CBS (formerly the Columbia Broadcasting System) as an executive producer and president of the company, and nine-time Emmy winner. This experience led Sony to recruit him as president of its U.S. operations, eventually naming him as chairman and chief executive officer in 2005. Stringer oversaw such businesses as Sony Computer Entertainment, Sony Music Entertainment, Sony Electronics and Sony Pictures. His selection was driven by company losses and by competition from such rivals as Apple, Samsung and Sharp.

The problems at Sony involved various issues representative of Japanese companies, many of which have been organized as *keiretsu*, groups of companies that act together for mutual support.[167] Unfortunately, the lack of totally

---

166 For a revealing interview with Hahn, see Bernard Avishai, "A European Platform for Global Competition," in *Leaders on Leadership* (Warren Bennis, ed.), *Harvard Business Review*, 1992, pages 91 – 108.

167 Business functions included in the largest *keiretsu* are industrial companies, distributors and banking institutions.

objective and profit-oriented decision-making led to some very questionable investments by the *keiretsu*, and, according to some observers, was a major cause of the Japanese recession that began in the early 1990s.

The attitude of collaborative decision-making allowed others to seize market share from Sony (as well as from other Japanese companies). Aggressive competition came both from the industry leaders noted above and from new competitors (such as Amazon in the e-reader business). The culture of group consensus allowed bad (or no) decisions to continue, and it was not until the global recession beginning in 2008 that Springer began to take aggressive action to realign his senior management.

The losses Sony experienced finally led to reconfiguring the company into two new core groups with new, younger senior managers. Cost efficiencies of $3 billion were sought through closing several production facilities and eliminating nearly 10% of the workforce, and by reducing the number of Sony vendors by half based on the most aggressive pricing offered and fastest delivery times. However, company revenue dropped by more than 15% from 2009 to 2012, and losses quadrupled to $5.8 billion during that period.

Most products experienced a decline in market share in markets in which Sony had a major presence or for which had previously had technological domination. According to Gartner Group, a marketing research firm, Sony had less than a 2% share of the worldwide mobile phone market in 2011, far behind Nokia's 24% and Samsung's nearly 18%. Sony's shipments of LCD televisions fell by more than 14%. Home game devices are similarly struggling, with PlayStation unable to meet Xbox sales (Microsoft), while games have become a major attraction of the iPhone (Apple).

Howard Stringer could not fix the Sony brand problem or develop innovative products like its competitors. Web-based intellectual property was never properly developed or exploited. Furthermore, the Japanese 20-year recession forced Sony and its Japanese competitors to reduce research and development and inevitably, market share. Investors have observed these problems, and Sony's American shares (American Depository Receipts [ADRs], stock symbol SNE) have lost nearly three-quarters of their market value in the five years from 2008 – 2012.

During his tenure, there were various public relations problems that affected Stringer's attempts to pursue a successful management strategy. Some examples:

- The planting of malicious software code by joint venture Sony BMG in its CDs in an attempt at copy protection
- The same joint-venture had been caught in a payola scandal for which it paid a $10 million fine
- The recall of nearly ten million laptop batteries because some spontaneously burst into flames
- The exposure of personal data of minors who used Sony BMG websites, for which a $1 million penalty was assessed

Stringer started his chairmanship as a conciliator and cultural transformer when Sony needed an authoritarian, forceful leader. He reverted to a tougher Western style once the 2008 recession began, remarking at an internal meeting that "If the captain hits rough seas, he looks after his crew. When you hit an iceberg, you worry about the ship."[168] Observers believe that this aggressive attitude may have worked three years earlier, but that the industry was innovating and changing so rapidly that the lost time was precious and far too costly. In early 2012, Sony announced that Stringer would be replaced by Kazuo Hirai, previously the company's executive deputy president.

Percy Barnevik, ABB (home country: Sweden)

Percy Barnevik created ABB in 1987 by combining Asea, a Swedish engineering group, with Brown Boveri, a competitor based in Switzerland. At the time of the merger, ABB had 210,000 employees and was active in 140 countries. Despite its imposing size, critics wondered if the merger was realistic and if the company's structure could effectively function. Various issues arose when the merger occurred: Could a company operate without a home country identity? Could a matrix organization (see Chapter 7) manage efficiently? Could Barevik's global vision be transferred to the senior managers of ABB? What would happen to ABB after Barnevik's departure (in 1996)?

---

168 Quoted by Richard Siklos, "Sony: Lost in Transformation," *CNNMoney*, June 26, 2009, at money.cnn.com/2009/06/24/technology/sony_digital_transformation.fortune.

Appendix A: Profiles Of Management Leaders

Barnevik is widely acknowledged to possess enormous energy, ambition and intelligence. His Swedish heritage provided a somewhat friendly and caring personality, ready for teamwork and conflict resolution. His focus was on benefitting all stakeholders rather than the short-term focus of U.S. companies on profit maximization. Furthermore, he did not believe in hierarchal organizations, and would pursue strategic management initiatives while involving himself at lower levels of management as problems and opportunities arose. His childhood experiences as a Swedish Lutheran in a small town made him into a demanding senior manager who showed little patience with subordinates who were insufficiently prepared.[169]

After various industrial assignments, Barnevik was named chief executive officer (CEO) of Sandvik Steel's American operations in 1975. He managed to triple sales and turn a company from losses to profits during his four year tenure. In 1979, he became CEO of Asea, one of the world's top ten electrical engineering companies but suffering from excess capacity in the markets it served, weak demand, and falling profits. The company was a typical patriarchal organization, providing assured employment and a focus on technical rather than business skills. Barnevik enjoyed the opportunity to make Asea into a competitor in its industry by radical changes, including eliminating the old bureaucratic organization and greatly reducing headquarters staff. His seven years as CEO resulted in an increase in earnings by eight times and a 20 times jump in market capitalization.

Following some smaller acquisitions, Barnevik was repelled at attempts at major German and later U.S. deals. He then approached Brown Boveri and was able to conclude a merger in 1987 allowing operations in complementary geographic areas of Europe. The cultures of the two companies were compatible, and the expected globalization of business would have inevitably forced each to be acquired/merged or to cease operations. As was his practice in his early years, Barnevik saw the need to proceed quickly to avoid conflicts and political disputes between the two managements.

The senior managers selected to make the merger successful had to have high energy and intelligence, possesses managerial and technical skills, and

---

169 A useful discussion of Barnevik's career during his tenure as chief executive officer can be found in Manfred F.R. Kets de Vries (with Elizabeth Florent-Treacy), *The New Global Leaders*, Jossey-Bass, 1999, pages 59 – 108.

be demonstrated leaders in multicultural situations. Barnevik implemented a matrix decision-making structure which required business area and country managers to collaborate on strategies, with the occasional irreconcilable conflict passed to an executive committee (*Konzernleitung*). As with any matrix organization, conflicts inevitably occurred despite attempts at role clarification and the development of procedural rules.

Economic opportunities appeared to be global as the recession of the early 1990s was ending, motivating Barnevik's acquisition of about 150 companies in geographic areas and businesses where ABB did not have a strong presence. Deals were made in Eastern Europe, the U.S. (Combustion Engineering), Great Britain and Asia. Barnevik made several changes to the management structure of ABB with the inevitable feelings of insecurity, stress, redundant flows of information and communications, cynicism, fear, a sense of inferiority, poor morale and exhaustion. His focus on profits and cost efficiencies drove ABB stock higher by forty times from the beginning of his tenure (almost three times the general stock market), equal to a return of about 30% a year. Net profit increased 60 times and sales 30 times during that period.

These results led to Barnevik's receiving a one-time payment of 148 million Swiss francs when he retired as CEO in 1996. Six years later under another CEO, ABB stock's market value fell from about $85 in 2000 to about $23. (In early 2013, the stock was trading at about $22¾ having reached nearly $35 just prior to the 2008 recession.[170]) The company announced a loss of $691 million as investors worried about the $4 billion of debt and were concerned over exposure to operating risks that have been poorly understood.

When ABB's board of directors made Barnevik's pension payment public, a scandal ensued and Barnevik was forced to resign as chairman of Investor, the Swedish investment company and to return back a large portion of his pension payment. An amazing fact about Barnevik's pension is that it was not approved by ABB's board; the company had no proper remuneration committee and Barnevik used an executive order to authorize the payment.

---

170 At the time, ABB principal trading market was in Zurich and so these stock quotes were converted from Swiss francs. ABB is now traded on the New York Stock Exchange.

The stated long-range perspective of Barnevik to managing a huge global corporation conflicted with short-term problems with senior managers, the cutting of corners in making various merger deals[171] and other situations. Barnevik's handling of his pension, and the failure to sufficiently review certain acquisitions led to a decade of problems and poor performance in ABB's stock price.

Al Dunlap, Sunbeam Corp. (home country: U.S.)

"If you're a little frustrated with the prior management [of Sunbeam], you're a tolerant man. I would have hung them." Comment by "Chainsaw" Al Dunlap the new Chairman and Chief Executive Officer of Sunbeam Corp.; New York Stock Exchange, at an analyst meeting, reported in September 1996. Al Dunlap was one of the first leaders of American business at the end of the 20th century who used unscrupulous business tactics and accounting fraud to deceive (at least temporarily) investors and the public. We mentioned others in Chapter 8 who came shortly afterward: Lay of Enron, Kozlowski of Tyco and Ebbers of WorldCom.

1996: On November 12, 1996, Al Dunlap announced that he was planning to eliminate 6,000 jobs (half of the Company's workforce), close 16 of 26 factories, sell off divisions making products inconsistent with the core product line, and annually launch 30 new products and save $225 million. Dunlap had formerly led Scott Paper (now part of Kimberly Clark), where he eliminated about one-third of that company's workforce. The plan at Sunbeam is to build up the international small appliance business based on the Sunbeam and Oster brand names. Some analysts are enthusiastic about the plan; others are skeptical because of the impact of the staff cuts on product introductions and other strategic initiatives. Sunbeam's balance sheet listed $200 million in debt.

1997: The cost cutting is about over and the stock price has doubled. Dozens of new products are promised, and the plan is to double revenues (emphasizing international sales) and improve operating margins ten times. However, the

---

171 In 2002, ABB announced charges of $1.4 billion, including a doubling of provisions for potentially ruinous asbestos liabilities to $940 million. Most of the liabilities arose from activities at Combustion Engineering that Barnevik purchased about a decade earlier without adequate due diligence. Stanley Reed, ABB: Huge Tremors at a Swiss Giant," *BloombergBusinessweek*, February 13, 2002, at www.businessweek.com/stories/2002-02-13/abb-huge-tremors-at-a-swiss-giant.

consumer appliance industry has been experiencing limited growth, with low margins due to the buying power of large retail chains. To raise cash, Sunbeam sells $60 million in accounts receivable and initiates an "early buy" program for gas grills, allowing retailers to "purchase" grills in 1997 but not pay until mid-1998. Once the retailers were loaded up with grills, Sunbeam starts a second sales program. A "bill and hold" plan permitted customers to buy and store their unpaid merchandise in Sunbeam's facilities. The two sales arrangements account for a major portion of the revenue gains in 1997, but are in fact future sales booked now.

1998: New products are launched, emphasizing such high-technology versions of electric blankets with sensors and high-end gas grills, all promoted with an advertising campaign boosted 25 times. To support growth targets of 25% compounded annually, Dunlap announces the acquisition of Coleman Co., a leader in outdoor recreation equipment; First Alert, a maker of smoke detectors; and Signature Brands, an appliance company. It is announced that more than 5,000 jobs, 8 factories and 33 warehouses would be closed. In April, Sunbeam shocks the stock market when it announces that it would post a first quarter 1998 loss on lower sales. After onetime charges of $0.43 per share, the loss per share is $0.52 in the first quarter of 1998 compared with earnings per share of $0.08 in the same 1997 period.

Domestic sales, representing 74% of total revenues in the quarter, declined 15.4% from the 1997 quarter due to lower price realization and unit volume declines. As the result of Sunbeam's alleged misleading actions, a series of class action lawsuits are filed on behalf of all persons who purchased the common stock of Sunbeam Corporation during Dunlap's leadership. The complaints charge Sunbeam with issuing a series of materially false and misleading statements regarding sales and earnings. The alleged misstatements and omissions were made in an effort to convince the investing public of Sunbeam's continuing double digit quarterly sales and earnings growth.

The three acquisitions permit a repeat of the 1996 tactics of downsizing and plant closings. Meanwhile, the balance sheet shows $2 billion in debt, a negative cash flow, and a net worth of a negative $600 million, on sales of more than $1.5 billion. The stock price falls nearly 50%. Sunbeam Corp.'s Board of Directors fires Al Dunlap citing poor financial results, marking the end of his two year stint at the company. The scorecard: 12,000 employees eliminated; significant losses; and a demoralized company. "We lost confidence in (Dunlap's) ability to move the company forward," said one of the directors.

Dunlap was also suspected of irregularities at Scott Paper, his previous chief executive officer position. He agreed to pay $500,000 to settle charges by the primary U.S. public company regulator, the Securities and Exchange Commission (SEC), and was banned from serving as an officer or director of any public company. In addition, Dunlap paid $15,000,000 out of his own funds to settle a related class action.[172]

In 2002, Sunbeam emerged from bankruptcy as American Household, Inc. (AHI), a privately held company. Its former household products division became the subsidiary Sunbeam Products, Inc. AHI was purchased in September 2004 by the Jarden Corporation, of which it is now a subsidiary. Al Dunlap: "[My] harshest critics call me a bastard and say I have no heart."

Figure A-1: Women Global Business Leaders

Name: Indra Nooyi
Nationality: Indian
Age: 53
Company: PepsiCo
Sector: Beverages

Name: Andrea Jung
Nationality: Canadian
Age: 51
Company: Avon Products
Sector: Personal goods

---

172 "Former Top Officers of Sunbeam Corp. Settle SEC Charges; Dunlap and Kersh Consent to Fraud Injunctions, Permanent Officer and Director Bars, Civil Monetary Penalties," Securities and Exchange Commission, Litigation Release No. 17710, at www.sec.gov/litigation/litreleases/lr17710.htm.

Name: Anne Lauvergeon
Nationality: French
Age: 50
Company: Areva
Sector: Nuclear Engineering

Name: Güler Sabanci
Nationality: Turkish
Age: 54
Company: Sabanci Group
Sector: Conglomerate

Name: Gail Kelly
Nationality: South African
Age: 53
Company: Westpac
Sector: Banks

Name: Dong Mingzhu
Nationality: Chinese
Age: 56
Company: Gree Electric Appliances
Sector: Household goods & construction

Name: Christina Gold
Nationality: Canadian
Age: 62
Company: Western Union
Sector: Financial services

Name: Cheung Yan
Nationality: Chinese
Age: 52
Company: Nine Dragons Paper
Sector: Forestry/paper

Source: "Top 50 Women in World Business," *Financial Times*, September 25, 2009, at www.ft.com/cms/s/0/bcfcdb2c-a716-11de-bd14-00144feabdc0.html#axzz278OSOjVF.

Appendix B: Cases On Management And Organizational Behavior

The ten cases in this chapter attempt to highlight specific business situations that need to be evaluated for purposes of resolving a management or organizational behavior problem. The cases are notated with a subject area descriptor, but as in real-life, situations in companies extend into various topics, even possibly beyond the material discussed in this text. Although not all of the facts you might want to know are provided (or in any situation), there is sufficient information to arrive at a resolution.

The purpose of these cases is to integrate the external environment with the company's situation. In other words, one cannot evaluate a business problem as if it were in management, finance, marketing, manufacturing or other business discipline. You must consider whether internal company functions are doing a reasonable job and if the organization is responding in an appropriate manner to known and likely changes in the global marketplace.

Cases offer realism in terms of understanding people problems in organizations. As in any situation one encounters, the reader/manager must work with incomplete information which must be extrapolated and summarized to suggest possible avenues toward a resolution. The data that is missing in a case is usually not available in actual interpersonal situations. We often do not know what people are thinking, what their hidden agendas are, how they feel about you and others, and similar matters. We can only develop educated solutions based on the facts in the case and on the theories presented in the text.

The cases and their topics are as follows (in alphabetical order):

- Balto/Nectis (decision-making)
- Chris Farr (interpersonal dynamics)

241

- Cran Fan Stan (change management)
- Dixon Products (leadership)
- Edward Gilmore (personnel/human resources)
- Jerry Monroe (individual motivation)
- Let Us Entertain You! (controlling)
- Recreation Sensation (group dynamics)
- Select Electronics (directing)
- We *Are* Computers! (planning)

Jerry Monroe (individual motivation)

Jerry Monroe is senior vice president of production and engineering for The Orange Box Company in Baltimore MD. Jerry has an M.S. degree in information technology and had been a supervisor, then middle-level manager and now the head of an extremely important department in this rapidly growing computer manufacturer. Jerry was from the old school of experience in managing employees (he had been a sergeant in the Army), and was used to giving orders and having them followed.

Orange Box was located in a technology park where other tenants included computer science and biotechnology companies. In addition, there are similar organizations, including the government and the military, located throughout Washington D.C. and the surrounding suburban area including MD and VA counties. As a result, higher than average wages and benefits were paid to try to keep turnover low and to prevent employees from accepting positions with competitors.

It was obvious to Jerry, to the managers who were his direct reports and to other key managers that many employees were only working their required 40 hours a week. There was no sense of a desire for a superior effort or to develop ways to make the production and engineering department more efficient and effective. Employees were not working anywhere near their full potential. Jerry was distressed with the situation because, in the current weak economy, the company could only prosper by increasing productivity.

Jerry hated asking for advice but was finally forced to confer with his personnel manager to request his help. Jerry was typically blunt: "Our people don't seem to get it. Our wage studies indicate that we provide wage incentives near the highest in this area, and our fringe benefits cost us a fortune. Despite these rewards, our people are still unmotivated. What can be done?"

The personnel manager replied, "Jerry, if you and the president would study a bit of management and organization behavior, you both would know that rewards (as you call them) are never enough to motivate workers. Employees want other incentives beyond scheduled wage increases, and their health insurance and pension contributions. Our employees state that they are discouraged because, no matter how hard they work, they get the same pay and chances for promotion as co-workers who are making a minimal effort." At first Jerry got angry but then responded, "Okay, genius, what would you do? Productivity *must* improve."

Questions for Consideration

1. Orange Box employees do not seem motivated to try to improve company performance. Why?
2. Discuss Jerry's seeming inability to better manage the workers in his department.
3. As personnel manager, how would you reply to Jerry's question: "Okay, genius, what would you do? Productivity *must* improve."

Cran Fan Stan (change management)

The route salesmen for Cran Fan Stan (Stan's) were talking during a coffee break in a one-day training session being held at company offices in Amherst MA. Seymour Harris was talking the loudest – and he was really angry. "All I want to do is to deliver the product to my route and make schedule. I'm not interested in providing additional services to the retailers, particularly since I'm paid for driving and distributing inventory. And the minute I'm late, guess whose pay gets docked?"

The other salesmen – at least the more experienced ones – simply nodded in agreement, while the younger route salespeople (RSs) were silent. "Stan's is changing our relationship with our customers," Seymour continued, "and we're the ones who will lose while the company gains." He was referring to the newly announced instructions for them to become marketing representatives (MRs) and not what had essentially been order takers.

The Beginning of the Business Concept

Cran Fan Stan, a healthy snack beverage leader, began in 1980 in Amherst MA. Dr. Stanley Darcy, a pediatrician, and Dr. Mary Black, a food engineer, joined forces to create healthier snack options. Dr. Stan (as he was known to his patients) had listened to complaints from parents that their children were drinking too many sugary sodas. At the same time, he observed a growing child obesity problem. In response, he created his own pure fruit drinks and provided them as treats for his patients. They were a big hit and parents began to ask where they could buy them.

One such parent was Dr. Black. She liked the taste of the fruit drink, but wanted to add even more vitamin and minerals. The two agreed to work together on a recipe for a healthy drink for children and young adults, and then to add other products as they went along. The company name they choose was partly an acknowledgement of the very important cranberry industry of MA and was the first fruit used in their new juice. Over the next 25 years, Stan's added more than ten healthy products sold across New Enland. The route salespeople became the face of the product as they stocked the shelves and spoke to the owners of the small, independent shops that were the majority of their customers.

The Competition

In the early 1990s, the business was sold to a European food manufacturer and distributor. At first, annual sales for Stan's products increased significantly. The drinks were in almost every major supermarket and drug store chain throughout the U.S., Canada and parts of Europe. The public had increasingly become aware of healthy eating, and there was a large increase in the proportion of snacks sold in such outlets such as fitness clubs and school vending machines.

The total healthy food industry has over $6 billion dollars in revenues. Many competing businesses were more generous to retailers, offering larger profit margins and promotional support. As a result, Stan's began to lose retailers to other brands, and Cran Fan Stan experienced a large loss in market share.

The Distribution System

Initially, Cran Fan Stan organized its distribution through its own route salespeople (RSs) who called on smaller, specialty shops and outlets, and later added independent wholesalers who called on supermarkets and grocery stores. The parallel methods operated throughout the countries served. The wholesalers promoted Stan's products through their own selling efforts, from taking orders through delivery and stocking shelves, and were the contact point for invoicing, credit issues and returns. The wholesale process was used by Stan's competitors and was standard in food retailing.

Recently, Stan's changed its structure so that distribution is now handled by Stan's employees. Previously responsible only for insuring that deliveries to specialty shops and outlets occurred efficiently, now the RS position will become a marketing representative (MR) function. A MR will now be expected to deliver merchandise, manage the retailer's inventory, assist with displays, market through promotional activities, and discuss healthy eating with retail customers. To provide this additional level of effort, MRs will be provided with computers that will allow them to process most of the paperwork of the old RS and new MR at the store. Each MR will service only about a dozen retailers per day, rather than the 18 or so that the RS currently visits.

"No other company in the food industry can match this level of service once the transition to the MR system occurs," said Warren Fields, Stan's marketing manager. "It would take our competitors several years to catch up. We are clearly providing total service and not merely stocking shelves."

The Area Manager

Cran Fan Stan created a new job position of area manager (AM) to educate, encourage, supervise, and assess the MRs. The AMs and MRs will work jointly and have responsibility to manage the routes that are assigned. The AM positions have been filled by internal candidates with RS experience and by outside hires that have a background in similar large company activities such as Ocean Spray or Snapple. Five Beta sites (test locations) were set up to evaluate alternative methods of offering the MR service. Although the first site has only been operating for four months, there has already been a 15% increase in sales for the same locations. Furthermore, the enhanced service has motivated some retailers to drop competitive beverage products.

It is expected that all U.S. distribution will convert from a RS to a MR-based system within the next three years. Over the coming twelve months, each RS will be offered the choice to become a MR by the AMs, which will include a promotion to a higher pay grade, or to accept a position in company headquarters or field locations at approximately the current pay grade. Each AM has a different approach and opinion on how to manage this transition. Here is a sampling of what they have to say:

- Stuart Walker: "These MRs are going to have to succeed or they are out. We may be able to keep a few of these people in another capacity, but there wouldn't be many in that situation. The MR is the future of this business and we must proceed toward that objective."
- Maria Lopez: "Most of the RSs can deliver as MRs. With proper training, they will perform well. The AMs just need to make sure that the MRs are adequately supervised and motivated, and that they don't try to go beyond their knowledge and job responsibilities."

To begin the conversion to the MR model, all RSs now working for Stan's have been given some marketing training. At present, they have been told to sell basic promotions and provide merchandising activities for Stan's customers. Prizes have been arranged for superior performance, with football tickets, gift cards, or sportswear for the top performers as additional incentives and to show company support.

The Reaction

After the training session, some of the attendees had mixed feelings.

- Bob Sherman: "I'm looking forward to these new MR opportunities. Just delivering product can get pretty boring. I've only been here for five months, but once you understand the route and the delivery system, it gets fairly repetitious."
- Seymour Harris (who appeared at the beginning of the case) wasn't so certain. "Yeah, I guess so," he replied. "Hey, I gotta go." As he headed for his truck, Seymour began to think. In talking with the other RSs, he'd learned that those near the top could really relate to the retailers, listen to their problems and complaints, and represent the company.

He was wondering if he had the skills to be a MR or whether he should find a new job. There wasn't an AM yet for his area, so the training had been haphazard. Seymour wasn't sure if he had a future at Cran Fan Stan.

Questions for Consideration

1. What do you see as the differences of the management approaches of Stuart Walker and Maria Lopez? As an area manager for Cran Fan Stan, what would you do to incentivize the RSs to become MRs?
2. How can managers use the company's history and/or the present situation in the food industry to motivate the RSs both now and as they assume greater responsibilities as MRs?
3. What would be the best way to motivate the RSs (like Seymour) who may be nervous? Would pairing Seymour with a motivated employee like Bob be a good idea? Why or why not?

Recreation Sensation (group dynamics)

Janet Maron, CEO and president of Recreation Sensation was confused. She could not understand why senior staff meetings often accomplished very little. These meetings consisted of Janet and the company's vice presidents and division directors. The intended purpose of these meetings was to develop and discuss creative ideas for new products and marketing.

Recreation Sensation manufactures various recreational products for outdoor and indoor use. The company started with a light-weight all-terrain bicycle developed by Janet's late father which can be folded and carried in a luggage bag. The bicycle quickly became popular in urban areas, allowing train and subway riders to pedal from their stations to their place of employment or to school. Although somewhat difficult to learn to fold and stabilize, once mastered the Recreation Sensation bicycle offered exercise, mobility and convenience.

The company expanded to produce and market leisure goods for active land, water and snow sports, such as advanced bicycle concepts, kayaks, surfboards and snowboards, and has begun to test a radical design for skis. Products are sold globally – the bicycle is particularly popular in Asian cities

— and enjoy a receptive market. However, recreation companies are constantly developing innovative ideas using advanced materials, and a new concept is usually met with a competitive product by the next season.

Recent staff meetings have focused at identifying new products, modifying existing products, and working on solutions to problems in innovative design, development and manufacturing. After a recent meeting, Janet spoke to one of the meeting attendees, Sandy Greenwood, the vice-president of marketing, of her concerns regarding the apparent lack of progress. Sandy was a highly effective manager and respected in the company, and she had a solid reputation in marketing to the recreation industry.

Janet told Sandy that there was a lack of candid discussion by some participants. Sandy answered: "Why don't I speak confidentially to the others and see if I can get a handle on the problem." On the day prior to the next meeting, Sandy arrived in Janet's office to discuss what she had heard. Without mentioning names, Sandy read from the various statements made by the senior staff.

- Janet often projects that she really knows our industry. The ideas of the staff are reasonable, but Janet has to put her own interpretation on things that are said. People would appreciate credit or recognition for their ideas.
- All senior staff members are not equal. Some are interrupted while they are speaking, and not just by Janet. Others get rejected regardless of their ideas. This isn't civil behavior — it's just being rude.
- Does Janet really care about our ideas? After all, she is the daughter of the company's founder.
- Do we really intend to enter or leave certain markets or products? Should we bring in outside designers? Should we consider new marketing methods, like a tie-in with a professional sports team or an Olympic champion? How has the Internet changed our distribution system? These changes are on our minds, but no one brings them up in the staff meetings.
- The industry and our markets are dynamic, and we've got to adjust. We need to completely review what we are and where we need to be in the future.

Janet was uncertain about these comments and what was actually meant. She wondered what to do.

Questions for Consideration

1. What do you think is going on at Recreation Sensation?
2. How do you feel about Sandy's conversations with the staff? Did she do the right thing?
3. What should Janet do? Why?

We *Are* Computers! (planning)

The We *Are* Computers Company is a $30 billion company that manufactures computer products for business and personal use. At the most recent management meeting, a joint committee of Marketing and Product Development proposed a new type of tablet computer with various innovative features. These include three USB ports and a battery life of six hours. Marketing believes that it can sell 10,000 units at $700 in the first year after development, and that this level of sales will continue for four years.

Research and development will cost $7½ million. Manufacturing and distribution are expected to involve the following per unit costs: materials - $125, labor - $150, selling costs - $75, and administration (packaging, shipping, invoicing, the collection of remittances and general overhead) - $75. Corporate taxes are paid at the combined rate of 40%. The president of We *Are* Computers asks you, the Chief Financial Officer, to comment on the feasibility of this proposal. *He is particularly interested in what could go wrong.* We *Are* Computers! must earn at least 17½% on any new investment that it considers. What is your analysis of the situation? What additional information would be useful?

Dixon Products (leadership)

Daniel Fergus is the president and chief operating officer of Dixon Products Inc. (DPI), a privately-held manufacturing company in the lawn and tractor business. There is considerable competition in this industry with Lawn Boy and Toro among the largest companies. DPI has annual sales in the $50 million range with most mowers retailing for about $300, and has created a market position with its mulching mower that eliminates the need to bag and dispose of grass clippings. The mower mechanism shreds grass into tiny particles, which are released back into the lawn as a form of fertilizer.

Fergus bought the business from the founder Richard Dixon after working at DPI for ten years. Dixon wanted to retire and devote his energy to developing farm gardens for small homes to replace the flowers and plants seen at many houses. After Fergus took over the company, he told the 200 employees that they now had a new boss who would make all major decisions and accept no arguments about procedures, production quotas or the budget.

Fergus' Management

After a few early "discussions" with some of the more senior Dixon managers, the staff realized that Fergus was in charge and that the only options were to accept the situation or leave. Some employees did leave – mostly motivated and experienced managers – but many stayed because of the weak job market, the fair wages and benefits being paid, their friendships with fellow workers, and the realization that the DPI product line was superior to many other mowers.

Fergus was true to his word regarding how the business would be operated. He did seek advice from his accountant, his attorney and his chief technology manager on specialized questions, but on all other matters he was in charge. Over time, customers – mostly lawn equipment retailers and large home supply stores like Lowe's and Home Depot – began to expect new innovations on the mulching mower design. For example, some grasses (like Zoyzia) did not shred easily or were unsuitable for fertilizing lawns. Another request was for a mower that could mulch leaves in the Fall season to avoid raking and bagging, and to use the resulting organic material as a protective ground cover for lawns. However, no adjustment or product idea was provided to the market for these situations.

Fergus came to realize that product development would be essential to maintaining his company, and to explore the insights of his senior employees, a meeting was called to discuss the situation. After a presentation by an outside consultant on developments in the industry, Fergus told the group that their recommendations would be expected in one week. As one manager remarked on leaving the meeting, "I see this as a strictly no-win situation. If I make any suggestions, I'll be criticized. If I don't make any suggestions, I'll be criticized and possibly fired."

Questions for Consideration

1. Would the situation described in this case likely have occurred in a large public corporation? Note that Dixon Products is a small, private-ly-held company.
2. If you were a senior employee, how would you respond in this apparently "no-win" situation?
3. If you were an outside advisor to Daniel Fergus (perhaps his attorney), how would you counsel him?
4. What were Richard Dixon's responsibilities to the firm after the sale of the business to Daniel Fergus?
5. What do you see as a positive outcome?

Balto/Nectis (decision-making)

Balto Ltd. is a privately-held Canadian corporation that manufactures and distributes electronic products. The headquarters and factory are located near Toronto. Although the majority of sales are domestic, more and more attention is being given to sales within NAFTA (the North American Free Trade Agreement, which allows trade between the U.S., Canada and Mexico without such restrictions as tariffs). Two major customers, one domestic and the other in the U.S., take 20 per cent and 35 per cent, respectively, of Balto's output.

The company manufactures more than 1,500 different items for stock or to order. Total annual sales are $40 million Canadian (roughly $40 million U.S.). Vendors of raw materials are constantly asking for shorter periods until they are paid, and at present the inventory of most finished products is small. Current orders will take about six months of production. Balto employs about 1,500 people but has difficulty getting enough skilled labor. Space is not a problem, however, since the factory was recently enlarged.

The senior management of the company consists of a president and his direct reports in sales, manufacturing, finance and information technology, who form a board of managers that meets every Friday. Manufacturing is responsible for a small research and development department and for purchasing.

The president was in charge of sales before taking over as his current position, and he still takes a special interest in sales (rather too much interest, in the view of the heads of other departments). He has worked to improve relationships among the senior managers, which was formerly not good. He insisted on job descriptions for members of senior management and ten other principal executives. Introduction of these descriptions has eliminated the confusion about responsibility and authority that was formerly an impediment to cooperation.

Balto is profitable, but its financial structure leaves much to be desired. It has loans from large shareholders outstanding and has negotiated bank credit facilities. However, the banks are objecting to extension of the loans, yielding only reluctantly to Balto's wishes, and they have recommended the sale of additional equity to existing and possibly new shareholders.

The Proposal

On Wednesday evening, the sales manager returns from Boston with a proposal from one of the company's most important U.S. customers, Nectis (New England Computer Technology Innovative Solutions). Nectis is a fairly large wholesaler, purchasing materials from manufacturers like Balto and selling them to industrial and business companies. Until now it has made a significant portion of its purchases in Asia rather than from Balto or other North American companies.

Nectis's Japanese suppliers have recently formed a cartel, which is an anti-competitive agreement among companies in an industry. As a result Nectis must purchase on much less favorable terms than formerly. Moreover, the general manager of Nectis knows that some of the companies in the cartel are strongly in favor of eliminating wholesalers altogether.

The purchasing manager of Nectis has proposed that he buy primarily from Balto. He has drafted detailed specifications of the items that will be required, including the yearly quantities. He proposes to purchase about 25% of Balto's annual output. However, the Nectis manager has some demands. The quality of the items supplied by Balto must be better than previously. Products are often insufficiently finished, they show too much variation, and some items are too easily broken. Further, 17½% of the initial order must be delivered as soon as possible, with 7½% to then be delivered each month following. Invoices will be paid three months after they have been received, although Nectis will try to reduce the delay over the next few years.

For the time being, the Nectis manager is not in favor of a merger of the two companies. Since he is being pushed by the Asian suppliers to sign new contracts, the Nectis manager wants Balto to decide as soon as possible on his proposals, within three weeks at the latest. He states that he has had some discussions on the subject with other suppliers, including an important Balto competitor, but that he has made his firm proposals to Balto first.

The sales manager of Balto is very much in favor of accepting the Nectis proposal. Nectis is a reliable firm with which his company has had long and satisfactory relations. He has told the Nectis manager that he will return to his office, discuss the proposal with the board of managers, and give him a tentative answer within a week. Back in Toronto, the Balto sales manager is about to inform the president of the proposal when the manufacturing manager phones, so the sales manager reports on the Nectis discussions.

The manufacturing manager says immediately that it's impossible to accept the contract. There is a shortage of foremen and of all-round skilled employees. Further, his employees are becoming very irritated with complaints about quality. Then, he's having trouble getting raw materials, and just yesterday the finance manager had objections to the fast payments Balto was being asked to make to vendors. He ends by saying: "We have numerous regular customers who we rely on. Let's try to find a way to provide better service and products to them before considering the Nectis proposal."

Following this conversation, the sales manager calls the president. He remains excited because of the company's focus on sales, but his enthusiasm has been somewhat affected by the manufacturing manager's remarks. After reporting on the Nectis developments and his conversation with the manufacturing manager, he asks the president: "Shouldn't you come to Boston with me next week?"

The president finds it hard not to say "yes" immediately, but the remarks of the manufacturing manager, who he believes is doing a good job, worry him. So he congratulates the sales manager on the proposal and says he will call a special meeting of the board of managers for the following morning.

Questions for Consideration

1. Discuss the management issues raised by the Balto/Nectis case.
2. What is the definition of the critical problem? How should it be evaluated? List specific points of analysis.
3. What should Balto do?

Edward Gilmore (personnel/human resources)

While growing up, Edward Gilmore knew that his parents highly valued independence, and they forced him as much as possible to get to school, activities, friends' homes and church using his feet, his bicycle or public transportation. This character translated to his performance both in the classroom and whenever there was an opportunity for extra credit, as when crossing guards were needed to help the littler children, or when a teacher needed a classroom monitor during brief parent meetings or discussions with the principal.

His father was concerned because he believed that this self-reliance prevented Edward ("don't call me Ed or Eddie") from making many friends. Edward always maintained that he did not need a lot of friends. "They take up too much time and energy that I could better use to learn and improve." And he was not just saying these words: he became the first Eagle Scout in the Boy Scouts in his town; earned numerous commendations for academic excellence; was on two sports teams; and was considered by nearly everyone as a future leader.

Edward excelled at university. He graduated in the top 5% of his class and was a swimming champion in his event, the individual medley (butterfly, backstroke, breaststroke and freestyle). He did not join a fraternity ("too much silliness and drinking") and lived by himself in an apartment. After graduation, Edward joined a manufacturing company, quickly mastered the important orientation and training material, and chose a product development position so that he could demonstrate his initiative and ability to succeed. He became one of the best people at understanding sales reports, and at working with engineering and manufacturing to innovate on the existing product line. He was even able to develop a few new product ideas that seemed to have potential.

Corporate marketing was becoming concerned about the performance of the North Central region, which included corporate customers and retailers in the states of MN, ND, SD, MI, IN and WI. As the sales manager for that region was being reassigned due to his mediocre results, the personnel, finance, marketing and engineering vice-presidents met to consider the best person for the vacancy. The sales management job is not an easy assignment given the size of the territory, the slowdown in general business activity, and the stability of the populations of the region making it hard for new vendor representatives to easily gain customer confidence.

The personnel vice-president was asked to begin the meeting by commenting on the qualifications of the leading candidates. After briefly reviewing the file documentation including recent annual reviews, she concluded with her recommendation. "As all of us know, our company requires a strong personality to manage the North Central region. That person must be energetic, a proven success, unafraid to deal with initial rejection from customers, and willing to work with underperforming salespeople. And we must assist that person with a training budget for the salespeople, sufficient time to make the necessary changes, an expense account, and any other support we can provide. The outstanding candidate for this critical assignment is Edward Gilmore."

Questions for Consideration

1. Has the personnel vice-president adequately described the situation? Should she have been given the responsibility to present these conclusions?
2. Does Edward's history suggest that he would be a person who can succeed in the sales manager's position?
3. Other than the qualifications of the other candidates, what additional information would assist the four vice-presidents in making a decision?

Chris Farr (interpersonal dynamics)

The Last National Bank of Somewhere was a medium-sized financial institution in commercial banking, specializing in providing credit (loan) and non-credit products to businesses. The latter category included services that enabled a company to conduct its financial activities, including treasury management (the collection and disbursement of funds), trade finance (for international activities), information systems (to update company databases and execute transfers), and numerous other support services. The bank was organized into various business segments, including several credit groups organized by industry or client size. Chris Farr headed one of these groups (Segment G), and had just been selected by senior bank executives to become the manager of several business segments, organized into a division (to use the bank's terminology), and to receive a promotion to senior vice president.

One of Chris' first assignments was to choose his successor to manage Segment G to continue and expand on the success that had been experienced over the past three years. As in other organizations, Chris' "success" was really due to the efforts of his first-line subordinates, who actually did all of the hard work in visiting clients and prospects, marketing the bank's products, writing proposals, answering objections, closing sales and supervising implementation. Few of the clients and prospects had ever met Chris, and when his name was mentioned, they had to ask who he was.

Chris was extremely good at managing "up", that is, in claiming credit for the hard work of his subordinates. In fact, he deliberately placed himself between the senior executives and his staff, and as a result the bank did not realize who was responsible for creating the strong partnership between the business community and the bank. To prevent any serious rebellion among his subordinates, Chris would occasionally request a promotion or bonus for his best performers. However, his ability to retain good employees was one of his weakest metrics (compared to other bank managers), which gave concern to the senior executives when they considered whether to promote Chris.

The First Manager Candidates for Segment G

Chris reviewed the candidates for promotion to manager of Segment G. All four people under consideration had the necessary technical skills, had completed at least one certification in their fields, and had earned MBAs from good universities. Furthermore, they had been successful with clients and prospects, had received various commendation letters from Chris, and had no known personal issues. The candidates are described in the following sections.

- Ruth Jacobs, 43 years old, married, two children, husband recently hospitalized although his diagnosis is not yet known. Ruth had loyally worked in Segment G for six years and was considered as very intelligent and focused. She had not been previously considered as manager "material" because of her lack of congeniality with her peers and superiors, and because her technical skills seemed to take precedence over her management skills.
- Donald Armour, 44 years old, married, three children. Donald (call me "Don") was a fairly recent hire from a competitor, and had brought a portfolio of client contacts along with excellent presentation skills.

Don was concerned about his subordinates, managed their various activities in the attempt to improve their career potential, and was willing to do the promotional activities necessary to market the bank, including seminars and speeches.

The Second Manager Candidates for Segment G

Two other candidates are described below.

- Judith (Judy) Conway, 37 years old, single but seriously dating. Judy had been with the bank for eight years after being recruited from a smaller bank. She was considered as the most physically attractive of the management candidates, and there were rumors that Judy had been very friendly with Chris at various meetings and on overnight sales trips.
- Thomas (Tom) Ward, 45 years old, married, two children. Chris had recruited Tom two years ago from a larger competitor with the promise that he would be the next Segment G manager if Chris were transferred or promoted. Tom was successful but to some it appeared that, like Chris, his subordinates did most of the hard work. Tom was in something of a difficult role, because he was operating out of a regional office of the bank and was not visible to senior managers much of the time.

Chris Interviews Each Candidate

In order to develop a more complete picture of the four candidates, Chris decided to interview them individually. Here are excerpts from their responses to questions about why each should get the job and how his or her management style would be implemented.

Ruth Jacobs: On why she should get the job – "I think that my record speaks for itself in terms of technical innovation and product development." Chris admitted that this was true, but asked Ruth how she would manage the Segment G staff. Ruth replied: "I am convinced that clients partner with our bank because of our superior products and our skilled people. The only way to continue our success is more of the same – more innovation, more staff de-velopment, more excellence in delivery. The management issue is not a major component of this job, because our people are professionals who need little hand holding or motivation."

Donald Armour: On why he should get the job – "This segment of the bank has been largely self-motivated for a while, although my approach has been to assist and support people to develop themselves through training, consultation with me and role playing of client situations. We constantly try to anticipate what could happen at a client or prospect's office, and then script the best response to each question or objection." On how he would manage Segment G - "I'd do more of the same for the entire group just as I'm doing now for my team. This approach has been working, we've been beating our goals and I'll simply extend the process to everyone in Segment G."

Judy Conway: On why she should get the job – "Well Chris, we've been p-r-e-t-t-y close, so you know that I'm the person most qualified to lead this group. You certainly don't need me to review my qualifications. In fact, I'm assuming that this meeting is largely a formality." On how she would manage Segment G – "I've watched you over the past several years and I would do what you do best. The people in Segment G are professionals and require little direct supervision. However, it is important to keep senior bank executives informed of our situation – just as you've done – so that we receive the visibil-ity and respect that we deserve."

Tom Ward: On why he should get the job – "As you know, I was prom-ised the manager position at the time I was recruited, so I'm not sure that I need to review all of my accomplishments. However, I have worked with several bank clients to enhance our relationship, and I have moved the market footprint (marketing language for territory and industry coverage) in various new directions." On how he would manage Segment G – "I would supervise fairly directly. I think a close relationship is the motivating factor in a profes-sional environment. People want to do the right thing – they just need regular direction."

Chris Considers His Decision

Chris thought about the four candidates, but soon began to focus on what he really hoped to accomplish with his promotion – to use his new position to raise his visibility within the bank. Maybe someday he would be the president or a board member! He realized that the performance of Segment G would reflect on him and could affect his career. So this decision was important.

But what was the most important characteristic to look for in the new manager? Was it technical skills, which would seem to point to Ruth? Was it careful preparation for client situations, which would favor Don? Was it a personal relationship with Chris as the division senior manager, which would clearly give preference to Judy? Or was it Tom, who was promised the job when he was hired and seemed to be doing a good job. Chris never really liked these hard choices, and usually deferred to the others on his management team when deciding on new strategies, new products to develop (Ruth always had strong opinions), new hires and other important business issues. He did not want to spend too much time on this; after all, he had to choose furniture for his new office.

Questions for Consideration

1. Explain how the five individuals in the case differ as to how each person appears to manage others.
2. What decision do you think that Chris will make? Why?
3. Do you think that Chris' new senior managers will accept Chris' choice?
4. Discuss the management and OB issues presented in the case. How would you change the management processes at the Last National Bank?

Select Electronics (directing)

Select Electronics ("Select Elect") has 40 organizational units that provide $30 billion of electronic products to global business customers and retailers. The skills of Select Elect's 8,000 employees range from highly advanced engineering and design to basic manufacturing and clerical processes including the assembly of components. All new hires must meet rigorous aptitude and special test requirements at the time of hiring, and for skilled positions, graduates of good business, engineering and computer science programs are given preference.

The personnel department has responsibility for all compensation and benefits decisions, with each salaried employee assessed on an MBO contract basis and rated from superior (for outstanding performers) to unsatisfactory (for employees who are not meeting minimum standards). The distribution of ratings and the impact on the following year's compensation in a typical rating period is as follows:

Rating	Distribution as a % of All Employees	Impact on Base Salary
Superior	5%	+ 20%
Exceeds expectations	20%	+ 12%
Commendable	35%	+ 8%
Acceptable	30%	+ 5%
Unsatisfactory	10%	No increase

Unacceptable employees are placed on probation for the next year, are coached and counseled, and if performance does not improve, are terminated with a generous severance.

Hourly employees require less education and/or experience, often some high school, as long as they possess tenth grade mathematics and English competency. They do not have a job evaluation similar to that of the salaried workers, and are paid on an hourly basis depending on the job skills that are required and seniority (the years of employment at Select Elect).

Compensation at Select Elect is slightly above the industry average so that employees will not be motivated to leave for a position with the competition. Fringe benefits are quite reasonable and the health insurance provided is more than adequate.

Questions for Consideration

1. Is Select Elect likely to have a morale problem with its employees? Explain your logic in answering this question.
2. How might you advise management on changing personnel policies or other matters relating to directing at the company?

Let Us Entertain You! (controlling)

Let Us Entertain You! has operations in various aspects of the entertainment industry including cable television, cellular telephones, movies, music, theater and theme parks. While the stock market is impressed with its mix of businesses and diversification, the company's 16% return-on-equity is 2% points below that of the industry average. As Chief Executive Officer, you are concerned that your managers may not have the necessary strategic vision of the company in providing a complete package of services to customers. Some recent examples:

1. Two of your businesses competed for the same contract and undercut each other's price to the point where money was lost based on all-in costs.
2. Your auditors are concerned about certain of the expenses of the movie and music groups, such as lavish client entertaining, including golf games, dinners at 5-star restaurants and excursions to Las Vegas.
3. Your semi-annual manager conferences, designed to review progress toward business unit objectives, seem to focus more on excuses and promises and less on evidence of specific business successes.
4. Your profit forecasts are aggressive, but you have been experiencing serious cash shortages and have had to draw down perilously close to the limit against your $1 billion lending agreement from your banks.

Your financial department has prepared the following statistics to highlight the current position of Let Us Entertain You.

Strategic Businesses (SBUs)

10 SBUs with
19-23% Return-on-Equity (ROE)
1,500 Employees

10 SBUs with
14-18% Return-on-Equity (ROE)
2,500 Employees

20 SBUs with
9-13% Return-on-Equity (ROE)
4,000 Employees

What actions should you take to satisfy the financial markets and provide a long-term growth strategy for your company?

INDEX

Significant Authors Cited